My Dear Good Rosi

Letters from Nazi-Occupied Holland
1940–1943

My Dear Good Rosi

Letters from Nazi-Occupied Holland
1940–1943

Judy Vasos

Pen
Stroke
Press

Oakland, California

My Dear Good Rosi: Letters from Nazi-Occupied Holland 1940–1943
Judy Vasos

Published by
Pen Stroke Press
3048 Madeline Street
Oakland, CA 94602
www.judyvasos.com
judyvasos@gmail.com

Text copyright © 2018 by Judy Vasos
Illustrations copyright © 2018 by Judy Vasos

All rights reserved. No part of this book may be reproduced, transmitted, or stored in an information retrieval system in any form or by any means, graphic, electronic, or mechanical, including photocopying, taping, and recording, without prior permission in writing from the publisher.

ISBN: 978-0-9997425-2-5 (print)
ISBN: 978-0-9997425-3-2 (ebook)

Library of Congress Control Number: 2018931061
Publisher's Cataloging-In-Publication Data

Name: Vasos, Judy.
Title: My dear good Rosi : letters from Nazi-occupied Holland, 1940-1943 / Judy Vasos.
Description: Oakland, California : Pen Stroke Press, [2018] | Includes bibliographical references.
Identifiers: ISBN 9780999742525 (print) | ISBN 9780999742532 (ebook)
Subjects: LCSH: Netherlands--History--German occupation, 1940-1945. | Political refugees--Netherlands--Correspondence. | World War, 1939-1945--Personal narratives, German. | LCGFT: Personal correspondence.
Classification: LCC D811 .V37 2018 (print) | LCC D811 (ebook) | DDC 940.53492092--dc23

Editors: Susan Rawlins, Leona Weiss, Amy Rothman
Book Design: Robert Aulicino, www.aulicinodesign.com
Book production coordinated by To Press & Beyond, www.topressandbeyond.com

Printed in USA.

Lovingly Dedicated to

CLEMY AND HUGO MOSBACHER
with great appreciation for the hundreds of letters
written to your only child, Rosi, during a long, painful
separation that ended in your murder at Auschwitz.
Your letters were preserved and held close to Rosi's heart
for over seventy years. Eventually, she passed them
on to her children, Tony and Steve.
As grandsons, they never got to know you and thought
grandparents were reserved for others.
They referred to you as their mother's parents.
The legacy of your letters made you real.
They now call you their grandparents.

Contents

Introduction	ix
The Mosbachers in Germany	x
The Mosbachers in Holland	xiv
The Mosbachers in Westerbork	xix
A Legacy	xxi
Acknowledgments	xxiii
Notes on the Text	xxv
Descendants of Ignaz Adler	xxvi
Descendants of Sigmund Mosbacher	xxvi
Letters	1
Letters from September 1935 through December 1940	1
Letters from January 1941 through December 1941	113
Letters from January 1942 through January 1943	224
Ari Knoller's Post-War Letters	257
Mentioned in the Letters	273
Frequently Mentioned	273
Also Mentioned	274
Emigration and Immigration Visa Requirements	281
Documentation Required for Emigration from Germany	281
Documentation Required for Immigration to the United States	282
Rosi Lisbeth Mosbacher Baczewski	284
Stolpersteine/Stumbling Stone	298
Resources	300

Introduction

The first time Judy Vasos and I met, in 2010, was to discuss the project that ultimately became this book. The project, then in its infancy, centered on Judy's husband Tony's grandparents, Hugo and Clemy Mosbacher, German Jews murdered in Auschwitz, and their daughter, Tony's mother, Rosi Mosbacher, who died in 2009, aged ninety-three. Rosi was still alive when Judy and Tony came across a thick folder containing the letters the Mosbachers sent to their daughter in the course of their separation induced by Nazi persecution. "Don't throw them away," Rosi said, and beamed when they said they planned to have them translated and published.

Fleeing Hitler, the Mosbachers crossed from Germany into Holland in February 1940. In Holland they would wait for their American visas, completing the process initiated in Germany. By then their only daughter was already abroad and employed in England as a maid with a family that took in refugees and subsequently as an au pair with another family; Tony was named for Anthony, the child in Rosi's care in England. In the 1920s, the US established quota numbers for applicants seeking entry based on country of birth. Rosi's number came up later in 1940, enabling the twenty-four-year-old to enter the United States in August. The Mosbachers were looking forward to joining their daughter in New York after the acquisition of their visas.

The visas came through and the Mosbachers purchased tickets for the Atlantic crossing. On May 8, Clemy wrote to her daughter in England: "I can still hardly believe that we are going to America." The *Veendam* was scheduled to leave Rotterdam on May 12. On May 10, Germany invaded Holland, breaching Dutch neutrality. Five days later Holland capitulated. Queen Wilhelmina fled to England, along with the government.

In Germany, the Mosbachers had German exit visas but lacked American visas. After the German occupation of Holland, they had their American visas and steamship tickets but no exit visas, and from then until their end by gassing, the Mosbachers strained every muscle to break the deadlock, a quest documented in the 100-plus letters contained in this volume. They make for painful reading, but they also attest to love, compassion, and the strength of familial bonds. Sadly, Rosi's letters have been lost. Most likely they suffered the fate of their recipients.

The letters collected by Judy Vasos, with their explanatory notes and background, go some way toward explaining what is a complex history. My task is to add some additional shading. I, too, am part of this story. I was born in Transit Camp Westerbork in 1943 and spent a good part of my life researching and writing about the Holocaust, including a book about the camp from which the Mosbachers, like my grandparents, were shipped to their deaths in Poland. It was this book, *Boulevard des Miséres: The Story of Transit Camp Westerbork*, that prompted Judy to seek me out.

The Mosbachers in Germany

German Jews were Hitler's first victims. Within months of taking power on January 30, 1933, the Nazis organized a boycott of Jewish services and businesses. On April 1, crudely painted Stars of David and the officially sanctioned "yellow spot," ancient symbol of degradation, stigmatized Jewish storefronts and name plates in Berlin, home to some 160,000 Jews (the entire Jewish population in Germany in 1933 was roughly 500,000). Stationed in front of Jewish-owned department stores, Brownshirts dared passersby to enter.

"The thousand year history of German Jewry has come to an end" declared Germany's foremost rabbi Dr. Leo Baeck.

Less than a week later, on April 7, the first of some four hundred pieces of legislation designed to eliminate Germany's Jews from the political, economic, social, and cultural life of the nation surfaced in the *Reichsgesetzblatt*, the official register of laws promulgated by the government. Paragraph 3 of the Law for the

Restoration of the Professional Civil Service stated: "Civil servants of non-Aryan descent must retire," and the Law Regarding Admittance to the Profession of Law threatened Jewish lawyers with the loss of their practices. Other laws excluded Jewish physicians from panel practice with the National Health Insurance, while the Law against the Overcrowding of German schools introduced a numerus clausus in the public school system.

How would one characterize this history? Viktor Klemperer, dismissed from a professorship in romance languages, kept the most compelling journal of life in the Third Reich by a German Jew (he was married to a non-Jew and a highly decorated World War I veteran, enabling him to remain in Germany throughout the war). On January 10, 1939, summarizing the history of German Jews, Klemperer writes.

> Until 1933 and for at least a good century before that, the German Jews were entirely German and nothing else. Proof: the thousands upon thousands of half and quarter, etc. Jews and of Jewish descent, proof that Jews and Germans worked together and without friction in all spheres of life. The anti-Semitism, which was always present, is not at all evidence to the contrary. Because the friction between Jews and Aryans was not half as great as that between Protestants and Catholics, or between employers and employees or between East Prussians for example and southern Bavarians or Rhinelanders and Bavarians. The German Jews were part of the German nation, as the French Jews were a part of the French nation, etc. They had their place in German life, and were in no way a burden on the whole. Their place was very rarely that of the worker, still less of the agricultural labourer. They were and remain (even if now they no longer wish to remain so) Germans, in the main intellectuals and educated people.[1]

---

[1] Viktor Klemperer, *I Will Bear Witness: 1933-1941* (New York: Modern Library, 1999), p. 291.

But the Nazis did not care to make distinctions, at least not those. The Laws of September 15, 1935, the Nuremberg Laws—"the laws," Hitler boasted, "whose full significance will only be recognized hundreds of years from now"—and the supplementary decrees defining who was a Jew signified the end of the so-called German-Jewish symbiosis, reducing Jews to virtual pariahs. Among other things, the laws robbed Jews of their German citizenship, prohibited "Aryan" women under the age of forty-five from working in Jewish households, and criminalized sexual intercourse between Jews and non-Jews of "Aryan" descent.

Until the end of 1938, the persecution of Jews proceeded in three big waves: the boycott and non-Aryan legislation of April 1933; the Nuremberg Laws of September 1935, and the pogrom of November 9/10, 1938, the Kristallnacht or the Night of Broken Glass. The Nuremberg legislation was a turning point. Now even the most optimistic of Jews were convinced that the end had come, despite official Nazi declarations that the discriminatory legislation had been designed to clarify the relations with Jews, not encumber them. For the first time emigration was accepted as a given, and wherever the hope for a Jewish future on German soil still flickered, Kristallnacht extinguished it for good. Where in the past Jews had had the option of defining their relationship to Judaism, including the option of rejection, those days were over. A Jew could no longer choose not to be Jewish.

At the time of the promulgation of these laws Rosi was no longer living with her parents in Nuremberg, the site of the annual Nazi rallies celebrated in Leni Riefenstahl's *Triumph of the Will*, but employed in a home for Jewish children elsewhere in Germany. She was nineteen-years-old and living on her own for the first time. So it's hardly surprising that the first letter in this volume is filled with paternal advice, urging their daughter "to remain pure and undefiled," to strive for maturity, and expresses the hope that all of her wishes may come true. (Hugo wrote the bulk of the letters, especially the longer ones, often followed by some additional input from Clemy.) Not a word about the Nuremberg Laws, promulgated some twelve days earlier in their very backyard; Nuremberg had been the family home for hundreds of years. Understandably—caution was necessary. The only indication that something was amiss (and Rosi surely would have understood) was a vague reference to the absence of "a truly good mood that has made correspondence hard for me at this time." That very day, the Mosbachers were getting ready for the Rosh Hashanah celebration, Jewish New Year. The Mosbachers were Orthodox Jews and assiduously kept the Jewish calendar, somewhat of an anomaly among German Jews. The latter, like their American counterparts, were highly assimilated. They might show up in synagogue on the High Holidays, but no more.

Hugo Mosbacher, born in 1880, grew up in Wilhelmine Germany. Clemy, six years Hugo's junior, was Austrian by birth. They married in 1911 in Nuremberg. In retrospect, the period between the founding of the Reich in 1871, coinciding with the full emancipation of the Jews, and the outbreak of the war in 1914 was the economic highpoint of Jewish life in Germany. Jews prospered, breaking new ground with department stores, book publishing and newspapers, to mention but a few areas in which they became dominant, hence more visible, hence more at risk. Hugo was a junior partner in a metal firm in Nuremberg. He got along well with his Gentile partner and stayed with the company until after Kristallnacht. Like most German Jews, the Mosbachers were decidedly middle class, with all those strengths and weaknesses: they believed in progress, property, and the rule of law. Class conscious, Hugo counseled his daughter to mix with the "*upper ten thousand*" (italics in the original) in New York.

The Kaiserreich collapsed in defeat in 1918, to be succeeded, after a tumultuous revolutionary period, by the Weimar Republic, named for the city of its founding. In the Weimar Republic, the situation of the Jews, especially in its crisis-ridden initial and final phases, took a sharp turn for the worse. There was much talk of a "Jewish Republic," of a "Jewish press" and culture; worse, a "Jewish plot" to bury Germany through revolution; of Jews stabbing Germany in the back while the "unvanquished" army in the field was homing in on victory, and of Jews selling Germany out at Versailles. Even relativity was assailed as a deus ex machina of a perverted Jewish mind. These were the years when new anti-

Semitic parties and movements began to flex their muscles, culminating with the victory of the Nazi Party at the polls in 1932, laying the groundwork for Hitler's accession to power on the second to last day of January 1933.

Frustrating and bewildering as life was in the opening years of Hitler rule, Germany's Jews by and large clung to the hope of riding out the storm in Germany. If 1935 was a turning point, 1938 was the point of no return. That year, dubbed by Hitler "The Year of Understanding," saw a spate of anti-Jewish measures and a hardening of Nazi policy, completing Jewish isolation. In August, Jews were required to add "Jewish-sounding" middle names, "Israel" for men and "Sara" for women, and in October their passports were marked with the letter "J"—to mention but two of many new restrictions. Kristallnacht was next. The night the synagogues went up in flames Hugo was one of thousands of Jews hauled off to concentration camps. Hugo wound up in Dachau, the concentration camp built shortly after Hitler came to power. Several months later he was back in Nuremberg, released on condition that he quit Germany. On April 1, 1939, American visas pending, the Mosbachers were forced to live in a Nazi-designated Judenhaus—Jew House—which they shared with Hugo's sister, Frida, their maid Lina, and several other acquaintances. Eight months later, the Mosbachers stashed their belongings into a handbag, boarded a train for Holland, and crossed to safety at Oldenzaal, a border town sympathetic to refugees fleeing from Germany, on February 21, 1940.

The Mosbachers in Holland

Dutch authorities were not nearly as welcoming as the townspeople of Oldenzaal. No sooner had they crossed into Holland than they were arrested and detained in separate detention centers in Amsterdam, where they spent the next two months, from March 1 through May 1—going without a change of clothes for ten weeks. Upon their release—they still had to report to the authorities every day—they lived with their relatives the Knollers in the Beethovenstraat until October 1940, when they moved to

Rijnstraat 102. "We moved into a small but very nice room with heating and warm water," Clemy wrote to her daughter on October 27. They lived on the first floor with the Sabel family, the Knollers on the third floor. They remained at this address until their arrest in February 1943. Most of the letters to their daughter were written in this flat.

The Dutch, contending with the worldwide Depression and fearful of stepping on Nazi toes, did not do well by the refugees. As in every other country, it became increasingly difficult, if not impossible, to secure the necessary work and/or residency papers—or find nations willing to receive them. In depression-ravaged Holland, Dutch nationals enjoyed priority in the labor market. In 1937, a new law prohibited the establishment of independent businesses or professions by foreigners. Many of the regulations issued in the course of the thirties did not apply to the Mosbachers. They were not looking for jobs nor, as far as can be determined from the letters, dependent on government handouts.

To absorb the flow, the Dutch built a camp in Holland's inhospitable northeast to house roughly 3,000 victims of Nazi persecution while they arranged to get the visas that would enable them to move on. The Mosbachers avoided internment in Westerbork, or Central Camp for Refugees, Westerbork, to give its official designation, because they were able to demonstrate being on track to receive the necessary documents in the near future.

On the whole, German Jews were not well received by the Dutch. Some Dutch Jews disliked them as well. Many thought that the better educated and more prosperous German Jews looked down their noses on their western neighbors. In Amsterdam, they moved into apartments located in well-to-do neighborhoods—the "German-Jewish ghetto of the Beethovenstraat," for example—out of reach of many locals suffering from a chronic housing shortage. The hatred of foreigners was strong. The Jewish Council employed a number of German Jews, who favored friends and relatives over the Dutch-born Jews when the deportations to the East began in mid-July 1942.

The great majority of emigrants, documented and undocumented—by the time the Mosbachers set foot on Dutch soil, they numbered 15,000—had a hard time of it, and the Mosbachers were no exception. It appears that financial support, at least some, came from relatives in the US. Additional support may have come from monies administered by various agencies dedicated to helping refugees find their feet but increasingly ineffectual as the Nazis clamped down. The letters, however, are for the most part silent on this. One of the letters mentions a *seder* evening in which the hostess was hardly able to take part because, absent outside help, she had to do everything herself. Another letter indicated that money was scarce. The Mosbachers survived on hopes of joining their daughter in the US, and prepared by taking English lessons. For two years, the weekly letters from their daughter kept them going, month after month after month—until the letters were reduced to a trickle, then stopped altogether.

It makes sense that the Mosbachers downplayed their suffering. What parent wouldn't? Even so, there are numerous instances, often couched in no more than an offhand remark, that things were in fact rather terrible. Early on, Clemy mentions having her stomach pumped, diagnosed as caused by nervous tension. In addition, she suffered from gallbladder attacks, unrelieved itching, and other stress-related symptoms. Being confined in a single room, forced to interact with company not of one's choosing, the uncertainty about their fate, the never-ending rumors passed off as fact, and other pressures took an increasingly heavy toll. "Not knowing anything increases our nervousness," wrote Clemy on the last day of January 1941. Hugo, optimistic by nature, tried to put the best possible gloss on things, but there is no mistaking a gradual unraveling as time passed and the future looked increasingly hopeless.

Communication with the outside world was strictly monitored, and the Nazis made no bones about it. While this practice had been going on for months, it was not until October 1940 that the occupier assigned a censor number to every letter sent abroad. The first Mosbacher letter with a censor number—2327-996—is dated October 16. Needless to say, Rosi's parents had to be extra careful if they wanted the letters to reach their destination.

INTRODUCTION — xvii

On June 27, 1941, Hugo mentions that the American consulate was

> "no longer taking applications and that no visas are being issued.... Now that the U.S.A. is out of the question, the Committee [for Jewish Refugees) is talking to us about Cuba.... [W]e are always clinging to new projects.... The same reasons that caused us to leave the Fürther Straße [that is, the Judenhaus] would also now cause us to depart from here.... During recent months," Hugo continues, "exit visas have been issued here, but not to all those who are waiting for them. On the other hand, the consulate has not in any way expedited the granting of visas. The reasons for this are unknown to us."

We, however, do know.

On June 26, 1940, the State Department circulated a memo instructing its representatives abroad to do everything possible to stop refugees seeking entry into the US. "We can delay and effectively stop for a temporary period of indefinite length," wrote Assistant Secretary of State Breckinridge Long,

> the number of immigrants into the United States. We could do this by simply advising our consuls to put every obstacle in the way and to require additional evidence and to resort to various administrative advices which would postpone and postpone and postpone the granting of the visas.

The Mosbachers took the physicals, filled out paper after paper, bought another round of ship tickets, secured affidavits attesting to their character and guarantees from American sponsors that they would not become dependent on the dole—a paper chain whose weakest link was unpredictability. As soon as one condition was satisfied, another surfaced, raising hopes only to crush them.

With the American embassy no longer part of the equation,

the Mosbachers considered other ways of getting out—Cuba being one, as noted—but none materialized. They were trapped. Paradoxically, had Rosi's parents stayed in Germany they might have gotten out in 1940, causing the Mosbachers to second-guess the decision to leave for Holland. But in the war on the Jews decisions that seemed utterly logical when made rarely panned out, coming to grief against America's impenetrable "paper walls," the implacable dictates of the New Order, a compliant Jewish Council, and last, and certainly not least, what has been called the "administrative cooperation" with the Germans on the part of the Dutch. The Dutch banks played their role in the "Aryanization" of Jewish businesses, as did the Dutch civil service, the police officers of the Dutch SS, and the Dutch railways. Respectively these agencies helped expropriate, register, collect, and transport the Jewish citizens and refugees. At his trial in Jerusalem in 1961, Adolf Eichmann stated that the task of making Holland Judenrein ("Jew-free") was never a problem. Hannah Arendt has called the destruction of Dutch Jewry "a catastrophe unparalleled in any Western country," a disaster comparable only to the extinction of Polish Jewry.[2]

Holland's longstanding reputation for tolerance, and the expectation of bringing the "racially compatible" Dutch around to their way of thinking, led the Germans to proceed slowly. The gloves started coming off in 1941, but it was not until the spring and summer of 1942 that anti-Jewish decrees reached a new level.

> Anne Frank's diary entry, June 20, 1942.
> Anti-Jewish decrees followed each other in quick succession. Jews must wear a yellow star, Jews must hand in their bicycles, Jews are banned from trams and are forbidden to drive, Jews are only allowed to do their shopping between three and five o'clock and then only in shops which bear the placard "Jewish shop." Jews must be indoors by eight o'clock and cannot even sit in their own gardens after that hour. Jews are forbidden to visit theaters, cinemas and

---

[2]Hannah Arendt, *Eichmann in Jerusalem: A Report on the Banality of Evil* (New York: The Viking Press, 1963), p. 81.

other places of entertainment. Jews may not take part in public sports. Swimming baths, tennis courts, hockey fields, and other sports grounds are all prohibited to them. Jews may not visit Christians. Jews must go to Jewish schools, and many more restrictions of a similar kind.[3]

Only four letters reached Rosi in 1942. The last one is dated May 29, 1942.

The Mosbachers in Westerbork

The Mosbachers managed to hold out until the end of January 1943. Arrested in their home, they were taken to the Joodse Schouwburg (Jewish Theater) in Amsterdam, a holding tank for Jews about to be deported to Westerbork. The Mosbachers entered Westerbork shortly thereafter. "There is no lack of acquaintances here," wrote Clemy to relatives in Amsterdam on January 26. "We are no better or worse off than all the others. Greetings and kisses. Stay well—Clemy and Hugo." The next day Hugo sent a change of address card to Clemy's sister in Asti, Italy—the final sign of life.

By the time the Mosbachers entered Westerbork, the camp had long ceased to be operated by the Dutch authorities. Its official transfer from Dutch to German hands took place on July 1, 1942. Renamed Police Transit Camp Westerbork, the compound entered upon its last phase as a storehouse for Jews to be "resettled in the East." The first transports, consisting primarily of foreign Jews, left Holland in mid-July. From then until the end of the war, ninety-three trains carried some 104,000 Jews to their deaths, out of a total Jewish population of roughly 140,000. The transport list of February 2, 1943, indicates that the cattle train that carried the Mosbachers left Westerbork on February 2. They were gassed upon arrival in Auschwitz three days later.

Jacob Boas, PhD

---

[3]Anne Frank, *The Diary of Anne Frank: The Critical Edition.* Prepared by the Netherlands State Institute for War Documentation. Trans. Arnold J. Pomerans and B. M. Mooyart (New York: Doubleday, 1989), pp. 182-183.

A Legacy

My mother-in-law Rosi Baczewski gradually let it be known that she wanted the story of her parents to be told. Our telephone calls, letters, and visits with her were more and more devoted to talking about her parents' lives and their deaths at the hands of the Nazis.

I had known her for over twenty years when she brought out boxes of photographs and encouraged my husband, her son Tony, to write down the names of family members she identified in the pictures. She showed us letters in German, pulled out one and told us it was from her father, written from Amsterdam in the early 1940s. Her father and mother addressed her as "My dear good Rosi," she said. She gave us the photographs, but put the letters back in the folder.

Rosi was eighty-eight when she left New York and moved to San Francisco. Some years later, helping to sort her belongings, I discovered the folder of her parents' letters that she had saved for more than sixty years.

We had several of the letters translated and began to read about Hugo and Clemy Mosbacher, whom she always called "such good people," often adding, "I wish you had known them." The letters were filled with their frustration, patience, hope, questions about family members running from the Nazis, and expressions of love for Rosi and all the "dear ones."

Her parents had been at the center of a close-knit Jewish family who had celebrated life together at the Mosbacher home in Nuremberg. None of them could have predicted that the Nazis would shatter their lives, scattering the survivors all over the world.

Holocaust survivor, Elie Wiesel said of the Shoah, "For the dead and the living, we must bear witness." Hugo and Clemy

Mosbacher bore witness in life. They continue to do so now, more than seventy years after their deaths, in the letters their daughter preserved and passed on. And, as a result, we know them.

Judy Vasos
September 2017

Acknowledgments

My deepest gratitude, of course, is to Rosi for saving her parents' letters for over sixty years and encouraging me to tell their story.

Judy Janek, former archivist at Tauber Holocaust Library and Archives, confirmed the importance of the letters and introduced me to the excellent translator, John Bass. Joining John in working on the translations were Gerhard Jochem of the Nuremberg City Archives, Louise van de Ven, Barbara Sommerschuh, and Leona Weiss, each of whom also played other essential roles in the making of this book.

Gerhard Jochem encouraged me to write Rosi's biography for the Rijo website and answered my questions about life in Nuremberg before and after Hitler's rise to power.

The people on the JewishGen website helped enormously with the research—thanks for your generosity, especially to the research wizard Evertjan Hannivoort and to Louise van de Ven, who translated the grim documents from the Westerbork transit camp.

Barbara Sommerschuh of Sütterlin Project in Hamburg transliterated the letters written in Sütterlin script, an indispensible assistance.

Jason Mundstuck was an early supporter of the project whose suggestions were very valuable.

Thanks to Jack Boas and Yoka Verdoner, Dutch friends who wrote about life in Holland and Camp Westerbork.

The editorial team of Susan Rawlins, Leona Weiss, and Amy Rothman turned a pile of letters into a professional manuscript. Janice Sellers created the beautiful genealogical charts.

To Gail M. Kearns, Book Sherpa at To Press & Beyond for her steadfast help guiding me through the intricacies of book publishing.

And to Robert Aulicino of aulicinodesign.com who worked his creative magic to design the cover and interior of the book.

Linda Mayo and Cheryl Bartky helped me remain open-hearted enough to compile this book.

Many thanks to the United States Holocaust Memorial Museum's Survivors and Victims Resource Center; René Pottkamp of NIOD (Institute for War Documentation in Amsterdam); José Martin of the Name and Face project of Camp Westerbork's Archives; Frank Harris, networker extraordinaire of Jewish families from Nuremberg; and to Hans Kremer for his postal history skills.

The Mosbacher and Adler family members filled in missing pieces of Hugo and Clemy's life and gave me strong encouragement and support. Thanks especially to "cousins" Marianne Flack, Ruth Schottman, Marion Frolich, and Ruth White.

My family helped me deal with the darker parts of this story and maintain balance. My sister Linda and brother Joe took a deep interest in that story and were my steadfast assistants.

Thanks to the dear friends who cheered me on from the conception of this book to its birth.

And to Tony and Steve Baczewski, Rosi's sons—I hope these letters have helped you know and appreciate your grandparents whose voices can now be heard, telling their story.

Notes on the Text

Both Hugo and Clemy used the older Sütterlin script in their early letters. After the German occupation of the Netherlands, Hugo used mostly modern cursive German and Clemy at least tried to write a clearer hand in order for the Nazi censors to read and approve their letters. The Nazis banned Sütterlin in 1941.

Die Sütterlinstube Hamburg, The Sütterlin Project of Hamburg, has provided enormous assistance in transcribing the earlier letters into standard German. Still, there remain illegible words that are indicated by [?] in the letters.

Words in English, Yiddish, or other non-German languages in the original German letters appear in italics in the English translations. A few untranslated German words are also rendered in italics. However, "the Doktors," by which Hugo refers to his brother Dr. Emil Mosbacher and his wife Rosl, is not italicized since it is used as a name.

All the letters were written on back and front of a single sheet of paper. Every available space was used and paragraph divisions were dispensed with, giving the impression that the German authorities may have limited them to one-page letters. The editors have added paragraphing to the letters for ease of reading.

We have written out numbers below 100 per English convention, although Hugo and Clemy used Arabic numerals per European convention.

Descendants of Ignaz Adler

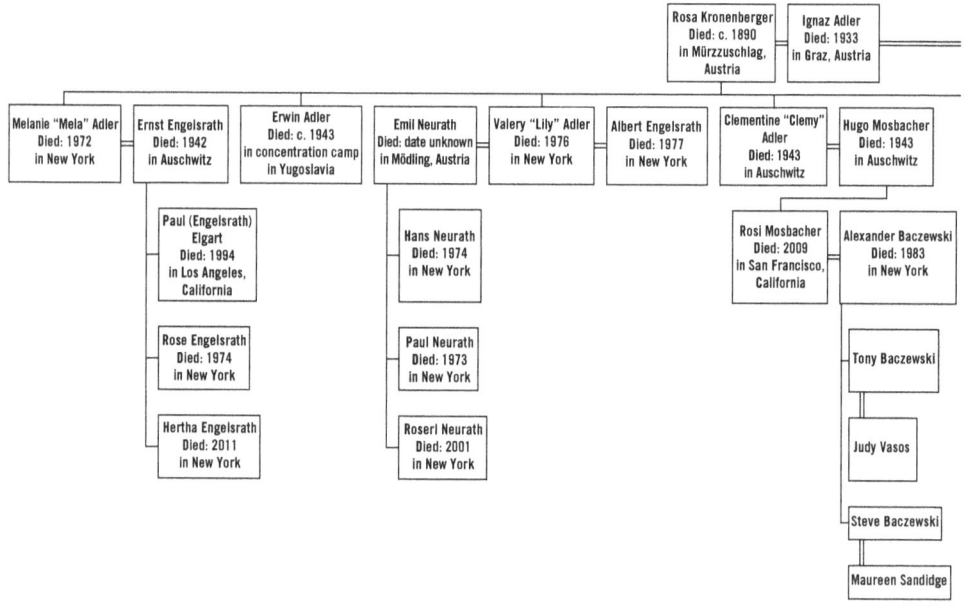

Descendants of Sigmund Mosbacher

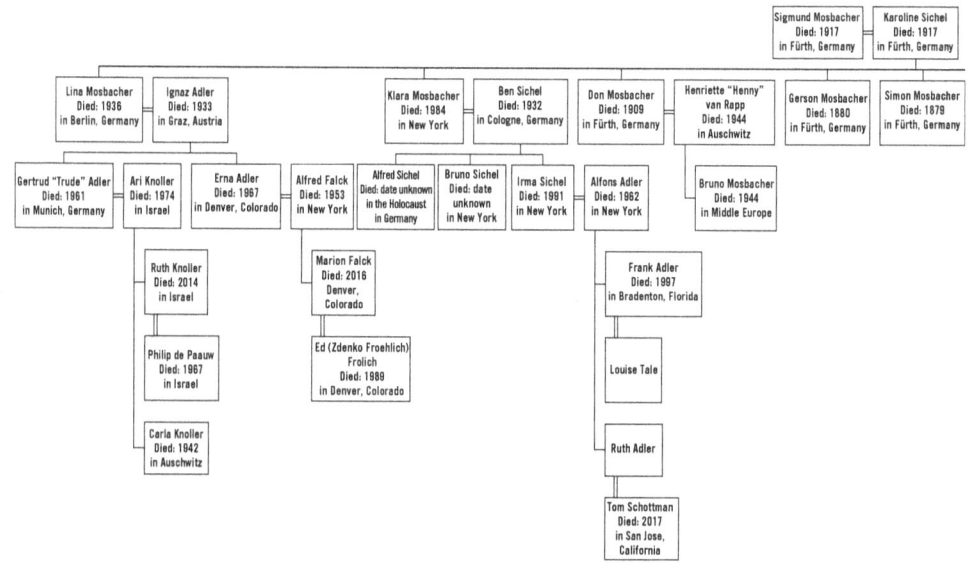

Lina Mosbacher
Died: 1936
in Berlin, Germany
Alfons Adler
Died: 1962
in New York
Irma Sichel
Died: 1991
in New York
Fredl Adler
Died:
in Denver, Colorado
Luise "Lusi" Garam
Died: 1991
in Denver, Colorado
Gertrud "Trude" Adler
Died: 1961
in Munich, Germany
Ari Knoller
Died: 1974
in Israel
Erna Adler
Died: 1967
in Denver, Colorado
Alfred Falck
Died: 1953
in New York
Frank Adler
Died: 1997
in Bradenton, Florida
Louise Tale
Ruth Adler
Tom Schottman
Died: 2017
in San Jose,
California
Ruth Knoller
Died: 2014
in Israel
Marion Falck
Died: 2016
in Denver,
Colorado
Ed (Zdenko Froehlich)
Frolich
Died: 1989
in Denver, Colorado
Gabrielle Adler
Jonathan Adler
Ann Schottman
Elly Schottman
Wendy Schottman
Tim Schottman
Kate Schottman
Philip de Paauw
Died: 1967
in Israel
Carla Knoller
Died: 1942
in Auschwitz
Alan Frolich
Lindy Frolich
Larry Frolich
Hugo Mosbacher
Died: 1943
in Auschwitz
Clementine "Clemy"
Adler
Died: 1943
in Auschwitz
Helene Mosbacher
Died: 1943
in Auschwitz
Philip van Gelder
Died: 1950
in Amsterdam,
Netherlands
Frida Mosbacher
Died: 1943
in Sobibor
Gustav Roederer
Died: 1925
in Nuremberg,
Germany
Max Mosbacher
Died: 1886
in Fürth, Germany
Anna Schweizer
Died: 1926
in Nuremberg,
Germany
Emil Mosbacher
Died: 1973
in New York
Rosl Neumann
Died: 1997
in New York
Rosi Mosbacher
Died: 2009
in San Francisco,
California
Alexander Baczewski
Died: 1983
in New York
Elisabeth "Els"
van Gelder
Died: 1995
in Switzerland
Alfred "Freddie"
van Gelder
Died: 1993
in Switzerland
Anna Roederer
Died: 2010
in Emeryville,
California
Philip "Fips"
(Seligsberger) White
Died: 1978
in Israel
Stephen (Sigmund)
Mosbacher
Died: 1945
in Holland (KIA)
Marianne Lore
Mosbacher
Peter Flack
Stephanie
Flack
Jennifer
Flack
Tony Baczewski
Judy Vasos
Steve Baczewski
Maureen Sandidge
Leon White
Dan White
Ruth White

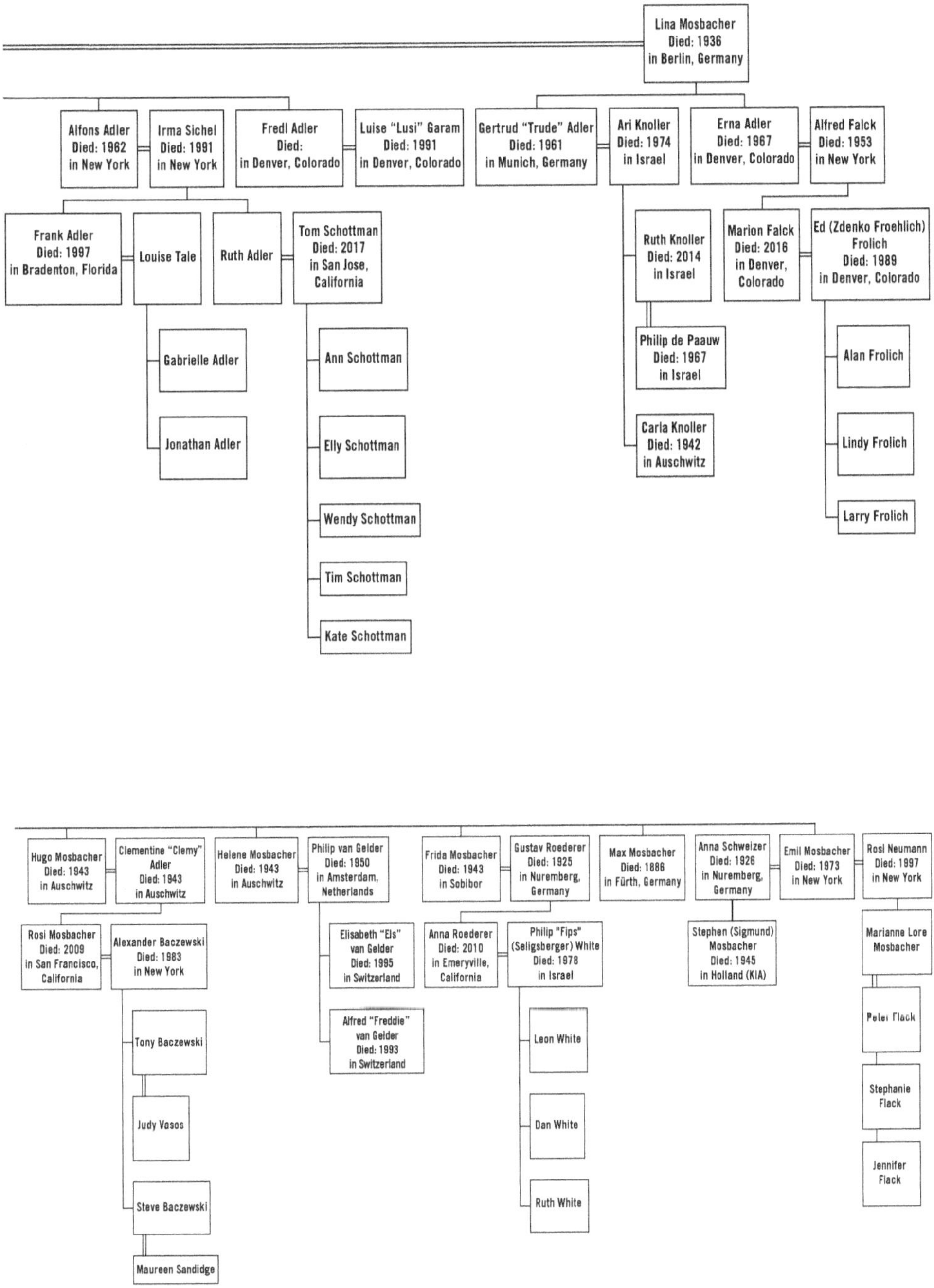

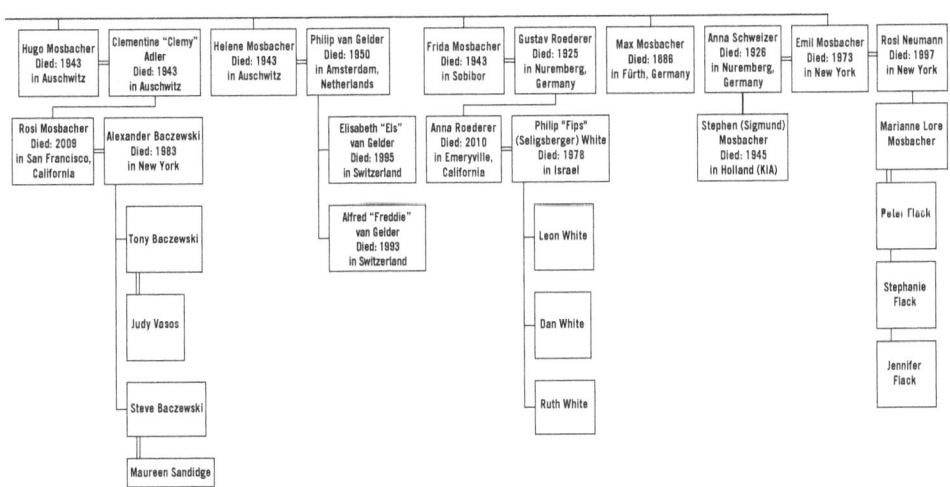

LETTERS

Letters from September 1935 through December 1940

Nuremberg, September 27, 1935

My dear good Rosi!

In honor of the day of preparation for the *Rosh Hashanah* celebration, I'm going to start off the morning by talking to you, my dear Rosi. Your letter that arrived yesterday pleased us very much. I hope that in the meantime a large package has reached you undamaged. My lack of a truly good mood has made correspondence especially hard for me at this time, and I was glad to receive your mail. With the very active assistance of your dear mother, I wrote, *inter alia*, to the bank in Amsterdam, to Clara [Mosbacher Sichel] in Graz, to Ludwig Mosbacher and his wife in Merano, to Simon in Barcelona, to [Clara] Fenigstein in Zurich, Cecile Mosbacher, Lenchen Mosbacher in Frankfurt on Main, Frida Maier in Nauheim, Jettchen Neumann in Nuremberg, Rudolf Strauss in Cologne, Erwin [Adler] in Graz, and also to uncles and aunts in Ermershausen,[4] Kleinheubach, Eschau, Miltenberg, Fulda, Vienna, and Zagreb.

For you, it is now exactly as if you had seen mail lying out at home. We will forward to you any interesting letters that may arrive. And now to you, dearest Rosi. What do parents wish for their child? What does the father wish for his daughter? What do I wish for my dear Rosi? It is pointless to answer these questions, for you know and

---

[4] First five towns are in Bavaria. The Mosbacher family's roots in southern Germany can be traced back to 1611.

feel the answer yourself. You know how your parents feel about you, what they want for you, and what they wish for you, and how strongly they wish it. Of course, I don't mean that we long blindly for the fulfillment of all your wishes. There may be some among them for whose fulfillment we do not strive. For the first time in your life, dear Rosi, you are in a strange environment. You are making the acquaintance of all sorts of people and all sorts of characters; you are gathering experiences of the most varied kind, and these impressions will, in the course of time, help you to attain a higher level of maturity. And I am convinced, once you have attained this new maturity, that we—parents and daughter—will be in agreement and that your actions and the goals you set for yourself will always correspond to what we want for you. As parents, we want to go with the times and not be considered old-fashioned. Nevertheless, there are traditions. My father, of blessed memory, constantly etched into his children that one must remain pure and undefiled (I have told you already that, in particular, he compared the female sex to the finest silken cloth), and so this, too, is a wish that is very close to my heart. For the rest, I believe that our Rosi will never disappoint us and will keep the promises that we have made to ourselves concerning her.

Dear Rosi, you are our happiness, and for this reason you also have an obligation to us that this happiness always outweighs the care that, God willing, we shall constantly have for you, for a very, very long time to come. Stay well, and pray that we stay well. We are, as always, with you, and this feeling makes the separation easier for us. Receive our blessing and a genuine *Rosh Hashanah* kiss from your father who loves you.

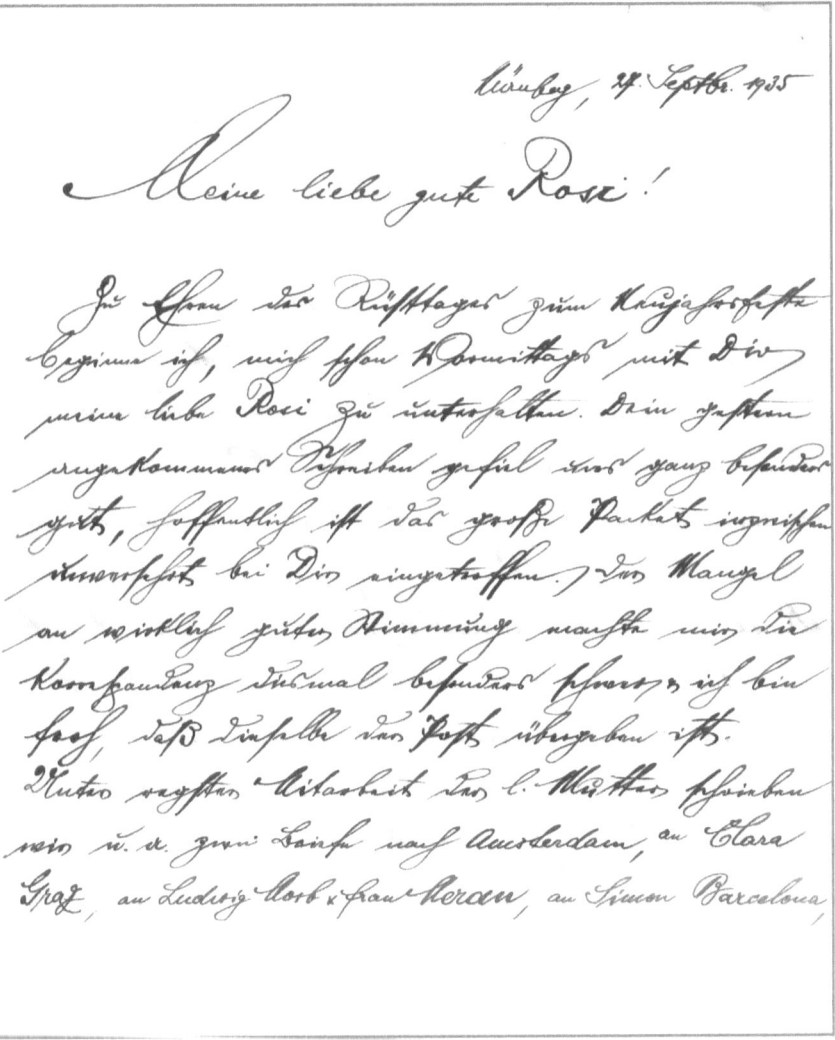

First page of Hugo's September 29, 1935, letter to Rosi.

Germany in 1935

By September of 1935, Adolf Hitler and his National Socialist German Workers' Party (NSDP or Nazis) had been in power for two and a half years, having won a majority of Reichstag seats in March 1933, and then quickly consolidating dictatorial control.

The Nazis began passing laws to deprive Jewish citizens of their rights, thus isolating them from German economic, civil, and social life.

The Nazi Party "Rally of Freedom" was held in Nuremberg, September 10–16, 1935, and the Nuremberg Laws of September 15, 1935, codified Nazi racial ideology. These laws deprived Jews of their citizenship and forbade them to marry Aryans, to have sexual relations with Aryans, or to employ young Aryan women as household help.

The Mosbacher Family in 1935

Hugo and Clemy Mosbacher were still living in their home at 27 Hallerstraße, third floor, in Nuremberg at the time of this letter. Hugo's "lack of a truly good mood" at the time of the Jewish holidays probably is his response to deteriorating conditions for German Jews.

Hugo was writing to family members and close friends in honor of the Jewish New Year. It is not clear if he was writing to the Bank in Amsterdam in an effort to transfer funds into or out of Germany.

Rosi had left Nuremberg to work in a home for Jewish children and later to attend a teacher training program in Würzburg until it was closed by the Nazis. She was nineteen at the time of this letter.

Nuremberg, June 5, 1939, Monday, 11 a.m.

My dear good Rosi!
Now that I've finished talking on the telephone[5] and

---

[5]Hugo and Clemy had just spoken on the telephone to Rosi in Amsterdam, where she was visiting her aunt and uncle, Ari and Trude Knoller, on her way to England.

have a postcard in hand, my mood has completely changed. It's dark at my writing table today, despite the sun. This enormous sheet of paper comes from your Sabel portfolio, and that's why I'm using it. The mail delivery brought a postcard from Hammelburgers, your cards to us and Fischel; Aunt Frida got congratulations from Johanna Rindsberger in Würzburg to whom we did not speak yesterday. Early this morning I filed a return at the tax office for Frida R[oederer];[6] beforehand I had kohlrabi and potatoes. Mother had already gone into town. Last night Franz Schweizer[7] told us that he would come by this morning. He will bring me the English translation. Hirsch-Fischel said yesterday that they had a box of candy ready for you; Lina[8] is skeptical as always and insists that she had given you her gift several days previously and that it had nothing to do with your departure. She made the right decision.

Yesterday I also calculated a delay of one hour and told myself 8:20 + 1 hour = 9:20; and distance to the apartment = 10:00, and then I was still somewhat off. It's really a shame that you didn't teach me to write Hebrew; I could have learned it really well from you, and then I would be able to understand Paul Fleischmann's[9] long lists of data, *Sidra*,[10] and so on. Dear Uncle Ari is a maven in this field, while dear Aunt Trude is at about my level. My telephone call gave dear Mother the greatest possible happiness. It would have been nonsense if you had called. Also it could have been a mistake; you didn't know if we were already back from Würzburg. But, if you

---

[6]Frida Roederer was Hugo's widowed sister.
[7]Franz Schweizer was the cousin of Hugo's brother Emil's deceased first wife, Anna Schweizer. Paula Schweizer was Franz's mother.
[8]Lina was the family's maid.
[9]Paul Fleischmann was Rosi's second cousin, the son of Hugo's first cousin Jacob Fleischmann and his wife Heddy. The Fleischmanns also lived in Nuremberg and the two families were very close.
[10]A sidra is the weekly Torah portion read during the Sabbath service. Rosi had been learning Hebrew in the years before she left Germany. It's not clear why Hugo interrupts his discussion of the phone call with this seeming digression.

need to or simply wish to call, then do it like Paula Schweizer, on a collect basis. We don't want to argue about whether Uncle Ari has more in guilders than I do in marks, but, however that may be, we'll stay with return calls.

The intermezzo with the water closet could have turned out even more embarrassing if you had used it in a different way from the one I was thinking of. We were of course enormously happy to hear from you that everything was going well, and today with Phanodorm we slept somewhat longer than usual. At 7:05 I was the first in the bathroom, and, because at 7:35 Mother was still preoccupied with your card that had been stamped in Düsseldorf, I was just able to smuggle her into the bathroom while Aunt Frida was on her way to the same place. Disappointed, as so often, she had to withdraw with her remarks about waiting so long already. You're familiar with this, or rather our, early morning daily radio show. Fellheimer was here with me early, at the desk to settle accounts and mainly to ask about you. I calculated 36 marks + the cost of water + baths at 75 pfennigs each. If I had left it at the old price of 40 marks, he would have been satisfied. At least Mother helped me out with a mark, since I only came up with 35 marks. Today, as an exception, I'm writing down all the details so that you won't miss a thing, although I know that you particularly enjoy dispensing with everything trivial and unimportant. It's not going to be said about my reports, "One must read it daily, one must wash him daily,"[11] and so on.

Fränkel called while I was out and told Mother that he will come this afternoon at 3:45; he was happy and enthusiastic. Because last night we wanted to enjoy our conversation with you quite alone and undisturbed, we carried the telephone into the bedroom. It was still there this morning, and since it's a long climb up the stairs, by the

---

[11]Hugo's meaning is unclear. He and Rosi might have been sharing a private joke.

time I got there, the phone had stopped ringing and we missed the call. I'm sure the caller was Ludwig Mosbacher,[12] wanting to tell me that he's leaving this morning. Aunt Frida received a summons for four o'clock this afternoon to fulfill her duties as a valiant *Chevra* woman.[13] It's almost 12:00, and Franz is still not here.

And now, my dear Rosi, I believe I've reported all the events of the day. We're happy to be in touch, through you, with all our loved ones there, and, even though every visit involves more or less work, and, if we also infinitely regret that Aunt Trude is not as well as she should be and without help, we are nevertheless enormously pleased that the dear aunt has this work with you because we are firmly convinced that she and all her loved ones are sincerely pleased with you. It is too bad that the times have so hardened us that we pass by many situations where it should be our duty to stop and that we almost have to force ourselves to be uninterested, because we lack the possibility of coming up with something that might help the other person. Still, these deficiencies must not be allowed to spread, something of the old tradition has to remain, and love and mutual affection between siblings and their children, etc., must still be cultivated insofar as nothing stands in the way. Give our most sincere greetings to every single one of our dear ones there.

Franz was just here, at 12:30, and brought the English that I, of course, have to copy as clearly as possible if it is not to turn into some other foreign language through Miss Fränkel. Now, dear Rosi, the only thing I have left to do is to shout out the old watchword: Be careful! And you know quite well, dear Rosi, how I've always wanted you to be careful in all your actions. Not only when you're crossing the street and in heavy traffic. I know, too, that you understand well what we mean by this because you,

---

[12] Ludwig Mosbacher was Hugo's first cousin. He and his family were leaving Nuremberg for England and later the United States.
[13] Frida volunteered to wash the bodies of the dead for a Jewish burial society (Chevra Kadisha).

dear Rosi, have called out the same watchword to us. I don't know whether I've already told you this once, or more than once, or not at all. When I was a young chap and was with some friends at an especially lively party where perhaps more was drunk than was advisable and customary and where more money was spent than I could afford and the conversation and a number of other things went a bit too far, I excused myself for five minutes, stepped out of the tavern, and thought about my life and about my unassuming parents, who at that hour had already long been in their beds, and I also thought of all the things of that they, quite justifiably, would not approve, and I preached a moral sermon to myself. Because of this and this alone, I never again overstepped the boundaries that had already been violated. I came to my senses that evening because I asked myself: Who are you, from whom do you come, what are you? I always recollect the late, clever Schorsch Cahn from Mainz who so often told me, in his Mainzer dialect: "One man's permissible pleasure is another man's great crime." What I'm trying to say with these expostulations is that, once you are no longer beneath the parental roof, you have taken a greater responsibility upon yourself than if you were still at home. You have to look after your health, you must not overexert yourself, you must exercise caution in everything you do and undertake, be it in eating, drinking, swimming, canoeing, working, sleeping. In all activities and inactivities, in a word, or perhaps two: "Have the greatest sense of responsibility" or "Be careful." The two are identical.

And now, after this outpouring, the warmest greetings and heartiest kisses to you, my dear good Rosi, from your father.

[Franz's note on the reverse side.]

Rosili:
Good that you're gone. "How pleased I am, how pleased I am."[14] Your faithful and devoted servant, Franisme [?]. *Dei gratia*.

[Also on the reverse side.]

My dear Rosi,
When Father handed me his letter to read, I had to laugh heartily at his thoroughness. It's unbelievable; you've barely been gone and Father already has so much to report. However, dear Rosi, you will always be with us. How happy we were when we heard yesterday that you had arrived safe and well, and how much I would have liked, together with you, to talk longer to my good Trudl. If only.... When we got home last night it was so quiet and empty, and early this morning how I missed hearing you call out "Breakfast, Mother!" We'll slowly have to become accustomed to being alone. I was in town this morning, which caused me to miss Franz's visit, but Frida says that he'll come to see us tomorrow evening. You must have been astonished, dear Rosi, when you saw your cousins. I doubt that you recognized Ruth and Carla at all.

Dear Ari, we were very pleased to get your recent letter. Now you can hear all the details from Rosi. Dear Trudl, don't exert yourself so much; we hope you'll get some help soon. I had a most enjoyable bath early this morning. The warmest greetings and kisses to all of you and most especially to you, dear Rosi, from your mother.

---

[14] From *Three Sisters* by Russian author Anton Chekhov.

The Mosbacher Family in June 1939

By the time of this June 1939 letter, the Nazi government had deprived German Jews of their citizenship, prohibited them from practicing professions or owning businesses, and barred them from schools, public transportation, and public venues. All Jews had to carry identity cards stamped with "J." The Nazis registered the middle names of all Jewish men as "Israel" and of all Jewish women as "Sara."

On Kristallnacht, the Night of the Broken Glass, November 9, 1938, the Nazis sacked and looted Jewish shops and synagogues. They arrested nearly 30,000 Jewish men and detained them in concentration camps. Hundreds died there, but most were released in the next three months on the condition that they apply for emigration from Germany. Hugo was sent to Dachau on November 12, 1938, and released on December 19, 1938.

Rosi remembered having to deliver the family's silver and other valuables to a municipal office after Kristallnacht as part of the punitive fine of one billion Reichsmark (some 400 million US dollars at 1938 rates) demanded of the German Jewish community to pay for the damage done to their property. The Reich government confiscated all insurance payouts to Jews whose businesses and homes were looted or destroyed, leaving the Jewish owners personally responsible for the cost of all repairs.

According to Rosi, Hugo's relationship with his non-Jewish business partner lasted until November 1938, when a Nazi decree prohibited Jews from employment. She said that her parents lived on an insurance policy of Uncle Emil's after Hugo was forced to leave his job. The details remain murky. No one knows how the Mosbachers were getting by in this difficult time, but they seem to have had enough money for food. Perhaps they were slowly selling off valuables.

In April 1939, the Jews lost their rights as tenants and the remaining Jewish population of Nuremberg was forced into fifty-two "Judenhäuser" in a designated area of the city. Unrelated people had to share overcrowded apartments. On April 1, 1939, the Mosbachers had to leave their home at Hallerstraße 27 and were relocated to a "Jew house." The National Occupational and Workforce Census of May 17, 1939, enabled the Nazis to register all Jews in Germany. According to census records at the Nuremberg city archives, the Mosbachers were living at Fürther Straße 16 as subtenants of the Schmitt family. As head of household, Hugo completed the census forms, listing eight people: himself, Clemy, Rosi, his sister Frida, their maid Lina, and three other people—Herman Fellheimer, female [?] Hirsch (age 66), and Melanie Fischel née Hirsch (age 56).

Hugo's letter provides a glimpse of German Jews on the move. Rosi is on her way to England; Ari and Trude Knoller are living in Amsterdam, having fled Berlin; Franz's mother, Paula Schweizer, is also a refugee in Amsterdam; and Ludwig and his family are immigrating to the United States.

Rosi's Departure for England

Rosi applied for immigration to the United States in September 1938, at the American Consulate in Stuttgart. Her exit visa from Germany was finally issued in Nuremberg on March 24, 1939, and was valid until March 24, 1941.

In 1939, England began granting emergency refugee status to 70,000 mostly young German Jews, and Rosi took advantage of this opportunity. The British Consulate in Munich issued her visa on April 18, 1939. She left Germany on June 3 or 4 and stopped in Amsterdam to visit her aunt and uncle, Trude and Ari Knoller, and their daughters Ruth and Carla. She left Holland on June 11 and landed in Harwich, the usual port of entry to England, on June 12, 1939.

Meanwhile Hugo and Clemy were still waiting for their valid German passports and exit visas. The Nazis encouraged Jewish emigration and confiscated the assets of those who left; the problem was finding a country to accept Jewish refugees. Like Rosi, Hugo and Clemy had applied for American visas and were waiting for their American immigration quota numbers to come up.[15]

Rosi spoke with them by phone in early June when she was passing through Amsterdam. Her parents called her in England for her twenty-third birthday, July 14, 1939. That was the last time they heard one another's voices.

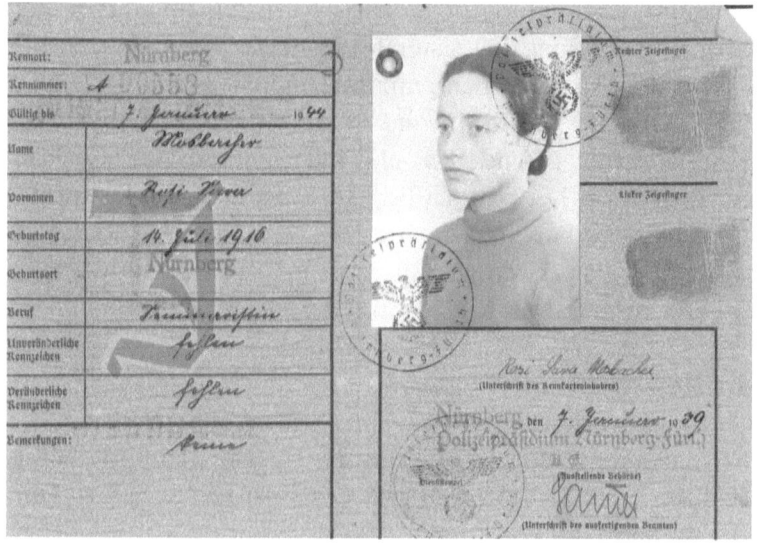

Rosi's German ID card was issued in 1939. It has the large "J" for "Jude"—Jew.

---

[15]Even though the Nazis initially encouraged Jewish emigration, they did not make the process easy. See "Emigration and Immigration Visa Requirements" for a complete list of required paperwork. The annual number of immigrants from Germany to the United States was restricted by the Immigration Act of 1924 (Johnson-Reed Act). If an applicant's name appeared on a list for the year, s/he received a number and waited until the number was reached before appearing at the US Consulate with his/her paperwork.

Rosi's German passport. Rosi's middle name was actually Lisbeth.

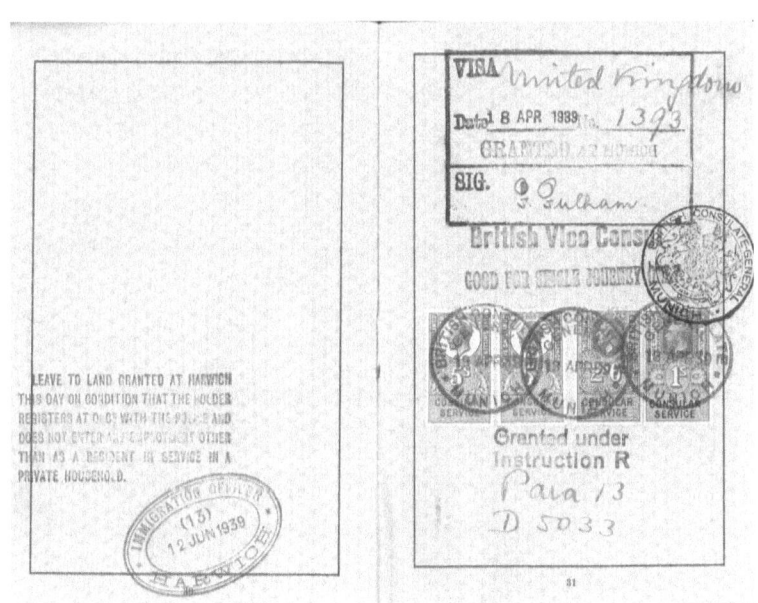

Rosi's British entrance visa. Note that this special visa restricts the holder to employment in domestic service. The British issued these emergency visas under this condition.

[By airmail, postmark unreadable; probably late July 1939.][16]
To: Miss Rosi Mosbacher
c/o Mrs. Eulalie Heron
76 Brockswood Lane
Welwyn Garden City
Herts / England

Friday afternoon

Dear Rosi!

When I returned from the post office where I mailed the letter to you, your two postcards of Wednesday and Thursday had arrived. The communicated reference number is also noted on the letter from Woburn House,[17] Upper Woburn Place, London W.C.J. If people are separated from each other, they think differently. In any case, things will not work out as you imagined, and, if the situation is not clear, nothing will come of it at all. On June 25, Woburn House wrote that, calculating four weeks time at the Home Office, the permits could arrive within the next couple of days. I am sorry to learn of Emil M.'s[18] sickness. With God's help, everything is fine with us, and so, if it's His will, it shall stay like this. Greetings and kisses, Father.

---

[16] Postmark details from postcards are noted. Envelopes for letters were discarded, so postmark details cannot be included for letters.

[17] The Jewish Refugees Committee office in London's Woburn House assisted adults in finding jobs and accommodations. Hugo seems to have been forwarding a letter from Woburn House to Rosi that had come to Germany. Perhaps the permits mentioned have to do with Rosi's temporary visa, employment, or luggage. It's unlikely that Woburn House would be communicating with Hugo and Clemy, as older people were not receiving these temporary work visas. Hugo's concerns are not clear.

[18] Refers to another Emil Mosbacher, Hugo's older cousin, who was in London at the time and who helped Rosi while she was in England. He paid for Rosi's steamship ticket to the United States.

[Postmarked August 25, 1939, in Nuremberg.][19]

My dear Rosi!

It is just now [?]. I came directly from the doctor and am sitting in the train station from where I am sending you my Saturday's greetings. I just had my stomach pumped out, and I have to call in the afternoon to learn the results. The whole thing is surely not serious, but you, dear Rosi, know how upsetting the most trivial things can be. One's nerves certainly play a part. I hope that I can soon report to you that I am well again. For some time I have wanted to ask you whether you have been to the dentist. Have you ever needed suppositories? Please reply to all my questions. Recently I asked how the Ludwigs' dress fits you, but you did not answer. Miss L [refers to Ludwig Mosbacher's wife, Johanna] often inquires about you. She is very agreeable and always extends her greetings to you. We now have very much to do in order to [?]. Everything has to be taken care of step by step. This evening Aunt Dina will be with us. She invited herself. She moved in with Mother Jettchen[20] and hasn't been here. We were satisfied, as was Mother Jettchen. Mrs. Hichenberg received her [immigration] certificate. We hope that Aunt Frida will go to Miltenberg-Würzburg for a few days. This would give me a break from the extensive schmoozing about people that I can hardly endure. Nowadays one is busy with totally different matters. It's fine that you can live with the Rs.[21]

Again, many greetings and kisses from your mother.

---

[19]The upper right corner of the card is torn, so several words are missing.
[20]Jettchen Neumann was the mother of Rosl Neumann and thus the mother-in-law of Emil Mosbacher, Hugo's brother. Hugo refers to her in other letters as "Mother" or "Mother Jettchen." Dina Schweizer was the mother of Emil's first wife, so Emil's two mothers-in-law were living together after they had been forced out of their former homes.
[21]Probably Michel and Selma Rosenstock, cousins who were briefly in England, en route to the United States.

Rosi in England

Initially Rosi worked as a maid for the Heron family in Herts, near London. By the time Rosi received Clemy's August 25, 1939, postcard, she had moved to Penzance in the southern tip of England where she stayed with Heron relatives for several months. The war began in early September 1939, and she moved away from the London area to avoid possible bombing by the Germans.

In late 1939 or early 1940 she began working for the Sudweeks family in Ealing, caring for their infant son Anthony, who was born on October 23, 1938. Anthony and his mother left London in September and, at the insistence of Mr. Sudweeks, moved to Wiltshire to live with his relatives. Mrs. Sudweeks was teaching school in southwestern England. Mr. Sudweeks, however, worked for the fire department and remained in London during the war. Rosi took care of Anthony up until her departure for the United States in late July 1940. Rosi named her first child Anthony.

[Postmarked August 31, 1939.]
To: Miss Rosi Mosbacher
c/o Mrs. Eulalie Heron
76 Brockswood Lane
Welwynn Garden City
Herts / England
[Address above is crossed out and replaced by:]
c/o Mrs. Barr
Mosmond, Greenbank
Penzance, Cornwall

My dear Rosi,

We miss your letters very much, but we hope that something will come soon. There isn't much to report. Father has already written you the main news. Stay well, dear Rosi, and receive many warm regards and kisses from your mother.

[Postmarked August 31, 1939, in Nuremberg.]
c/o Mrs. Eulalie Heron
76 Brockswood Lane
Welwyn Garden City
Herts / England
[Address above is crossed out and replaced by:]
Miss Rosi Mosbacher
c/o Mrs. Barr
Mosmond, Greenbank
Penzance, Cornwall
Thursday, August 31, 1939

My dear Rosi!
    We are happy and satisfied once we can write to you. I think that the mail will gradually start to arrive again. On the occasion of his mother's birthday, Franz was able to talk with A[msterdam?][22] by telephone. I am supposed to write her a letter again. According to Dina, her sister Bloch had news from her grandson Peter, who writes that Fritz Roederer and his young wife will spend eight days of their honeymoon at his home in New York. What I found still more interesting in this story is the legitimate prospect that we, too, will hear from America. In the meantime, have you heard anything about Emil Mosbacher's condition? Right now Lina is particularly busy with urgent shopping for the household. Frau Gugg[enheimer] in Basel had surgery and is bedridden and seriously ill. Yesterday I made a condolence visit to a family named Feuchtwanger (Richard, Paul, Fl [?]), and they asked about you, dear Rosi! They have an eleven-year-old in England and two others, somewhat older, in Palestine. How does it happen that these people know you? The question didn't occur to me until later. Otherwise I'd have asked the Feuchtwangers themselves. Stay well and be heartily greeted and kissed by your father.

---

[22]Probably Amsterdam, indicating that Franz's mother, Paula, was already living there.

[Postmarked September 1, 1939, in Nuremberg.]
To: Miss Rosi Mosbacher
c/o Mrs. Barr
Mosmond, Greenbank,
Penzance, Cornwall
Friday, September 1, 1939[23]

Dear Rosi,

What a great surprise today in the early morning to receive your postcards of Monday 28 and Wednesday 30 about which we were very happy, as you can imagine. We tried it in many ways, also airmail, which is no longer possible.[24] From your notes I see that you received part of our mailings, also that Frida's permit has been sent and, if Berlin is processing it, it will arrive soon. If it will be here, ours are sure to follow. For God's sake, may they be used again in the near future. Even if one had the passports, one would need the visas first, and this probably would make the whole matter fail. There is no doubt that some cases proceeded very quickly and many permits were served a lot faster. But it is useless to bother: Don't complain about things you cannot change! Though I still hope everything will turn out well, despite the gloomy outlook. Whether Franz will visit us today is questionable because his presence is required at the house by the absence of Mrs. Gugg[enheimer]. From Albrecht[25] you probably will hear good news on a very regular basis. From time to time we talk to his parents. Accept many, many greetings and kisses from your father.

[23]On September 1, 1939, Germany invaded Poland, precipitating World War II.

[24]They were not able to send mail. There are long, unexplained breaks in the Mosbachers' correspondence between June 5 and August 25, 1939. Perhaps Germany was restricting mail delivery to England due to increasing tensions between the two countries. Hugo mentions difficulty sending mail to Rosi, and Clemy also mentions problems in her brief note of August 31. After this postcard of September 1 there is another long break until Ari's February 21, 1940, telegram from Amsterdam, suggesting another breakdown in mail service to England after the outbreak of the war.

[25]Albrecht was a beau of Rosi's. His location is never clear, but he seems to have been safe and able to work and to write to Rosi.

Dear Rosi!

This morning we felt immeasurable joy when we received your postcards. Today we are unable to do anything, but everything will be all right. Stay well. Greetings and kisses, Mother.

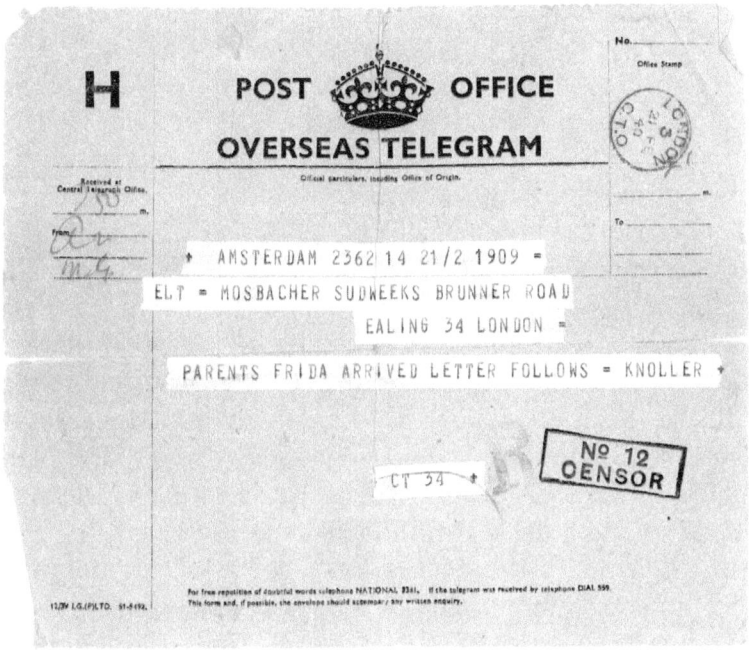

Ari Knoller's telegram to Rosi, dated February 21, 1940, telling her that her parents are in Amsterdam.

Detention in Amsterdam

Increasingly intolerable conditions prompted Hugo and Clemy to change their plan to wait in Germany for their American visas. Hugo's later letters indicate their American immigration quota number came up in early 1940, and they decided to leave Germany while they still could and to complete paperwork for their American visas at the American Consulate in Rotterdam rather than in Stuttgart.

Hugo, Clemy, and Frida deregistered as residents of Nuremberg on February 18, 1940, and they arrived in Holland on February 21, 1940. They had valid German exit visas and passports, but did not have visas to enter Holland, a neutral country. They crossed the border illegally on foot at Oldenzaal, a Dutch border town known to be helpful to refugees fleeing persecution. Their plan was to stay briefly with family members (the Knollers) while their American visas were processed, and they made arrangements to sail from Rotterdam to the United States.

For crossing the border from Germany into Holland without permission, Hugo, Clemy, and Frida were arrested and placed in temporary detention in Amsterdam from February 21 to April 21, 1940. They spent these two months in separate facilities, Hugo in room 54 of the police station at Oudezijds Achterburgwal 185, Clemy and Frida in a women's shelter at Keizersgracht 646.

Hugo describes sitting at a desk all day, walking around the yard once a day, and receiving two visitors a week. Clemy kept busy sewing and knitting for the guards and their families. The formerly shy Clemy became more outgoing during this interlude. Hugo, who usually tried to be positive and upbeat, grew downhearted. It was the first time they had been separated since their marriage in 1911.

[Postmarked February 28, 1940; mailed from the women's detention shelter.]
To: Mr. Alfred Falck
Rue de Palais 23
Brussels[26]
February 26 [1940]

My Dear Ones and dear Rosi!

Not having Rosi's address, today I have to write to you. Surely the dear siblings have informed you that we are here for a few days now. We are well which we hope about you, too. I have not read your recent letters, dear Rosi, but I will catch up. Trudl and Ari are looking very good; the daughters are lovely. I hope that I will be able to write more soon. Today primarily I wanted to send a sign of life. My dears and dear Rosi, accept many hearty greetings and kisses from your Clemy/mother.

Also from me and particularly to you, dear Rosi, many hearty greetings, Frida.

---

[26] Clemy sent her first postcard from Amsterdam detention to Rosi by way of her half-sister Erna and brother-in-law Albert Falck, who had fled Berlin in 1939 and were living in Brussels. Apparently Clemy did not know Rosi's English address since Rosi had moved. She was also letting Erna know that she and Hugo had reached Holland. This postcard was the first communication from her parents that Rosi had had since the beginning of the war between England and Germany the previous September, so they had reason to want to communicate with her quickly.

Photo courtesy Royal National Archives

The Women's Detention Shelter (Tehuis voor Vrouwen) at Keizersgracht 646. This photograph dates from the 1920s. Clemy and Frida were detained here from February 21 to April 21, 1940.

Photo courtesy of Jack Boas

The police station at Achterburgwal 185 where Hugo was held in detention in room number 54. The photo was taken in 2012.

March 1, 1940
Amsterdam
Achterburgwal 185
Kamer 54[27]

My dear Rosi!

On the afternoon of Sunday, February 18, we left [Nuremberg], arrived in K[öeln] at 12:30 at night, and spent the night in the waiting room until the morning. Then we continued our journey for several more hours and spent the remainder of Tuesday, until seven in the evening, partly in D[üsseldorf] and partly in another town. In the meantime you will probably have heard about our arrival and subsequent events. I visited Mother last Sunday and have permission to visit her again on the coming Sunday. Thank God, she is well, [unlike?] Aunt Frida who, at the moment, unfortunately, doesn't look at all well. Of course, we imagined that the beginning would be very different and never had the slightest notion that we would encounter such difficulties. Sometimes it's good not to know everything ahead of time; our decisions would have been quite different. Still, we hope that our problems will soon be resolved. After all we do have a waiting number[28] and the consulate in Rotterdam has already gone past it. I am staying here with a married couple and observing the [Jewish] rituals. We can buy extras like butter, cheese, and fruit with the money[29] we placed on deposit. I'm using the time to learn English, something I totally neglected at home. It's high time that I catch up so that I won't be totally ignorant.

I haven't yet read your letters that just arrived here, but I hope to get to them soon. Mother and I are completely

---

[27]The address of the local police office where Hugo was being kept in temporary detention.
[28]They had finally received their American immigration quota numbers, no doubt another reason they decided to leave Germany and wait for their number to come up in Holland.
[29]Apparently they were able to take some money out of Germany.

out of our wits and will be happy to get some stability in our lives again and to start getting news from you as we were doing. Our friend who stayed behind, for whom I would have had to do a lot of work, will also find out over time what is causing the problem. He has already communicated with us several times, but we still don't know what's going on.[30] Of course, we thought that Lina would be able to carry out our instructions from here, a little at a time, but she will be able to manage the closure without us. I believe that it's possible that our baggage and some of Frida's has been forwarded in the meantime. We received the packing permit accidentally, while Frida has not gotten hers. In the last months they were only issued to those who could show a visa at the Deviezen[31] office. Of course we would be greatly helped if we could get just a little of our wardrobe; right now we have only the clothes that we were wearing when we arrived. We left the furniture behind, except what we could sell. I already received a few visitors. Lenchen, Henriette, Bruno were here already; Trude was here yesterday because I had to fill out a questionnaire for the consulate.

The day ends at 7:30 p.m. and starts again at 7:30 in the morning. We are treated in a very humane and proper manner. If I were a young fellow, the stay here might be quite beneficial. However, since I already have a lot behind me and worries about what is ahead of me, this intermezzo is quite inconvenient. I feel especially sorry for our dear mother and Aunt Frida who have never experienced anything like this in their whole lives. Also, it's especially distressing to the feminine temperament. Still, the main thing is that we all get through it in good health and then recuperate. Today I already feel quite calm and collected, and we aren't lacking for company.

---

[30]Franz was the friend in Nuremberg. Hugo was obscure about the "problem" that Franz had to see to.

[31]The Foreign Currency Office. They needed to show a Dutch or American visa, which they did not have in hand, to ship their luggage to Holland, but somehow they were given the permit anyway. Frida was not so lucky.

I'm sorry that you have to go without the usual exchange of letters, but the knowledge that we have moved somewhat closer to you will have to serve as a consolation to you for now. I hope Cousin Ludwig is up and around again. Special greetings to him and his family. I would also like to send our special greetings to Cousin Emil. During the final days, when Franz and I were discussing the "what ifs" and the "howevers," he said, quite correctly, that one should never imagine that one is going to go from an extremely unsatisfactory situation directly into Paradise. I completely understood that. Nevertheless, my notion of a mediocre situation was rather different. But this too will turn out well! With many, many warmest greetings and kisses from your parents who love you.

What cannot be cured must be endured.[32]

[Postmarked March 4, 1940.]
To: Miss Rosi Mosbacher
c/o Sudweeks
34 Brunner Road—Ealing
London W5
March 1, 1940

My dear Rosi!

How nice that I can directly write to you. I think about you constantly. Today Aunt Trudl visited us and told us about your letters. To me the most important thing is that you, my dear, are well as we are, too. Also Father is looking good. Maybe we will talk to each other [on the phone?]. We hope for Ludwig to have recovered. Things are moving along, dear Rosi. Write to us often and receive many greetings and kisses from your mother. To your employers best regards and kisses for the baby.

---

[32]In English in the bottom left corner of the page.

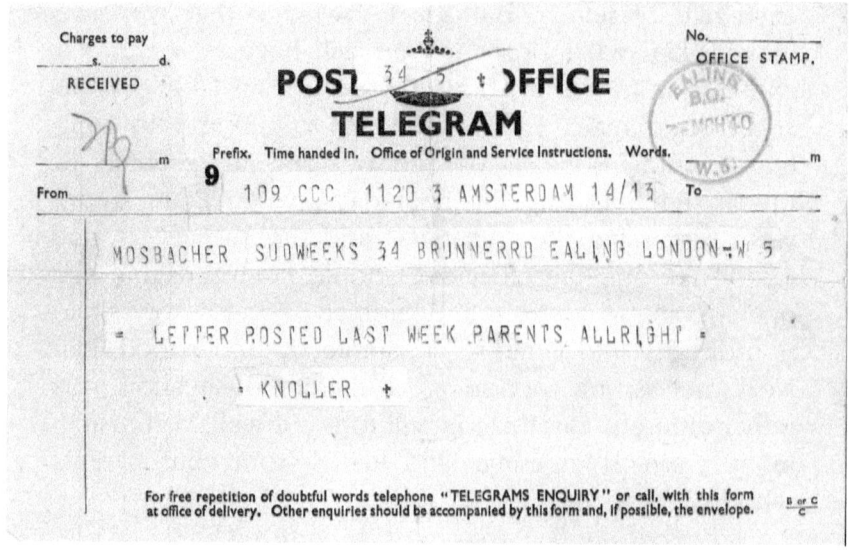

Ari's telegram telling Rosi to expect Hugo's March 1 letter.

March 6, 1940

My dear Rosi!

There is, to be sure, not much to report from here, but still you ought to hear something from me. Father told me on Sunday that he had written you a complete account; he is certainly able to do that. Above all, I don't have your mail, that Trude received and has partially read aloud to us, but to respond to it I ought to have it here. I hope, dear Rosi, that you're doing well and likewise your little charge. Now that spring is approaching you'll surely be going out more with him to take the air. We can see the sun so nicely through the window here; if only we will soon be able to enjoy it. Aunt Lenchen[33] was here today. I've never seen her looking so well. Her visit was unfor-

---
[33] Lenchen was Helene Mosbacher van Gelder, another of Hugo's sisters.

tunately very brief, but we were happy to have talked to each other. Trude will come at the end of the week. I believe she is going to go to the dear Falcks on Sunday. Lina will find it hard to understand why we haven't written. She'll have a lot to do in the next few weeks since she has to break up the household. I think Franz will help her. We have received various communications from him here, in the mail that we haven't yet read. We haven't heard anything from his mother. Trude was here together with Ella Cohn (Goldberger)[34] this week. There is no lack of acquaintances.

We often long to be with you, dear Rosi, and I'm sure the feeling is mutual. I hope, God willing, that we find a way to see each other again. Stay well—that's the main thing. Aunt Frida is my bedfellow. She sends her regards. My good one, receive many warm kisses and greetings from your mother.

[Postmark date illegible.]
From: Hugo Mosbacher
O.Z. Achterburgwal 185
Kamer 54

To: Miss Rosi Mosbacher
c/o Sudweeks
34 Brunner Road—Ealing
London W5
Friday, March 8, 1940

My dear Rosi!

For some time I hesitated to reply, hoping maybe to do it from another place, but unfortunately it seems to take a very long time until a decision is made. On Sunday I will be with Mother again, and I assume that she is as well as I am. Twice this week I received visitors, and they

---

[34] Ella Cohn Goldberger was Clemy's good friend from Germany.

are optimistic, as I would be in their situation. I am looking forward to reading all your letters soon that arrived in the meantime. I haven't heard from Lina and hope that over there everything is also developing normally. Even if not, it's none of my business. I think that the correspondence between the consulates in Stuttgart and Rotterdam will take a fortnight.[35] Those gentlemen have no mercy with us. Tomorrow the *Rosh Chodesh*[36] will be solemnized, but not at our place. The gentlemen we have to deal with here all are obliging and nice; I am used to different treatment.[37] Ari is in Brussels at an exhibition for a couple of days. The miserable appearance of Aunt Frida is worrying me a little. I think as soon as she is released she will recuperate quickly. By now I've gotten used to the never-ending nights, as I am no longer afraid of them after seventeen days. What do you hear from Albrecht? His parents and many others must have been astonished about our secret departure. Franz had to explain it to Dina by telling her that we were summoned to the consulate. It's not good to have reason to worry so much about oneself. Dear Rosi, accept heartfelt greetings and many kisses from your *father.*

---

[35] Another indication that Hugo and Clemy had received their American immigration quota number through the American Consulate in Stuttgart while they were still in Germany, but had decided to complete their immigration paperwork in Holland.
[36] Literally the "head of the month" in Hebrew; the first day of the month is celebrated as a minor Jewish holiday. Rosh Chodesh of Adar II was on March 10, 1940.
[37] Probably refers to the treatment of Jews in Nazi Germany.

[Postmarked March 16, 1940.]
Miss Rosi Mosbacher
c/o Sudweeks
34 Brunner Road—Ealing
London W5

C. Mosbacher
Keizersgracht 646
March 14, 1940

Dear Rosi!

I heard through Lenchen, who visited us yesterday, that mail had arrived from you, dear Rosi. I hope to hear something from Trude tomorrow, since Friday is her visiting day. On Wednesday it will be three weeks already that we are here. The time is passed with knitting and reading. Once a day I repeat my English vocabulary that still is pitifully poor. I think a lot about you, dear Rosi, and all our beloved ones. Days are so long. Soon the Ludwigs will start their long journey—where will it end? Our belongings have arrived safely;[38] Aunt Frida is still waiting for hers. I hope for you, dear Rosi, to be well and cheerful. Receive many greetings and kisses from your mother.

My dear Rosi,

We are so close and yet so far apart. I hope we will see each other before we depart for the U.S.A. Lovingly yours, Aunt Frida.

---

[38]Hugo and Clemy had shipped their essential household items and clothing to Rotterdam to await loading onto their ship for the United States.

[Postmarked March 16, 1940.]
to: Miss Rosi Mosbacher
c/o Sudweeks
34 Brunner Road—Ealing
London W5
Friday, March 15, 1940

My dear Rosi!

    The situation, unfortunately, remains the same. However, praise God, we are well and we shouldn't lose confidence yet. From visitors, I have also heard news about you, dear Rosi. I won't be able to comment on everything until my hands are free. I hope we hear soon when our turn is going to come in Rotterdam. Our baggage is there already, and I hope that Aunt Frida's will also arrive. Next Friday I have *yahrzeit*[39] and the Sunday after that is *Purim*. Will things have changed in our favor by then? I have never been separated from your dear mother for such a long time, and I am looking forward to the day after tomorrow, although we can only spend an hour together. The Doktors[40] have written a letter filled with expressions of gratitude. Unfortunately they will have to dampen their enthusiasm somewhat when they learn about the affair. Mother Jettchen[41] is said to be well and situated safely with a family, surely Belgians. We don't know, either, where the Doktors will finally settle down. I wish Ludwig's family a good crossing. I would be happy if I could start getting your reports again soon. We still hope that everything will work out in the end. Best wishes and many warm greetings and kisses from your father.

---

[39]The anniversary of his father's death.
[40]Hugo referred to his brother Emil, an obstetrician, and Emil's wife Rosl as "the Doktors." He often used a husband's first name to identify a couple, for example "the Ludwigs." Perhaps because there was another Emil Mosbacher, he distinguished his brother and sister-in-law as "the Doktors." Emil was not aware that Hugo and Clemy were being held in a Dutch detention center. Emil, Rosl, and their children had been in the United States since October 1938.
[41]Jettchen (Rosl's mother) was temporarily in Belgium, on her way to the United States.

[Postmarked March 21, 1940.]
To: Miss Rosi Mosbacher
c/o Sudweeks
34 Brunner Road—Ealing
London W5

From: C. Mosbacher
Keizersgracht 646
March 20, 1940

Dear Rosi,

Father visited us on Monday and brought us your letter, dear Rosi, which pleased me very, very much. You can imagine how I keep expecting Father from one week to the next. It's a long time since we were separated like this. Aunt Lenchen was here today, and Friday is Trude's day to visit. We hear very little from all the other dear ones, but we'll make up for everything as soon as we are back on our feet again. I brought along a calendar for you, dear Rosi; perhaps you don't have one yet. *Purim* is this Saturday, but we won't take much notice of it. We are well taken care of here in my women's shelter, and today it is four weeks that we have been here. Franz's mother[42] was asking about us. She will hardly be able to visit us now.

[On the address side of folding stationery.]

There isn't much I can report to you from here, but the main thing is that you know that we are well, and we hope the same for you. Dear Rosi, receive many affectionate greetings and kisses from your mother.
Amsterdam, March 21, 1940

---

[42]Franz's mother, Paula Schweizer, was in Amsterdam, apparently in poor mental health. Hugo frequently expressed his concern about her and about Franz's inadequate replies.

My dear Rosi!

On Monday, March 18, I received your letter of March 11, and yesterday, the twentieth, your letter written on March 13 and posted on the fourteenth. So one needs to allow for a delivery time of about six days. On Monday Mother had a visiting day, and I was able to bring her your letter. As you can quite vividly imagine, we are extraordinarily pleased with your good reports. It's too bad that we still can't write to you in such a satisfactory way. In the meantime it will have become clear to you that today is the fast day [43] and that the coming Sunday is *Purim*. It's too bad that now, for the second time, I am unable to keep the *yahrzeit* of my blessed father's death in a worthy manner. The first time was 1938 in Dachau.[44] Fortunately my current place of residence is not dangerous, but I understandably have the urgent wish that this sojourn, which is preferable to the former, may be ended very soon. My wish especially applies to dear Mother and to Aunt Frida; the latter looks still shockingly bad. So far this week I had only a visit from Aunt Lenchen, who at this time is in good shape.

Franz is corresponding a lot with Trude—more, I believe, than she likes. Of course I should have visited Franz's mother long ago. I regret very much that right now I cannot do it at all. I take it as settled that Els[45] is taking care of both my old and new affidavits and will see that everything gets to the consulate in Rotterdam.

---

[43]Ta'anit Esther fell on Thursday, March 21, 1940. The Fast of Esther is a Jewish fast from dawn until dusk on Purim eve, commemorating the three-day fast observed by the Jewish people in the story of Purim. If Erev Purim falls on the Sabbath, as it did in 1940, the fast is observed on the preceding Thursday.

[44]When Hugo was imprisoned for thirty-eight days at Dachau during November/December 1938, he probably missed his mother's *yahrzeit*. Sigmund Mosbacher died on March 5, 1917, and Karoline Mosbacher died on November 27, 1917, from an earlier, less virulent strain of the Spanish flu that swept through Central Europe.

[45]Els, Elisabeth van Gelder, was Lenchen's daughter who lived in Amsterdam and worked for the Committee for Jewish Refugees in the

It's regrettable that three-fourths of the Doktors' family is ill. When opportunity arises, we must take possession of our suitcases. Thank God that they arrived in Rotterdam. They left Hamburg as part of a shipment of general freight, and the final station on the route happened to be Rotterdam. Naturally we have to get it sent here [Amsterdam] because we arrived here with only a single handbag—you know that one of mine. Praise God, you will be well provided this *Pesach* [Passover] with matzos, salads, and fish. It would be nicer if we would sit again at the same table with you, my dear Rosi; *Pesach* is, after all, the most beautiful of the feasts. I have enriched my small vocabulary with "prunes." Unfortunately I have no one here to correct my pronunciation. Rutchen [Ruth Knoller], Els, Mau [?], and Freddy are the ones I haven't yet seen. It seems that I see more chocolate here than you do there. When I go to visit Mother it is always possible for me to be able to take her oranges, chocolate, figs, and so on. Does Ces,[46] more precisely known as Huntie, have an absolutely pleasant life there, or does she lack a lot of things? What does Frida Maier write from the U.S.A. to her brother Emil? I believe that she will hold her own anywhere, but Jettchen, who is so very different—what a marked contrast between these two women—leads perhaps a happier life. We are so happy to know that you are among decent people with whom you feel relatively

Netherlands, an organization that was established in 1933 to provide financial aid, emigration advice, and lodging to the stream of German and later Austrian, Czech, and Polish Jews seeking safety in Holland. This is the committee that Hugo refers to in his 1940 letters. Apparently Hugo has asked Els for her help with their immigration paperwork. She may have been able to help Hugo at this point, but later, after the German invasion, when Hugo asked for her help renewing their American visas and obtaining exit visas from the Netherlands, the committee had little influence.

[46]Cecile Mosbacher, Hugo's first cousin, was married to her second cousin, Sali Mosbacher, the younger brother of Hugo's cousins Emil Mosbacher (England) and Frida Maier (United States). Ces and Sali had been living in England since the late 1890s. Frida Maier provided assistance to Emil and Rosl.

good. I've already noticed that one can make a teacher into a butcher; the opposite is probably less frequent. That dear Anthony finds the "R" [in Rosi] difficult is much more understandable. Where could Ri[47] be? At the shelter, Mother has the opportunity to do a lot of knitting. For the shelter, naturally.

And now, dear Rosi, receive many greetings and fervent kisses from your father.

Many greetings to Uncle Emil[48] and the Ludwigs.

Just this afternoon I had a summons to the American Consulate in Rotterdam on Tuesday, March 26 (apparently this is, to begin with, for me alone).

[Written in pencil.]
March 26, 1940

Dear Rosi!

I suspect that Father has a letter from you; he went to Rotterdam today, and, as I heard, we have an appointment for an examination on April 4. Aunt Frida will also certainly get a summons within the next few days. You can imagine how happy this makes me. Father came to see me Saturday, and tomorrow I hope to get a report from him about Rotterdam since he promised to write to me. Trude did not visit on Friday, but we were compensated for it yesterday. You can imagine how happy every visit makes us. We are so cut off now and a pile of correspondence is waiting to be answered, but that can all be dealt with. I hope, dear Rosi, that the holidays weren't too stressful; I'm sure you cooked something good. Some recipes are enclosed; I'll send some more soon. Have Ludwig's[49] family already left or are they still getting

---

[47]Ri for Rosi? Perhaps a reference to a baby game that Rosi played with Anthony.
[48]Hugo probably meant his cousin Emil in London. He sometimes referred to this older cousin as Rosi's uncle.
[49]The Ludwigs were Ludwig and Johanna Mosbacher, who spent a year in London before immigrating to the United States.

ready? Trude tells me that a thick letter from Alfons[50] is waiting for us. He is earning eighteen dollars a week and has a job as a foreman at a construction site. He starts work at eight in the morning and stops at four, and he hopes to find a second job for the rest of his time. Fredl[51] is also earning; he's working in hides so it's in his trade. Dear Rosi, I have so little to write to you from here. Every day is the same except when we have a visitor. Right now I'm knitting a woolen blouse for Aunt Lenchen; I enjoy that very much. Little Anton[52] must be very sweet—can you send us a photo? Dear Rosi, accept my warmest greetings, stay well, and feel yourself being hugged by your mother.

[Written in pencil.]
Amsterdam, March 27, 1940

My dear Rosi!

When I returned yesterday from Rotterdam, your letter of the eigthteenth was there to greet me. It made me very happy and will make Mother very happy as soon as she gets it. First to Rotterdam. The consular review was carried out in my presence. First there were the various questions (where I plan to settle, what I plan to do, etc.) that I was only able to answer indecisively and not quite openly. After I had described my current situation, the Consul's young interpreter expressed the opinion that it would be a very good idea if my guarantor, Mrs. Rubens,[53] would set up a trust fund on my behalf in the amount of $3,000: that is $100 per month for two and a half years or thirty

---

[50]Alfons Adler, Clemy's brother, his wife Irma (who was also Hugo's niece), and their children Frank and Ruth were living in Columbia, South Carolina.
[51]Fredl Adler, another brother in the United States.
[52]The baby, Anthony Sudweeks.
[53]Pauline Rubens was a distant cousin living in Chicago whose sponsorship made it possible for Rosi to come to the United States. She also helped Hugo and Clemy. In both cases, she had to vouch that her financial resources would protect the US from any of the Mosbachers becoming "public charges."

months. I expressed my agreement with this suggestion because I have no doubt that Emil will be able to obtain this additional guarantee from Mrs. Rubens on my behalf without difficulty. The Consul is demanding this because Mrs. R. is already elderly, and in the event of her death I would have no security. Perhaps if I had laid more emphasis on Emil's position it would have been easier, but, in a preliminary discussion with the Committee here, I was advised against this.

Mother and I have been summoned to Rotterdam for Thursday, April 4, for a medical examination. Then, once the guarantee arrives, nothing—God willing—will stand in the way of our visa. I think that Aunt Frida will also receive her summons to Rotterdam soon, and that the much closer relationship (Mother) will not cause her any difficulty.[54] I was happy to hear from Brother Emil, confidentially, that my cousin, who is also Emil's namesake, has kept his promise to make three hundred available for us, and that New York is interested in seeing that we get these funds as soon as possible. I will write to Cousin Emil as soon as I have time. This is a very, very noble action! I beg you to speak of this to no one else, but you may refer to it when speaking to him.

You can well imagine that we are anxious and very desirous of a favorable decision. Today is the thirty-sixth day since our arrival. I was with Mother on Saturday; she is more than fed up. I saw Els yesterday for the first time, on the way to Rotterdam. She and Ari now have to send a telegram to New York. It is wretched when one cannot attend to one's most urgent affairs oneself. Mrs. Tuchmann's[55] contact to Ces is by way of Ces' sister-in-law

---

[54] Hugo's meaning is unclear.
[55] Mrs. Tuchmann was the wife of Hugo's former business partner. In 1911, at the time of his marriage to Clemy, Hugo became the junior partner in Montangesellschaft A. Tuchmann & Co., a metal wholesaler in Nuremberg. Mr. Tuchmann died around 1928, and a Gentile employee, Mr. Heubeck, bought out Tuchmann's interest. "Aryan" ownership enabled the firm to stay in business after the Nazis came to power. Heubeck died in 1935 or 1936 (Rosi was not sure), but somehow Hugo was able to keep the business going until shortly after Kristallnacht.

and other grievances, we are happy to have escaped many things of which to be legitimately afraid.[57]

We are not in touch with Lina, but I assume that she knows the reason for our silence. Aunt Frida is still lacking the first invitation to Rotterdam. I have not seen my brother-in-law [Philip van Gelder] since the day of our arrival and Bruno only one time also. Naturally we are wondering how you, dear Rosi, want to realize your plans and particularly what they comprise. Because we do not know them at this time, we cannot comment on them, as the late Hichenberg[58] always said. He would be amused if I could give him a regular daily report. Your reports are the only ones that we read. From the others coming in we only hear excerpts. God willing, we will soon be able to communicate good news. With most heartfelt greetings and heartiest kisses—your loving father.

April 3, 1940

My dearest Rosi,

Early today there were two letters from you: one of March 27 and the one addressed to me, of March 20, which gave me very special happiness. In the future, you need to write to me at Father's address since all the letters go first to Achterburgwal. By the way, as you may well believe, we would like to change this address as soon as possible. Father has to go tomorrow to an inquiry; we hope everything will go well. We spoke to Aunt Trude on Monday. She read portions of three of your letters to us. You are truly good, dear Rosi, and you know, too, how much joy your writings give us. Trudl told us that she recently visited Franz's mother. She is living quite modestly in one room and has her worries.

---

[57]Hugo did not often directly refer to Jewish suffering in Germany. This sentence indicates his awareness of the growing danger, which might account for their sudden, risky flight to Holland.
[58]Hugo quoted Hichenberg's comic wisdom several times in his letters. Hichenberg may have been a business associate or family friend. Clemy mentioned Mrs. Hichenberg in her August 25, 1939, postcard.

There are a lot of books available to me here, but I will only be able to read the book that you recommended to us when I am on the outside again. I find it extremely nice of the [Michels?][59] to invite you; they will certainly go to the U.S.A. soon. Has Ludwig's family left yet? God willing, we shall follow them soon. Rosi, day and night I think about how a reunion with you will be possible. Of course, when we are free it will be easier to discuss everything. Your reports of Anthony are very amusing. Dear Rosi, you are entirely right to have the zipper done properly by a seamstress. I used to have your other things mended by a seamstress from time to time. After all, all kinds of things do get damaged in the household. Father will have to answer your inquiry about the consulate. I was able to wash your colorfast pullover very nicely. I am amazed at the beautiful wool here; we are not used to it. Anthony's parents will probably think plenty about having such an operation. By the way, I believe that it hardly has success. I can understand that Ces is not your cup of tea, but she certainly means well toward all of us. People certainly have succeeded in coming together. Has her Mrs. Tuchmann been recommended?[60] Dear Rosi, you will hear from us again soon. Receive many greetings and many kisses from your mother.

Friday, April 5, 1940

My dear Rosi!

I hope you are well and in possession of our reports. Yesterday we traveled to Rotterdam and returned to our shelters at about five in the afternoon. Presumably the medical examination went well. The next stage of the process will be that the American Consulate will be informed of that fact. Then I must present the testimonials

---

[59] The name is unclear but may be Michels, Michel and Selma Rosenstock.
[60] Hugo may be asking if Mrs. Tuchmann has obtained a support affidavit from an American sponsor, part of the paperwork necessary for her United States visa application.

of good behavior during our stay in Amsterdam, as well as twenty dollars. By the time all these things have been done, the written bank guarantee will have arrived. We received the telegraphic notification of this yesterday before we left for Rotterdam. Aunt Frida will soon receive her first summons to come to Rotterdam also.

For the first time in many weeks I was able to have a long, pleasant talk with Mother. We complained to each other about our misfortunes, but obviously only briefly because we didn't want to spoil our day. Trude told me that reports have arrived there from you, dear Rosi, as well as some for us there from the Ludwigs. Because it always takes so long here until the letters have been censored,[61] the relatives prefer to hold them for us. Since we lack so many things, we also lack any topics of conversation. My only purpose in my letters to you, dear Rosi, is that you hear from us that, thank God, we are well. Since coming here I have written only one single card to the U.S.A. I have no desire whatever to correspond. All I can do is to hope from one day to the next that the day of liberation will come, especially since our own exodus is so near.

Perhaps it would have been more correct if, despite all fears, I had remained true to the principles for which I have always stood so emphatically. But, as Cousin Max[62] wrote long ago from the U.S.A., with reference to our situation, when you are confronted with such grave danger, what is there that you will not do? When the house next-door is on fire, one has to risk a leap from the fourth floor.

I've requested permission for another visit for next Monday.

Dear Rosi, we look forward with pleasure to the reports that are on their way from you. Accept the warmest greetings and most fervent kisses from your father who loves you.

---

[61]Presumably by the Dutch prison authorities.
[62]Probably Max Fleischmann.

From: Hugo Mosbacher
Amsterdam
O.Z. Achterburgwal 185

To: Miss Rosi Mosbacher
34 Brunner Road—Ealing
London W5
Tuesday, April 9, 1940

My dear Rosi!

Yesterday we received your lovely lines that pleased us enormously. In the afternoon I visited Mother for a chat. We particularly enjoyed your message that we may expect you coming here, dear Rosi.[63] After all the news that spread around the table at the time, I understand everything well. For ten days I haven't had a look into my English workbook. Often one has no quiet moment and the zest for studying is lacking. If only by *Pesach* there will be a change. Today I can stop counting the *Omer*[64] because forty-nine days—that is, seven weeks—are over. At least Mother is busy with the household chores. But Aunt Frida is around Mother the whole day long. Only after their arrival in the U.S.A. will they really be separated. On Friday Aunt Lenchen visited me, but my nephew Bruno still holds aloof. If I were free and had some money, I would have pleased some acquaintances with matzos. This had been my idea before our departure. Aunt Lenchen told me that Franz's immigration has been approved. Now I am curious whether he musters the resoluteness to comply. Will the Ludwigs settle in New York? Has Dr. Heilbronn found a position? If Cousin Emil wants to oblige our request, he only needs to charge his intimate friends with the matter. We hope that the written

---

[63]Apparently Rosi was planning to visit them in Holland. It's not clear why they wanted Rosi to take their belongings to England, but the plan was later abandoned.

[64]"Omer" refers to the counting of forty-nine days between Pesach (deliverance) and Shavuot (receiving of the Torah).

confirmation from America of our account will arrive this week at the American Consulate in Rotterdam to get our passports ready most quickly. Maybe Aunt Frida can take with her to Rotterdam what you recommended in your letter! If you, God willing, will come to us, we will not need to store our suitcases here. They will go along with you. Supposedly Erwin[65] has been lodged permanently near Belgrade. Albert and Lily Engelsrath with their family will move to Agram [Zagreb].[66] For a long time we have not received any immediate news. Since our failed affair with the Falcks[67] we have not read anything from the Doktors. We've got a lot to catch up with. Just now we had our daily walk in the backyard, but it is still quite cold. Do you have a garden around the house? My dear Rosi, be heartily greeted and kissed by your loving father.

[Postmarked April 11, 1940.]
April 10, 1940

Dear Rosi!

Today I have to confirm two letters from you. In the meantime you will have heard from Father about our trip to Rotterdam. You won't believe it, but yesterday, to our great joy, Aunt Trudl informed us of having gained a visa. Now we are hoping for the best. Aunt Frida is still waiting for a summons to Rotterdam. The events are overwhelming us, and I think a lot about Albrecht. How nice it would be, dear Rosi, if we could make the great journey together. What do you think? In earlier times I would have recommended to you to hand over our suitcases to the Ludwigs, though there are your belongings among them, your dark blue winter coat, etc. Also here I have difficulty to get my hands on our belongings because they are stored in transit.

---

[65]Clemy's brother Erwin left Austria to live in Yugoslavia.
[66]Lily was Clemy's older sister. She and her second husband Albert Engelsrath had been living in Vienna, but Albert was originally from Zagreb.
[67]Details unknown.

This morning we are expecting Aunt Lenchen who most of the time comes in the company of Henriette. The Ludwigs were lucky. They will be happy upon their safe landing. I hope soon I can write to you without restrictions, which is not possible from here. Stay well and make us happy by sending another message. Be greeted and kissed heartily by your mother.

[Postmarked April 13, 1940.]
From: Hugo Mosbacher
Amsterdam
O.Z. Achterburgwal 185
Kamer 54

To: Miss Rosi Mosbacher
34 Brunner Road—Ealing
London W5
Friday, April 12, 1940

Dear Rosi!

Your lines of April 1 to Mother have also reached me. We are happy to know that you are well, which, by God's grace, we are, too. I expect that Mother and I will receive our American visas next week. On Wednesday I again enjoyed a comforting visit from Trude, and this afternoon I am looking forward to Aunt Lenchen. As Trude told me, the Doktors wrote that they will settle in Ohio, in Cincinnati or another city. I assume that they will find it hard to leave New York. It's a good omen that Pauline Rubens settled our financial sponsorship so quickly. I did not expect it to work out differently, although the family here was somewhat skeptical. As a result of Uncle Emil[68] being so involved, it will naturally proceed more easily

---

[68] Pauline Rubens encouraged Emil (Hugo's brother) to open a medical practice in Ohio and helped him financially. Hugo felt that, because of Emil's intercession and Pauline's generosity, Pauline would help the rest of the family. Hugo's following reference to "Uncle Emil" was to his cousin Emil in London, who was also providing affidavits and financial assistance.

because, in her *noblesse*, she cannot refrain from helping the rest of the family. I think that Uncle Emil there will reply to Els and, depending on the outcome, I can answer later. I am very anxious about how our matters will go on here. There has to be an end to it sometime! With heartiest greetings and kisses, your loving father.

[Postmarked April 17, 1940.]
From: Hugo Mosbacher
Amsterdam
Achterburgwal 185
Kamer 54

To: Miss Rosi Mosbacher
34 Brunner Road—Ealing
London W5
Tuesday, April 16, 1940

Dear Rosi!

Your postcard to Mother dated the fourth arrived on Friday, the twelfth. Yesterday I received your especially long letter of April 8 that I was able to take to Mother when I visited her on Monday. When you are reading my lines I am always in the same situation: From 7:45 a.m. to 7:45 p.m. I sit at a table only with a short break. Every day goes by exactly as every other. The only breaks are the walk to the backyard and two visits a week. All your news was very interesting for us, both about Robert's engagement and your talk with Mrs. Tuchmann. I can understand that you do not dare to ask for days off. Here, too, I witness that those who always speak up prevail even with their small wishes, but mostly they become unpopular because of their steady demands. However, because of the holidays I myself have to ask for a vacation, not knowing whether it will be granted. I can well understand that you regretted Ludwig's departure because he was the closest one to you over there. A couple of days ago we learned that Aunt Frida's luggage is also on its way to Rotterdam. We were very relieved about this because we already had a packing permit when we departed, but Frida did not. For this sometimes she reproached Mother about why we did not take some of her belongings with us. Unfortunately Aunt Frida has not yet been summoned to Rotterdam. If the papers were lost in Stuttgart, this would be quite fatal, but I do not believe that is the case. That Ludwig resembles the Halle family is very likely because their kinship is close enough. Ari's present situation only results in losses, which is very regrettable. Recently Alfons sent Trude the first dollar. Here I would have time to play with Anthony the whole day through, and how much I wish I could do so. Some of my colleagues are playing Skat[69] constantly. Today it has been fifty-six days. To be with Uncle E.[70] does not seem amusing for the youth. That milieu would interest me. Dear Rosi, accept many thanks for the distraction you are giving us and hearty greetings and kisses from your loving father.

April 17, 1940

My dearest Rosi,

I still have to acknowledge your two letters of the third and eighth of this month. Dear Rosi, you must feel how much you please us with your frequent letters. I hope we can still celebrate the holidays with you and with the dear ones. It's now more than eight weeks that we've been here. Today Aunt Frida got a summons to go to the consulate on Friday; we are happy that she has now gotten this far. Father was here on Monday; on Tuesday, Trude, Frida, Lenchen, and Henriette. Those are the pleasures of the week. Lenchen said that Trude needed her assistance very much during the week. She has a lot of preparations to make and no help. Ruth has given notice and starting

---
[69]A German card game.
[70]Hugo again meant his cousin Emil in London.

May 1 will be at home again. We're very curious to know, dear Rosi, where you will spend the holidays. I find the Fischels' invitation to you extremely nice; will you make good use of it? In your last letter you wrote us something that interested us very much, about Mrs. Tuchmann, etc. Aren't the Tuchmanns going to America soon? I'm so pleased by your reports to us about your good appearance. I've got a number of things for you that I've had altered to your measurements. I hope you will be able to get away soon. So far, God willing, everything has worked out for us. Franz writes that Frida's arrangements are also underway. I'll write to you before the holidays in any case; today I wish you a pleasant *seder* in advance. Best regards to the Sudweeks family and kisses to Anthony. Dear Rosi, be embraced and kissed always by your mother.

[Postmarked April 20, 1940.]
From: Hugo Mosbacher
Amsterdam
Achterburgwal 185

To: Miss Rosi Mosbacher
34 Brunner Road—Ealing
London W5
Amsterdam, April 19, 1940

My dear Rosi!
    Today was "big mail day." With much joy I received your letters of April 12 and 15 and forwarded them personally to Mother. Because the photos you ordered for America were not all right, as we were told by the consulate only today (when we handed the photos over in Rotterdam no one complained about them), we had to be photographed again today. Tomorrow I have to go with these new photos to Rotterdam, hoping to receive the passports then. The photos from Nuremberg are not usable because they are stamped copies, and we need

photos without stamps. I write about this matter so extensively just in case you also have got such Nuremberg products. I agree with you that we will have to follow your recommendation. A short while ago we were visited by the rabbi for the first time. If I should not be free yet, I have been selected by him as reader at the *seder*. The news that the Doktors probably will settle in Cincinnati or Toledo I might have written to you before. Of course I know Mrs. Morgenthau well. Your walks are admirable. It is a pity that we cannot spend the *seder* evenings together, but, please God, we will do so in good health next time. I am sorry that you are also handicapped, but you are also smart enough to take things for what they are and to comprehend it as a smaller kind of sacrifice with which one has to deal. To me it has been interesting that you have read Goethe studiously and thus may compete with Cousin Ludwig. I congratulate Anthony's attempts at walking. During my English lessons yesterday I really had to think about him. I read a senseless verse that probably is meant for children: *"One, two, buckle my shoe. Three, four, shut the door. Five, six, pick up sticks. Seven, eight, lay them straight. Nine, ten, a good fat hen."* This afternoon I was at Mother's quarters. Frida returned from Rotterdam without things having been done because the affidavits must be of a more recent date, but they are in Stuttgart already and have to be returned immediately. Dear Rosi, stay well. I am with you, especially during the holidays, and send you my best wishes with many greetings and hearty kisses. Your loving father.

Hugo, Clemy, and Frida were finally released on April 20, 1940. They went to live with the Knollers while they completed their travel plans. They had their American visas and tickets to travel on the steamship S.S. *Veendam* on May 12, 1940.

[Postmarked April 22, 1940.]
To: Miss Rosi Mosbacher
34 Brunner Road—Ealing
London W5
Monday, April 22, 1940

My dear Rosi!

I want to follow up on our telegram of yesterday by a few lines at the beginning of the holidays. Last Saturday afternoon around three p.m. when I returned from the consulate in Rotterdam with the processed passports, Mother and Aunt Frida were already in the waiting room to be released. Upon my arrival naturally I received the same permission that had been ordered by a higher authority on Saturday morning. You can imagine our elation and the mutual happiness with Knollers, etc. During those sixty days a mountain of mail has arrived that I have not been able to sift yet. I am not ordered to leave, but of course this will be deliberated within the next days.[71] Frida's papers are not ready yet so her departure has to follow later. In the meantime, we have to register on a daily basis except for the holidays. Just now Ella Goldberger, formerly Cohn, sent us flowers as a welcome. She will join us tonight at Knoller's big *seder* table. We often talk about you, dear Rosi. It would be better if we could have a chat, but one cannot enjoy everything at once, and we have learned to do without. This morning a letter from the Doktors arrived. We also regret that they will not be able to welcome us on our debarkation in New York because the Doktors will already be in Toledo then. It is regrettable that Rosl is often sick, and the presence and help of Aunt Clara [72] cannot be overestimated and overstated. I especially like Ruth and Carla. Ruth is very brusque and exhausted. A short while ago my first visit was to Paula Schweizer, but she had already left. We will begin the holidays hoping for, with God's help, more satisfying and less troubling times together with you. With this wish and many, many kisses—your loving father.

My dear Rosi!

You will not believe how happy we are and grateful to dear God. By now we have learned what it means to wait, but together anything is easier to endure. Now we are able to enjoy the company of our loved ones properly. Until recently we were only allowed to talk under surveillance. Frida has a strained foot from falling down a few

---

[71]Hugo's meaning is unclear since he was already out of detention. He must have been referring to some aspect of their paperwork for departure. Frida's American visa was not ready and they planned to leave without her.

[72]Hugo and Emil's sister, Clara Mosbacher Sichel, lived with her daughter Irma and son-in-law Alfons Adler in South Carolina since immigrating in 1940, but she was also a frequent guest of Emil and Rosl in Toledo.

high stairs. She keeps Midri [73] company, which makes things easier for Trudl. All the best, dear Rosi. Happy holidays and many kisses from your mother.

[Postmarked April 26, 1940.]
c/o Aribert Knoller
Beethovenstraat 72
Amsterdam

To: Miss Rosi Mosbacher
34 Brunner Road—Ealing
London W5
Friday, April 26, 1940

My dear Rosi!

During our daily registration procedure your postcards of April 15 and 18 were handed out to us and today the one of the eighteenth. As arranged by dear Ari, we spent very comfortable *seder* evenings. It is only regrettable that Trude has no permanent help which is unpleasant for the visitors. We would also prefer to be accommodated somewhere else because Ruth and Carla have to sleep in one bed with their parents as long as we are here. One has to comply with everything that is proposed. Yesterday afternoon we spent with Lenchen and the evening with Henriette, just Mother and me! Aunt Frida still has to rest her foot and thus does not need to register. Our steamer and the day of our departure are still not certain. I thought you were supposed to have received the clothes from Stourbridge long ago. I will write to Gr. [?] asking them to send them to you. Freddy and his wife were with us the day before yesterday in the evening, and we liked them. Mrs. Cohn Gold[berger] is very happy. She visited us together with her husband whose looks have changed very favorably, which we applauded. If your meals are more

---

[73]"Midri" seems to have been a nickname for Ari's elderly mother (Klara) who lived with the Knollers.

expensive than regularly, one can assume that they comply with the rules for the holidays [Passover]. The difference has always been the price. I still have to ask Els if she really contacted Cousin Emil. I think she didn't because usually he responds quickly. The Knollers are happy about your messages. Yesterday Erna phoned us because it was her birthday. Right now we are in the post office, and Mother and I are writing simultaneously, maybe the very same thing. Continued good yontif [holiday] and most hearty greetings and kisses from your loving father.

[Postmarked April 26, 1940.]
Miss Rosi Mosbacher
34 Brunner Road—Ealing
London W5
April 26, 1940

My dear Rosi,
    Right now we are on our way to our former address,[74] which we have to visit every day. Yesterday we found there your replies of the fifteenth and eighteenth. The holidays were nice. I am only troubled by the thought that Ruth has to sleep in the same bed as her parents when she is with them and Carla on the couch, which is also in their bedroom. We are so happy to have come this far. The next part of our journey has to be talked through from A to Z. It's also a pity that I am coming to the U.S.A. with such a poor vocabulary. God willing, everything will turn out to be fine and we'll see each other soon. What is your recommendation about the suitcase? I have got coats, suits, and underwear, etc., in it, that I will need. Of course you could take it with you just in case it will take not too long. Hurry and tell me your opinion in order for us to schedule. Are we supposed to take your belongings with us? This is probably the best way because I don't even know if I can get to the suitcases.[75] The good food suits us well

---

[74]The detention center at O.Z. Achterburgwal 185, to which they had to report each day.

now because we are not used to it. Yesterday morning I returned from a meeting with Franz's mother totally devastated. I am sorry for her; she should be institutionalized. I also cannot understand why Franz isn't coming. We received so much mail that we only could read parts of it. Carla and Ruth are lovely and they particularly love you, Rosi. A simple recipe: From one egg, make strudel dough that you stretch and cut with a cutter into square pieces. Bake the pieces in a pot with boiling oil. Afterwards spread some sugar and cinnamon on it. I'll send you more recipes the next time. Kisses, Mother.

c/o Aribert Knoller
Beethovenstraat 72
Amsterdam
Sunday morning, April 28, 1940

My dear Rosi!

After mailing our postcards to you on April 26, dear Rosi, we received your letter of April 22 about which we were very happy. Yesterday we were summoned again and had to walk for approximately two hours. Also yesterday an old letter of January 12 from America arrived via Nuremberg. In the meantime we had a date with Paula again. She is such a poor thing, and Franz has no idea about her situation. Though I am not a psychiatrist, I am diagnosing her state as being far from normal. Things could probably become normal again if Franz were to turn up immediately. I expect to hear from him at any hour after he received my message from here. I hope his arrival is certain. One is happy about the holidays but also about them being over, particularly in your case because you must miss a lot. Our daily ways are predetermined. Today we also want to visit Els at the Committee to discuss various matters with her. With most heartfelt greetings and kisses—lovingly, your father.

[75] Because their luggage was in transit storage, Clemy didn't know if she could get to Rosi's belongings.

Dearest Rosi!

After yesterday's walk I was quite done in because, after the long time of sitting around, I am no longer used to walking. I hope you spent the holidays as comfortably as possible. Wednesday, May 1, is Carla's birthday. We talk a lot about you, dear Rosi. Of course Trudl is very busy now without getting any help, and so Carla who is on a break has to spend her precious time on the household. Ruth is still at her office. Many kisses for today from your mother.

[Postmarked May 1, 1940.]
May 1, 1940

My dear Rosi!

Today is Carla's and Rosl's birthday. We are writing this at the post office since we were in town with both daughters. Ruth is at home now, resting from her exhausting job. We spent the holidays very comfortably. On such days the Knollers have many visitors. Aunt Lenchen and Henriette spend much time with us. Yesterday Father and I met Els. Frida does not go out yet. We had a good time with Els.[76] She is looking well, as are her children, especially the boy. A short while ago in the streetcar we talked with Uncle Philip. He was very courteous. They are not supposed to know. Tomorrow Father wants to inform him about our journey, etc. You will be notified about our destination. The rumor here is that a ship sails via England where it will stay for two days. It's questionable whether there will be an opportunity to see each other. We hope to hear from you soon. There is so much to talk about. A letter from the Doktors arrived here very quickly. It is regrettable that they will not be there anymore when we arrive. Dear Rosi, can you imagine that we couldn't even change our clothes since our departure? It's ten weeks since then, but it's easy to take. Father's suit is very bad,

---

[76]Els had two children from her first marriage.

and I want him to get something tailored here. At home nothing could be obtained for months.[77] I hope you were able to entertain yourself to some extent. How were your holidays? Today Franz wrote a letter. One has to get used to his style. He often writes very foolishly. Stay well and accept many kisses—your mother.

c/o Aribert Knoller
Beethovenstraat 72
Amsterdam

To: Miss Rosi Mosbacher
34 Brunner Road—Ealing
London W5
Wednesday noon, May 1, 1940

My dear Rosi!

Today Franz's reply to our note about our release arrived. He is not hoping to come here until May. I do not know whether I may believe that. I hope that you, dear Rosi, are well and pleased as we are that the holidays are over. We will comply immediately and happily to your wish to write to S[tourbridge?]. A short time ago, when we were at the registration office, we met Meier Stern. This morning, as we mounted the tram together with Ari, Ruth, and Carla, we met Philip v. G[78] to whom we talked, naturally. Yesterday evening we visited Els for the first time. Allegedly she has written to Cousin Emil, but I doubt that because she has no answer yet and Emil usually replies very promptly, whether positively or negatively. Now I have to decide whether to turn to him myself. Brother Emil picked up Ludwig Mosbacher at the ship. He wrote that Ludwig looked horrible. With many greetings and kisses—your loving father.

---

[77] Clemy referred to difficulty purchasing clothing in Germany after the war began. During that time everyone was given food ration coupons, but Jews were denied clothing coupons.
[78] Philip van Gelder—Lenchen's ex-husband and Els' father.

Amsterdam, Friday, May 3, 1940

My dear Rosi!

Today your letter and your card of April 25 and 26 arrived, and we were again very pleased to hear from you. Both your *seder* report and the rendering of the menus, etc., etc., were amusing and interesting. Just now, while I was taking a noontime break, Mrs. Cohn Goldberger was here with Eva, who is supposed to resemble her father in speaking. She was making very urgent inquiries about him. After him, you were the one about whom Eva made detailed inquiries. Yesterday I went with Mother to the Committee to ask about various things. If all goes well, we (Mother and I) will sail on May 12, or May 15 at the latest. Aunt Frida's complete documents may also have reached Rotterdam. We would be happy if she could take this voyage with us. However, as a matter of principle, we don't want to wait for her. Els tells me that she wrote to Cousin Emil weeks ago. For my part I'm not inclined to believe it because, although he would not hesitate to deny her request, he would at least do so promptly.

During the last few days I have finally taken up my correspondence again. For two months I just ignored it. Today I wrote to Fellheimer, Dr. Herz, Grünbaums, Miltenberg, Leppert, Winckler, Ida Rau, Aladar Deutsch; yesterday to Franz and Dina, and there is still a lot left to do. I have been waiting for eight days for a call from Franz's mother. When I think about her and her condition, I start to sweat. If someone were to tell me she is no longer alive, I would not be surprised. If I call on her at home, the effort is wasted since she is always out. I wrote to Franz yesterday and told him the unvarnished truth about her condition in order to get him to arrive at long last now that he has permission to travel to Holland. It always takes Franz such an insanely long time to do anything. We are completely unable to explain Halifax. It's good that we know that Emil collected the Ludwigs.

Mother has gone to town with Aunt Frida and asks to be excused for not writing. Tomorrow we can tire ourselves out again with walking, when we go to report. Aunt Frida has the day free tomorrow. Fritz Roederer[79] recently wrote to Ari about financial matters in the meanest kind of way, completely unjustified. Ari answered him in corresponding fashion. Now Fritz has had the impudence to outdo himself. His letter will be returned to him today in its original form, since Trude only opens such items by mistake. I've seen acquaintances from Fürth-Nuremberg[80] here and spoken with some of them. I'm also expecting a letter from Lina.

I wish you a good *Shabbos*, even though I know that this wish can't reach you by tomorrow. Stay well and be most warmly greeted and most affectionately kissed by your father and mother.

May 8, 1940[81]

My dearest Rosi!

It's 6:30 right now. Father is still sleeping, while I want to talk to you, dear Rosi. It bothers me that we haven't written you in the last few days. Believe me, we aren't getting anything done here. Every day we have to make our way to our former dwelling, which takes up the whole morning. The afternoons are also pretty lively. It's quite a lot for Trude to accommodate three people without help. Frida sleeps across from our pension, of course, but during the day we're together.

Things are suddenly beginning to move very quickly with our departure. Just think—the ship is leaving Sunday evening. We're sailing on the *Veendam*, and today we're

---

[79] Frida's stepson.
[80] Hugo was from Fürth, a small city just outside Nuremberg. The city centers are fewer than five miles apart.
[81] This letter was written in pencil, apparently hurriedly. It is dated May 8, 1940; they were scheduled to leave Amsterdam for the United States in four days, on Sunday, May 12.

going to find out when we have to get ready to travel. It often happens that the ship sails a few days late. Yesterday Frida had to go to Rotterdam for an interview. We went with her to see about our baggage. Frida still doesn't have the 545 paper, and now it's questionable whether she can travel with us. God willing, it will still work out because Frida wants terribly to travel with us. It's good that we asked about our baggage. A suitcase and a crate are missing. We were told that they will turn up soon. We'll call this evening to see what's happening about them. These are just the problems that one has, and they have to be seen to. It's a shame that I don't have the suitcase that you have with you now. Frida could use hers; we've got our most important things in it such as our summer dresses and so on. Now we will just have to be patient until you come, dear Rosi.[82]

These weeks have gone by so quickly. Sunday afternoon we were with Ella Cohn (Goldberger). It was very nice and pleasant. We liked her very much. He [Mr. Goldberger?] asked for your address, which he wants to send to his sister Anny. I am sure she will give you a call: Dr. Friedländer, 30 St. Ann's Terrace, W8. She, too, would be pleased if you would get together with Anny. She has been in London for years. Eva G[oldberger] visited us on Sunday. I was amazed to see how well Eva has developed intellectually. I had to talk a lot about you; she looks up to you very much. We spent Saturday evening with Henriette; she is jealous of Trude. We will spend this evening with Freddy and tomorrow evening we'll have supper with Henriette. We're pretty nervous at the moment and, God willing, all will go well. I've got all your things for the daughters, dear Rosi, but unfortunately they're in the suitcase that wasn't there yesterday. They don't have

---

[82] Apparently Rosi had taken a suitcase with Hugo and Clemy's belongings with her to England. Clemy said that they would have to wait for it to arrive with Rosi since at that point they were expecting to arrive in New York before she did. Rosi also had one of their suitcases with her in England. They must have done this in case one of them arrived in the US without luggage.

much to change into, and, dear Rosi, whatever you're getting rid of, you can set aside for them. Ruth had her exam in Hebrew and passed with good marks. We enjoy ourselves enormously with the daughters; they are both darlings. The weather is bitterly cold again. Yesterday we really froze in Rotterdam. We called on Paula Knoller[83] in Rotterdam. She is the same as ever and was happy to see us. It's a shame that there is no possibility of calling you; I would have liked that so very much. My dear Rosi, just take good care of your health and always be on the alert, wherever you go. I can still hardly believe that we are going to America. Your letter of April 28 came today; it took a very long time to get here. And now, dear Rosi, I send you all good wishes. We'll write again before we leave. Many kisses from your mother.

My dear Rosi,

Today is Wednesday already, and Saturday evening at eight o'clock it's "All Aboard!" We were in Rotterdam yesterday with Aunt Frida, unfortunately without success.[84] Your dear letter written before the end of the holidays reached us today, and we are all very happy with your report. Sadly, things are not going at all well with Paula Schw[eizer]. Franz is taking a terribly long time to arrive although he has the great advantage to be permitted to immigrate.[85] With regard to an address in New York, I am still considering where you should write. I should have taken care of a number of things, but I believe we can manage without them. Many kisses from your loving father.

---

[83] Ari's sister-in-law, originally from Vienna, who had also taken refuge in Holland.
[84] They were unable to secure Frida's American visa so that she could travel with them.
[85] Apparently Franz had his American visa and they were expecting him in Amsterdam, where he would visit his mother before sailing.

The last page of Clemy's May 8, 1940, letter with
Hugo's postscript.

Hugo's Letters of May 1940

Hugo and Clemy had their immigration papers in order and their steamship tickets in hand. They planned to board their ship in Rotterdam on Saturday evening, May 11, 1940, to sail for the United States on May 12 or 15. Then the Germans invaded Holland on Friday, May 10. Holland had been neutral during World War I and had hoped to remain neutral during World War

II. However, the Germans bombed Rotterdam and threatened to bomb Amsterdam. Over 1,000 people were killed in Rotterdam and there was great damage to property. The Dutch government surrendered on May 15.

The Germans declared all existing exit visas invalid.

In Germany Hugo and Clemy had had German exit visas but lacked American visas. After the Germans occupied Holland, they had their American immigration visas and steamship tickets but no exit visas.

Friday, August 30, 1940[86]
Amsterdam

My dear, dear Rosi!

It was a fine discovery this morning before eight o'clock when I picked up your letter, together with other correspondence for the dear Knollers, that the postman had put through the slot in the door. This was your letter of August 15, and, of course, we are enormously pleased.[87] Several days ago we heard through Aunt Dina, who, in her turn, had heard from the Doktors that you have your visa and are getting ready. Now we were far from knowing with certainty whether you were still there with the S[udweeks] or were already gone. Every evening, when we lay our heads down, Mother asks, "Is our Rosi now underway?" You can imagine what your arrival means for us; it will give us courage and renewed hope.

I hope that in the meantime all our wishes, which I

---

[86] Note the long disruption in the correspondence between the German invasion of the Netherlands on May 10, 1940, and Rosi's arrival in the United States in August. The Germans suspended mail service to England, as the two countries were at war. In his September 12, 1940, letter, Hugo wrote that the Red Cross delivered a letter that Rosi had written from England on June 13. On August 31, 1940, the Dutch newspapers mentioned that mail to the US could be sent once a week, via Lisbon, on American ships.

[87] Rosi's quota number #1115 from American immigration came up on July 26, 1940. She sailed from Liverpool on the *Scythia* on July 31, 1940, and arrived in New York on August 12, 1940. Her initial plan was to join her Uncle Emil in Toledo, but she decided to stay in New York City.

posted to Toledo a long, long time ago, in a *Clipper*[88] letter, have finally arrived there—we also understand this from a letter of Dina's—and that it is possible for the Doktors to arrange everything. Ari's financial situation is just like Hugo's.[89] As you can imagine, the unwished-for prolonged stay is greatly irksome to both sides. The burden, of course, is greatly diminished if the financial part can be equalized, and I long to be in a situation in which I can do that. The Hugos' departure does not depend solely on securing their tickets and on obtaining all the visas for this long journey, but primarily upon obtaining permission to leave the country in which they now find themselves. In contrast to what was reported earlier, the Hugos, who have expired [American] visas in their passports, do not need to renew their affidavits and letters of credit. They will receive their new visas when they can show their ship's tickets and their visas for Portugal, etc.[90] Since we have so far heard nothing from the Doktors, I recently wrote at length to our mutual friend Franz so that he can pass everything on. Perhaps after the receipt of this letter you could write to Toledo that I do not need any papers or affidavits. Of course, it may be that Emil has already ordered them and Rubens has done the work. I think that the Doktors have already done something with Rubens about securing the ship's tickets for departure from Lisbon and the trip from here to Lisbon. So far nothing has been omitted, and the moment the Hugos have

---

[88]The *Clipper* was the Boeing 314 flying boat, built for Pan American Airways. It was named after the fast nineteenth century Yankee clipper sailing ships. On May 20, 1939, Pan Am began a transatlantic mail service from Port Washington, Long Island, New York, to Lisbon, Portugal, using the Clipper passenger planes.
[89]Hugo referred to himself in the third person and to Clemy and himself as "the Hugos." They were still living with the Knollers and money was scarce.
[90]Portugal was neutral during the war and never occupied by the Germans. If Hugo and Clemy had obtained exit visas from Holland and entrance visas to Portugal, they could have booked passage from Portugal to the United States. Ships no longer left Holland for the United States.

their exit permits they will wire the Doktors about seeing to the tickets in case it hasn't already been done.

We were very happy to get Michel's letter. Please give him and Selma our regards and our most sincere thanks for his goodness and their kindness. In the meanwhile, you may also have spoken to Uncle Fredl and Lusi. We can't list all those to whom we send our warmest regards, but you can give our regards to the dear Ludwigs to whom we are especially close. We are also thinking of Max and Berta[91] and, *last not least,* of Mother Jettchen. Dina wrote earlier that the Doktors are expecting you after a short stay in New York. Are you in contact with Pauline Rubens? The Hugos have to report daily, so they are in town every day by 11:30. They have lunch there and come home between two and three in the afternoon. Mother sits at the sewing machine every day; there is no shortage of work here at home. Aunt Frida helps out in the kitchen. Now that the children have gone away, Aunt Lenchen feels abandoned in every respect and is taking it badly. It doesn't make her any more likeable, but we do feel very sorry for her. I have to stop, because Mother wants to send her regards, too. And so, my dear child, keep on doing well, stay well, be very careful. My best wishes for everything you may undertake. With many sincere regards and affectionate wishes from your father who loves you.

My dear, good Rosi!

It has been a long time since we have known such happiness as we had today. I am infinitely happy and grateful to know that you, my good one, are at your destination and also happy to have the letter in our possession. If Elschen[92] had just said a word to me everything

---

[91]Max and Berta Fleischmann. Max was Hugo's first cousin.
[92]Apparently Els fled Amsterdam without telling anyone her plans. It's not clear if she took her children with her or sent them to England before the German invasion. Lenchen's son, Freddy van Gelder, and his wife also escaped. Thus Lenchen felt "abandoned."

could have been different. You can understand our nervousness. We regret very much that we are so cut off from the Doktors, but the main thing for us is that everyone is well. I hope we hear from you again soon. Give our regards to all the dear ones, especially Lusi, Fredl and the Ludwigs, and the dear Rosenstocks.[93] Stay well and receive many greetings and kisses from your mother.

Rosi's Immigration Visa No. 1115 showing her arrival on the *Scythia* from London into the Port of New York on August 12, 1940. The reverse side of this document states that Cousin Emil Mosbacher paid for Rosi's steamship ticket to the United States.

---

[93] Rosi lived with the Rosenstocks when she first arrived in New York City.

September 12, 1940

My dear good Rosi!

It is now thirty days since you arrived there, my dear Rosi, and we are so thankful for that and also for the fact that we know about it at all. We have been spared a great deal of anxiety in this respect. The last time we wrote to you—that is, the first time we wrote to you there—I used ordinary paper and only noticed my mistake at the post office when I paid the postage, which is why I'm correcting it today. I assume that this letter will be forwarded to you and that you have changed your residence and that further information is already on its way from you to us. Today we received through the Red Cross the message that you had written on June 13, 1940. Even though it came rather late, we were still pleased to have the handwritten original. It's natural to feel a certain longing. Even in normal times that would be appropriate, and in a strange place the feeling is still more intense. Even though the dear ones go to some pains to make our stay a pleasant one, we still feel keenly that we are a burden to them, which, given the length of our sojourn, is quite understandable.

We have still heard nothing from Toledo about our ship tickets. I have no doubt that the Doktors are now making an effort in the matter and that we will soon hear on what ship passage has been booked for us in Lisbon.[94] As I've already written, it's the prerequisite for obtaining

---

[94] The first new plan was to obtain exit visas from Holland and entry visas for Portugal where they would board a steamship to the United States. They were required to redo their paperwork in order to renew their now-expired American visas. Endless forms passed between Amsterdam and the United States. Though the Germans went through the motions of possible approval, it appears they had no intention of approving new exit visas. The delays were caused not only by the Nazis but also by the U.S.A. State Department. Breckinridge Long, the assistant secretary of state, ordered American consulates to sharply limit visas for Jews wanting to enter the United States. The Roosevelt administration's restrictive policies on Jewish immigration are a source of bitter controversy. For the text of a memo Long sent to State Department officials on June 26, 1940, see: http://www.pbs.org/wgbh/amex/holocaust/filmmore/reference/primary/barmemo.html

new visas. If we aren't yet ready to depart with the ship on which we are booked, the tickets can simply be used for the next voyage. Today I spoke to a gentleman who was supposed to depart at the same time as we were. He already has his tickets for a certain steamer from Lisbon. Dear Rosi, were you able to take all your baggage with you? Our baggage is still in storage in Rotterdam, but we are told that it's impossible for it all to go with us on a trip to Lisbon—first, because it's too much and too burdensome, and, second, because of the high cost. I don't know if all these stories are true, but it's certainly possible. You can imagine how intensely we are thinking of you: whether you have already found work, how you are adjusting, whether you intend to visit the Doktors, whom you spend time with. The main thing for us, dear Rosi, is that you stay well and lead a sensible life. We know nothing at all about Albrecht and we're curious to hear from you whether you hear from him regularly or irregularly.

I wrote you that we had to go through a lot with Franz's mother. For some time now she has been in a madhouse in Apeldoorn. However, her condition is not so bad and not hopeless. During my last visit I could converse very well with her. I have a much harder time reaching an understanding with her son to whom I have sent information by the meter, but unfortunately not in a form that he likes. To fulfill his requirements, I would need to be a qualified psychiatrist. My main activity here, aside from the work in connection with our departure, has consisted of visiting his mother, taking her to a local hospital, and the correspondence with Franz. Not one other person in the whole wide world shows any concern about this woman. Franz has already expressed some misgivings about the possibility that he may end up in the same situation, since he may have the same tendencies.

Aunt Frida accompanies us every day when we go to report. If just once she were to stay at home and do something besides what we do it would be so much smarter of her and so much better for her. We would be so pleased if she would behave more correctly, and it would be so much easier if just the two of us went to report. Due to the uncertainty about the arrival of our letters, it's already time to concern ourselves with *Rosh Hashanah* and *Yom Kippur,* by which I mean, dear Rosi, to send you in writing the good wishes that we would so much prefer to exchange with you in person. We were so close to doing that! When I recently wrote to the Doktors, I said that we knew what the closing year had brought, but what the coming year may bring is entirely unknown. For this reason we want to be thankful for the course of events in the old year, and pray to God that once more He may protect you and us and all those whom we hold dear. May the Almighty give you the strength to be able to carry out your plans, and, dear Rosi, may by His grace a part of your wishes be fulfilled as you wish them to be. Dear Rosi, we are grateful that you arrived safe and sound, and I am convinced that Fortune will smile on all your ways. We shall continue to trust and hope and to lead our lives in such a way that we can stand before God and our fellow human beings. During these high holy days, we feel ourselves united with you in our prayers, as I also feel myself to be every single day in my devotions. Arrange things so that you don't have to make any long journeys on *Yom Kippur* and fast well. And, along with the many good wishes, dear Rosi, I take your hand and kiss you warmly, thinking as I do that, God willing, in the not-too-distant future we will be united again and can make up for a great many things.

Due to conditions here, we have done absolutely nothing in respect to language. I know that's almost a crime, but it just wasn't possible. Give our greetings to Ludwig and family, the Fleischmanns, Fredl and Lusi, Hans and Paul Neurath[95] and their wives, etc., etc. I hope

---

[95] Hans and Paul Neurath were Lily Adler Engelsrath's sons from her first marriage to Emil Neurath. Hans had emigrated in 1938 and Paul in 1939. Both were living in New York City.

that our letters reach you in time so that we can give you at least a little happiness. With love and the warmest regards, your father.

Special greetings for Michel, Selma and Fani.

[The following two postcards were originally addressed to Rosi in Kew Gardens, Queens, New York. Someone wrote her new address over the old address.]
From: Mosbacher
Amsterdam-Z
Beethovenstraat 72/I

To: Miss Rosi Mosbacher
407 Central Park West, Apt. 3B
New York, U.S.A. 101W93
September 13, 1940

My dear Rosi!

Yesterday evening we mailed our second letter to your Rosenstock address. This morning we received your lines of August 28 and of course were very delighted again to hold something from you in our hands. I can imagine that the Doktors would be enormously happy to have you in Toledo, too. If you accept their invitation you do not need to be ashamed to ask to be separate within the apartment in case you have that wish at all. Being over here we cannot give any recommendations. Eventually you will have to decide which appointment is more favorable. I assume that Chicago is near Toledo and that you also have some options in Chicago. Meanwhile you have already talked to a lot of old acquaintances and friends. If you contacted Paul N[eurath], you surely met his little girl. Paul intervened successfully in Washington on behalf of his parents; one never gets to know any details. I also wrote to the Doktors that they are supposed to do something for us at the [State?] Department in Washington. No one wants to miss a chance and one passes on everything one hears, even if sometimes it is nonsense. Yesterday at the Committee I had to hand in our original passports, as did all the passengers of the *Veendam*. Currently efforts are being made so that those passengers obtain from the German authorities permission to depart. Were you put in touch with Helene Iglauer by Mrs. Tuchmann and is the latter also over there already? Today a long letter from Mr. Fellheimer arrived, mostly praising you, dear Rosi. We are very happy that Ludwig is feeling better. Thank God we over here are all well. We are very amused about what you wrote about Max and Bertha. We hope our two letters will reach you. Stay well, always be careful, and be heartily greeted and kissed by your father. All the Knollers send their kindest regards.

My dear Rosi!

I hope from now on our correspondence will continue again regularly. We enjoyed today's letter very much. All the beloved ones read your lines with great interest. Should Lusi change her situation, I would not mind if she would set aside her job for me. God willing, soon our most cherished wishes will come true. Stay well and accept many greetings and kisses—your mother.

Text side of Hugo and Clemy's 3.5 by 5.25 inch postcard to Rosi, September 22, 1940.

Address side of Hugo and Clemy's
postcard to Rosi, September 22, 1940.
Addresses for Rosi and her parents were obtained from the postcards.
The envelopes from Hugo and Clemy's letters and Rosi's letters
and envelopes to them were not found.

From: Mosbacher
Amsterdam-Z
Beethovenstraat 72/I

To: Miss Rosi Mosbacher
407 Central Park West, Apt. 3B
New York, U.S.A. 101W93
September 22, 1940

My dear Rosi!

On such a Sunday afternoon dedicated to writing letters, you, dear Rosi, should not be forgotten. Mother is sitting at her sewing machine and working today for Aunt Henriette. All the women prefer to order from her. Our beloved ones [the Knollers] intend to move to another, cheaper apartment on November 1. For this purpose today we participated in an inspection [of a future apartment]. October 3 is Pauline's [96] birthday. She would be delighted with your congratulations. Initially we thought not to live too far away from her this year. Franz vexes me with queries that are unnecessary because of my clarity.

---

[96]Pauline Rubens, Rosi's American sponsor.

He asked me about your first address "TH Bronx," whether the T is a "J" or "T."[97] He will receive a proper answer. He is good at teasing. It's obvious that he never has been an apprentice but for most of his life played the role of a master. One who never learned to subordinate himself will find it hard later in life. Dina writes quite frequently and amusingly. She seems to realize that we need to be cheered up a little. On Saturdays most often I attend a very small synagogue with an even smaller congregation to be summoned every fortnight. There are much more important things for which we want to be summoned. We hope all is fine with Ludwig, Johanna and their sons; our best regards to them. This year our correspondence on the occasion of the holidays decreased. It's no pleasure to write from here. Always with best wishes for you, dear Rosi, and much love—your father.

My dear Rosi!

I am so happy that we can write to you again, dear Rosi, but it would be so much better if we could talk to you very soon. I hope this most heartfelt wish soon will come true. Accept many kisses. Many greetings to the dear Ludwigs from your mother.

[Undated, but probably late September 1940.]

My dearest Rosi!

We yearn for your letters now. Your first letter went so quickly, and you can imagine how happy we are to know that you are over there and to be free of that great anxiety. We hope there will soon be some change in our situation. I am convinced that you have all left no stones unturned. Who would have thought that we would have to remain here for such a long time with the sisters? We

---

[97] Franz seems to have been fussing about the way in which either Rosi or Hugo wrote her address. She must have stayed briefly in the Bronx. Something is obviously missing or incorrect in "TH Bronx."

feel so depressed, but unfortunately, at the moment, there is nothing to be done about it. At the same time I'm happy to be able to make myself useful to Trude. I'm sewing and mending all day long, and Frida is also very busy and a great help around the house. Except for Mrs. Cohn-Goldberger and Mrs. Wechsler from Nuremberg, we talk to very few strangers here. However, we do go every Wednesday afternoon to Aunt Henriette for coffee, and on Sunday evenings Lenchen has her at-home day at our place. I enjoy the sewing and I also hope to be able to earn something with it. I've applied to the Committee for permission to attend a tailoring course,[98] and they will inform me as soon as there is a vacancy. It was a big mistake on our part not to keep on with our language study, but unfortunately we are both so nervous that our heads simply can't take in any more information.

Dear Rosi, I want to ask you so many things—how are you adjusting to life there, whether you have found a job yet, whether you are still living with the dear Rosenstocks. It is very good of Michel and Selma to have taken you into their home. In the meantime, you will have spoken to Fredl and Lusi. My dear Rosi, you will hardly have time to keep visiting the relatives constantly, even the closest ones. At Henriette's yesterday we read a long, detailed letter from Aunt Clara Hermalhaus. She does not appear to be in the best of health, for which I am terribly sorry. I'm really eager to know, Rosi, where we are going to pitch our tents someday. Even today I feel happy when I think about how we will be together again. I hope you were able to take all your baggage with you. Can you imagine that I've been running around in one single dress since

---

[98] Joodse Centrale voor Beroepsopleiding (The Jewish Center for Career Change), established in June 1940, offered a variety of classes in business, languages, electronics, machine work, tailoring/dressmaking, etc., advertised as "preparation for profession change for migration" ("*voorberelding van beroepsverandering voor emigratie*"). In February 1941, this organization was absorbed into the Jewish Council, which was under Nazi control. Continuing the class offerings perpetuated the hope of emigration in the Jewish community. See www.joodsmonument.nl/page/274170?lang=en

February? Our baggage is still in transit, and for that reason we want to leave it untouched. Of course, it's an open question whether that's the right thing to do.

Carla and Ruth are very interested in you, dear Rosi, and love their cousin very much. Ruth is at home now. She is busy learning Hebrew and wants to learn tailoring, also. Carla is attending a drawing school. Her main interest is in commercial art, which is certainly a good thing. The training lasts a number of years. It always amuses me to see Carla wearing your things. Please send us a picture of yourself. In the next days there will be a lot to write about, but, to tell the truth, it's getting hard to cope with things. I see that Lily and Albert [99] will get there before us. Haven't you heard anything from Albrecht? Before this letter reaches you, dear Rosi, it will be *Rosh Hashanah*.[100] I wish you everything good, my dear child—you know that. Stay well for us and, God willing, there will be a reunion soon. Give our greetings to all the loved ones you speak to and give them our best wishes. Write us often. That is the greatest happiness that we have. Aunt Trude and Ari and their daughters send greetings. Dear Rosi, be most affectionately hugged and kissed by your mother.

Lina has still not written us a word. We only hear about her through Franz.

September 30, 1940 [101]

My dear good Rosi!

I wanted to write you yesterday, on the first day of *Slichot*, but I was prevented from doing so by a visit from Aunt Lenchen, and today when Ari and I came back from the synagogue your very detailed report was there, which

---
[99] Lily and Albert left Yugoslavia for Italy and obtained their American visas in Naples in late 1940.
[100] October 3–4 1940, supporting the late September dating of this letter, since mail was taking two weeks to get to the United States.
[101] Selichot or Slichot fell on September 28, 1940. Beginning on the Saturday night before Rosh Hashanah, observant Jews recite penitential poems and prayers.

came at such a good time and gives us complete happiness at *Rosh Hashanah*. We can be satisfied with a transit time of fourteen days, and, as I said already, no present could make us happier than your entertaining letter does, putting us, as it does, in a *yontif* mood. If it hadn't arrived, its lack would have been sorely felt. It's the custom here that all our mail becomes community property so you should take that into account. However, we don't do it Michel's way here, either. Selma got herself in trouble once already that way. When she was visiting Clara's daughter-in-law, without any permission whatever, she picked up a letter from the table, that Irma had sent her mother and in which Selma's Michel was soundly excoriated. The affair was very embarrassing and had unpleasant consequences. If now our communications are often repetitive, the reasons are, first, that we're not always precisely sure what we've already written and, second, some letters never arrive, and then it's good if the subject in question is mentioned in the subsequent letter.

Concerning Toledo I recently wrote to the Doktors: You are who you are and that is totally consistent with your train of thought, which I must commend, because you can always go to Toledo/Chicago, but returning to New York is more complicated. Mrs. Schwarz was Pauline's sister; it's very important that you maintain a close relationship with the latter. It would be nice if the Schwarz nephew could be of service to you. I'm not sure what I think about the "Mother [Jettchen] Neumann" problem. I gathered that the Doktors were supposed to, or had to, take her in forever; and I believed that Sally[102] and his wife over there have not been what they should be for Mother. Now we are hearing how nice the daughter-in-law is to their dear mother. So why the move to Toledo or is it supposed to be just a visit?

How did our dear, late Hichenberg put it: "This is one

---

[102] Rosl's brother, Harry Neumann, was called "Sally" or "Solly" by the family. He went to the United States after World War I.

of my more middling days." By the time this letter arrives, the dear Fellheimers[103] will be with you, so I've been told. The old fool is as loyal to you as ever. There are some so-called friends or old acquaintances to whom I would like to send greetings, but I hear all the way over here that if I do so then they're going to say, "Those were the head *Chachamim.*"[104] So I'm not going to send greetings since my purpose was just to give them a bit of pleasure and not to be laughed at. The Fleischmanns' *"Take it easy"* sounds just like them. When you're sitting in a safe harbor, it's easy to give complacent advice. We were very happy to get Ludwig's and Hanna's address. You have probably given them my wishes in the meantime. All my dear ones are included in my prayers for healing. Helene Bergmann's father is also living here. Sometimes I see someone from home, but I avoid speaking to him because I have the impression that he may be afraid that I want something from him. People who don't have the slightest grounds for complaining begin to do so nonetheless, in advance, as a defensive measure. If you do go to Toledo, then insist firmly on taking a room outside their residence. And if your uncle insists just as emphatically that you do otherwise, then you can refer to me and say, "Separate living quarters can only serve to enhance our already outstanding relationship."

We still don't know if our ship passage from Lisbon has been booked. The travel agency here is waiting for confirmation by telegram. As I've already told you many times, as long as departure is not permitted, everything else is of secondary significance. Maybe—a very big maybe!—there will be a justifiable exception for the *Veendam* passengers who were ready to depart. Even if

---

[103]Although Fellheimer reported to Hugo about Rosi and other people in the United States, he was still in Germany. In his November 18, 1941, letter, Hugo wrote that Fellheimer had a visa but could not leave Germany.
[104]"Wise men" in Hebrew. Hugo seemed to think that both friends who had stayed in Germany and those who had made it to the United States would be laughing at his hasty decision to go to Amsterdam.

we have our share [of bad luck?], we must still be very thankful that the dear Lord gave you the insight that it was time to get out of there (there are probably many people who also had that chance and could not make up their minds). Further, that your visa came through, enabling you to travel, and you had a safe journey and arrived in good health. Even though we were enormously surprised by your arrival, I had often imagined such a happy solution, and so I believe that the three of us are under an obligation of gratitude. Albrecht's ideas and attitude resemble those that we once held and that were taken to absurd lengths. Before it's too late I hope he comes to understand that a change is absolutely necessary since germs can be contagious and can damage his health. Albrecht's parents are among the so-called friends to whom I referred above, to whom we haven't written so far, because I don't want to give them an opportunity for the kind of criticism I anticipate from them. Please do us this one huge favor and always be especially careful in big New York. And keep on writing to us so truly, so well, and so beautifully. With affectionate kisses from your father who loves you.

September 30, 1940

My dearest Rosi!
   Today we were able to take receipt of your letter of the sixteenth. We were enormously pleased by your thoroughness and with your beautiful writing. A letter from the Doktors came in the same mail. We don't want to describe it; the connection is very good at the moment. Your letter is a tonic for us. I just read it through for the third time. Your life, dear Rosi, is full of change at the moment, and you describe everything so well that we feel ourselves quite close to you. Dear Rosi, I'm eager to know what you've started doing again in the meantime; it seems that it will be housekeeping again. We hear with regret

that Ludwig is unwell. We hope that, God willing, he recovers soon. I can understand how much Hanna[105] has to do—it's no small matter. Our New Year's correspondence also includes a card for Ludwig's sister Clara [Fenigstein]. In general we're holding back on writing. First, because of the cost of postage and, second, because we don't feel up to it. I find it very nice that Gertrud[106] paid you a visit; please send her many greetings from me. In the meantime you will certainly have paid Paul Neurath a call. Has his wife had the second baby? I hope Paul's parents [Lily and Albert] can soon embark on their great trip; they've secured the necessary tickets. If only we could write about the same thing—the uncertainty and the whole business renders one's nerves *kaput*.

I'm so pleased that I always have something to do. At Trude's there's no lack of work. One would like to requisition Carla, but I get more done this way. It's crazy, especially since I see how slovenly she is and how useless it is to put things in order. Ruth is also annoyed by her sister. I get along very well with both girls. Carla can be especially loveable and nice. On November 1 the dear ones will move to the Rijnstraat. It's a modern apartment and substantially cheaper. We will probably rent a room and I intend to cook myself. It's not yet clear what Aunt Frida will do. Perhaps she will find a cheap boarding house. The weather here is already pretty cold, and I now have to see about getting a warmer wardrobe. Frida and Lenchen each helped us out with a dress during the summer. Our baggage is in transit storage in Rotterdam. Perhaps we ought to have it sent on, but, as I said, we are constantly thinking about leaving, and so we haven't done anything about the baggage. Dear Rosi, who is keeping your baggage for you? Aunt Lenchen will also dine on Wednesday with the dear ones. We will be with you in spirit, my good Rosi; unfortunately it will be the second

---

[105] Short for "Johanna," Ludwig Mosbacher's wife.
[106] Gertrud Nadel was one of Rosi's closest school friends in Nuremberg, and they remained friends in the United States.

Rosh Hashanah when we are apart. But, if we know that you are well and contented, then we will be so, too, as far as we can. With repeated good wishes, your mother kisses you warmly. This letter is for you only.

October 2, 1940

My dear good Rosi!

Even though we wrote you just a few days ago, dear Mother said this morning, "We want to write to Rosi again today," and then the same feeling came over me, to send a letter to you today on *Erev Rosh Hashanah*. We are so preoccupied with you, dear Rosi. We think about you so often, we share your cares, and as a consequence we converse with you in writing as often as possible. And I believe that this is an obligation for which we must be grateful because for such a long time it was not possible for us to keep up the correspondence.[107] People are so quick to forget obstacles that have been overcome and to take for granted what is new and good as easily as if it had always been there.

Yesterday I wrote to Toledo. According to a card from Aunt Lily, she and her husband received their American visas from the consulate in Naples, acting on instructions from the department in Washington. Rumor has it here that no visas are being issued in Rotterdam at the moment. That's obviously the same everywhere, but Paul N[eurath, Lily's son] would have arranged this exception through his connections. If Lily and Albert can do this, then I believe that this possibility is not closed to us. I think that in the meantime you will have heard about this event from Paul himself. In our case the situation is different insofar as it doesn't depend upon the visa, but upon the exit permit that has not been denied to those whom I mentioned. Still, it's good to be concerned about things that one doesn't yet have.

I can well imagine that dear Ludwig did not approve

---

[107]Most likely a reference to the long gap in mail service after the German invasion.

of your factory job.[108] Of course it is of great importance that you establish contact with the circles of the so-called *upper ten thousand*, and, given my attitude, you will surely not think that I am writing this so that you will become friends with rich people. But it's my wish that you don't remain away from your profession for too long and that you realize the value of what you have learned and achieved. I would like to see you become a tutor because you achieve worthwhile results in that field. With your knowledge of languages it would turn out well. And such tutors are only sought for by people who are especially well situated. To get a position of this kind, you will need to have relationships within those circles. If, after a fairly long time, you don't find the position you're looking for, you can turn your attention to Chicago where there is no shortage of such families. Otherwise, any job you may have is fine with me, if you find it satisfying. Those are my thoughts on this day before *Shabbos*, on which I wish you again and again the best and most beautiful things and pray most fervently to the dear Lord that he will always protect you, dear Rosi, give you good counsel, and keep you in good health. Your meeting with your old and best friend Gertrud brought pleasure to us, too, as did the Swabian's immediate recognition of your relationship.[109] "The cat never stops mousing"—I regret hearing this about the father of your friend. And now be soundly and ceremoniously hugged and kissed by your father who loves you.

---

[108] Rosi began working at the Gluck Knitting Mills (later renamed Reliance Knitting Mills) in Manhattan in September 1940 and continued working there, doing piecework at home after her children were born.

[109] The Swabian seems to have been Gertrud's father. It is not clear if the man recognized the relationship between the two young women or Rosi's physical likeness to her parents.

[Undated letter, probably October 11, 1940.]

My dearest, good Rosi!

I am so happy, dear Rosi, that we are again in written contact with you. God willing, it will stay that way as long as we are separated. I always hope that things will change for us soon, and this hope makes me happy. During the next weeks we will look for a room close to our dear siblings [the Knollers]. Carla and Ruth found it very amusing that you have been working in the factory. I hope you soon find a job that satisfies you in every respect. We think about you day and night, my good one, and tomorrow[110] we want to include everything in our prayers and pray for a reunion. Dear Rosi, if you have a new picture of yourself, then send it to us. I always carry your old one with me. What you write about Gertrud interested me very much; she has indeed remained a loyal friend.

I have all kinds of things to do this afternoon. At the moment I'm in the city, sitting in a lunchroom where we go every day for our noon meal that we buy beforehand, sardines, etc., and then we drink a coffee with it for ten cents. We have become so modest and frugal, but the main thing is to stay well. Carla is attending an art school and is very gifted. Both girls like you very much and read your letters with great interest. Ruth will begin sewing after the holidays. She is becoming a seamstress, as I always would have liked to do. The ladies in the family believe I have enough knowledge. I made a blouse for Trude that fits so well that I'm quite proud of it. I hope that I'll soon be able to attend a course. The Committee gives them free of charge, but at the moment they are all filled up. We've heard nothing from Franz for a long time; I'm sure he has a lot on his mind. Once again, all the best, stay well, and always look after yourself. Dearest Rosi, receive many kisses from your mother.

---

[110]Likely a reference to Yom Kippur (October 12, 1940) prayers, placing this letter on October 11. The next letter confirms the date.

[2327-996][111]
October 16, 1940

My Dear Ones and dear Rosi!

The letter from dear Sigmund[112] and the affection that it shows caused us true joy, and not less your added lines, dear Emil, in which, thank God, we found only good news. Yesterday, dear Rosl, we got your letter with Dina's address. Many thanks, dear Rosl, for your report, that once again provided us with some diversion and whose value was not enhanced by Dina's additions; what you wrote was intrinsically much better than any addition could make it. I believe that in the future we can dispense with that method. It's all quite unimportant, but sometimes it's amusing to concern oneself with less important matters.

We last wrote to you, dear Rosi, on October 11. You must have gotten several letters from us if you have collected them from all the different places. First we wrote to you in care of the Rosenstocks, then several times at Ludwigs', then also at Meltzers', and, now that we have your detailed letter of October 2 which arrived on *Yom Kippur*, we have the fourth address, c/o Schwarz, which we will use in the future.

Today I am writing to all of you together, my dear ones. When on *Yom Kippur* I came home in the evening, dear Rosi, your letter, which meant more to me than anything, was lying next to my place setting. Unfortunately this high holy day no longer evokes the same feeling as formerly. One no longer reaches that certain state of exaltation, and fasting means absolutely nothing, so that one returns home from the synagogue without the feeling of

---

[111]This letter is the first one with a censor number, indicating increased Nazi control of daily life in the German-occupied Netherlands. Hugo and Clemy had to be even more cautious about what they wrote if they wanted their letters to reach Rosi.

[112]Sigmund Mosbacher, Emil's son from his first marriage (to Anna Schweizer), changed his name to Stephen after immigrating to the United States.

inward satisfaction that one used to have. I don't know how to describe what I mean, but I'm sure, my dears, that you will understand me and improve on my description. Perhaps it wouldn't be a bad idea to create new holidays.

Aside from this, however, we have no cause to be especially downcast, because the Occupation Authority has approved the departure of the *Veendam* passengers, among whom we are included, although unfortunately Frida is not because, as you know, she was summoned to the consulate later than we were, and, when she was finished, Form 575 was missing, which may have been confirmed on May 10 by cable from Washington. This caused her to lose the visa that normally she might still have obtained and that would have enabled her to depart with us then, if not in some other way. Unfortunately, though, she was prevented from becoming a *Veendam* passenger. I am writing all this so precisely so that you will know everything in case there may be another way to obtain preferred treatment for her by the consulate. For us now the main thing is that the U.S.A. issues us new visas. We have nothing to do with the matter; both the exit permit and the business of the visas are processed by the local Committee on behalf of all those concerned. In regard to the ship's tickets, I acted on my own initiative and made reservations only for December 12 from Lisbon. When I did this, I knew nothing about the possibilities of departure; I took this step after I heard nothing from you. On October 2 the local travel agency sent a cable to the U.S.A. so that you might be requested to pay for the ship tickets. Previously I had inquired whether word had arrived saying that the payment was on its way. I was informed that no information concerning payment had been received. That did not disturb me in the slightest because I thought that the *Veendam* passengers, when the time came, would be embarked together, and that the New York Committee, acting on information from the local Committee, would already have told you what you had to do, whether the ship tickets had to be paid for or not, because in the end the reservations would be continued with a ship completely different from the one in which we had been assigned berths. I think that the Committee, when things reach that point—by which I mean when the American visas are granted—will also apply your payment to the voyage. You will remember that in an earlier letter I wrote that a certain sum had to be deposited with the Committee there for a possible voyage. I only reserved ship's berths because I heard from another passenger that he had done the same thing. I did it, as I wrote any number of times, in order not to neglect anything. So now you, too, are completely informed about this. May the Almighty grant that no complications arise, which they are so fond of doing whenever the Hugos wish to embark upon their travels.

Do you still remember how, when they [Hugo and Clemy] were on a visit here [Amsterdam] many years ago, they borrowed five hundred guilders, which Franz at that time was willing to lend because he knew that it would be repaid in installments. Today I am once more not writing at home because I am too much distracted there. At the end of October the dear ones are moving to 102 Rijnstraat, the address you should use in the future. We are once again looking for a room with kitchen privileges and hope that we will not have to make use of it and of the kitchen for very long. Yesterday Frida rented a small sleeping space from Wechsler of Fürth and his second wife (the first one is also here and lives separately). During the day until bedtime, she is busy at Trude's and takes her supper there. Lenchen was very lucky. On an especially stormy evening she went to her brother-in-law, where she is still living. She's also looking for a new room because the old apartment has to be vacated. Such stories do not belong to our middling days but to our main days, since Trude and Clemy suffer extraordinarily from them, while I remain somewhat calmer.

I celebrated Lenchen's birthday. On October 13 we went with Henriette and the jubilee child to a café. There were presents from all sides and it was quite satisfying. Phil [van Gelder], however, was apparently not satisfied. He telephoned us to say that he had to learn about the celebration from the newspaper.[113] He was amazed that we hadn't called him, and now he had to hear from us that Lenchen is well and in good spirits. He couldn't keep her on a shorter leash than he does. By chance Clemy came to the telephone while he was making a scene and acted accordingly. She told him that it was he, after all, who wanted to have nothing to do with her, and, as to financial matters, one had been forced to turn to him.

Now that the word is out that it may be possible for us to depart, we get telephone calls, partly from our hometown and partly from southern Germany, from people who have never called or only once until now. Of course I can understand the wishes that are expressed.#[114] Always the same. This Weilh[heimer] had the notion of inviting us to a cup of coffee some weeks ago. I agreed reluctantly. Yesterday he wanted to speak to me.

I hope, dear Rosi, that you will soon be able to give a favorable report about Ludwig. We still don't know where you are working, what kind of work you are doing, etc., etc., and once again we look forward with pleasure to your reports that are already underway. Today Mother really has nothing to add, and I'm going to send this letter right away. She always has work to do, just as she did at home, and not only for others but for us as well. Our baggage is still being held, untouched, in transit in Rotterdam, and we make do with the little bundle with which we arrived and with what we were wearing at the

---

[113] By September 1940, the only Jewish newspaper permitted was *Het Joodsche Weekblad* (the *Jewish Weekly*), which was produced by the Joodse Raad (Jewish Council) under the close supervision of the Nazi authorities. The paper mainly published Nazi propaganda, new Nazi orders, and community social items such as birthdays and marriages.

[114] Hugo's own addendum indicated with # in his letter.

time. That's not very nice, and it means constant repairing and patching; you'll understand. Stay well, my dear ones, and you, dear Rosi, and everything else, God willing, will turn out well. With many, many regards and kisses, naturally also from your dear mother. Your parents.

Requests to call on relatives and acquaintances and to arrange for affidavits. Weilh[eimer]., as it happens, had requests of a less consequential kind—just to pass on regards, including all of you.

[101 2331]
[Undated letter, probably shortly after October 27, 1940.]

My dearest Rosi!

On *Erev Simchat Torah*,[115] as we were starting to go home from Cohn-Goldbergers, I said to Trude, "Perhaps there's a letter from Rosi at home," and how happy I was that my intuition was right. I'm happy to hear all the good things from you. For us the main thing always is that you stay healthy. Father has certainly written to you that letters from you haven't arrived, and we don't understand the time differences.

Since Sunday[116] we have a place of our own. We moved into a small but very nice room with heating and warm water. We've already written you that it's in the same building with Trude. We are living with especially nice, decent people, but still we would be infinitely happier if our departure could begin soon. During the last few days I had a lot to do, due to Trude's and our moving, and there is still a lot to do, but I'm very glad to do it now that we're separate. Trude is very happy that, by chance, we found a room in the same building; we are on the first floor and the Knollers on the third. On moving day Father went very early to get Midri, who spent the whole day

---
[115] Simchat Torah fell on October 24, 1940, so the evening of October 23, 1940.
[116] Sunday would have been October 27, 1940.

with us. I cook for us, of course, and if I need something I can get it from Trude. If only Frida could have moved with us everything would have gone well. Her room is six minutes from here, and of course Father will have to accompany her home in the evenings. Aunt Lenchen has also found a place to live nearby; she has been through a lot. I assume that Lily/Albert are underway; also Hertha Engelsrath wanted to be in Lisbon by the end of October. The family is always making a fuss here, and jealousy reigns all the time. The weather is as cold as if it were deepest winter. Dear Rosi, always dress warmly. How is the fur coat holding up? Isn't it just about worn out? It was already threadbare with age. I hope that a letter from you is on its way. Greet all the dear ones, and receive the warmest kisses from your mother.

Photo courtesy of Jack Boas

102 Rijnstraat in the River District, where the Hugos roomed, was part of the old Jewish Quarter in the southern part of Amsterdam. Many Jews still lived in this section of the city in 1940. The building looks exactly as it did in 1940.

[106 232]
October 30, 1940

My dear good Rosi!

Your letter of October 10 reached us on October 24, the evening of *Simchat Torah*, to our great joy, and we were and are happy to have a report with good news from you in our hands once again. Perhaps a letter that you already sent us didn't arrive, or hasn't arrived yet, and we're lacking a context, which causes some things to be unclear to us. First of all, what is your position at Vieyra's like, whose name we hear for the first time? Are you there in the morning or the afternoon? When do you work in the glove shop?[117] Second, who is the Schwarz in your mailing address? Is Schwarz identical with Pauline Rubens' nephew? In any case, the umbrella was an act of great thoughtfulness.

In the meantime we have heard nothing more about our business. The Committee is working for all the *Veendam* passengers, and all we can do is to keep on waiting and hoping. Aunt Frida, who is not a *Veendam* passenger, because at the time she had not completed the process, has still heard nothing from Rotterdam. Yesterday a letter came from Oakland,[118] from which we gather that people are counting on Aunt Frida's prompt arrival, and of course they draw this conclusion from the fact that the ship's passage had been booked, which Uncle Emil arranged as a precaution. But we also reserved our passage, also as a precaution, and there is no guarantee that we will be able to sail with the steamer. That will only happen if all the conditions are fulfilled. We learned of the

---

[117] Rosi worked in the Vieyra home after she finished her day shift at the glove factory.

[118] "Oakland" is a reference to Frida's daughter Anna and her husband Philip (Fips) White, who had immigrated to Oakland, California, in 1936. The Whites in Oakland, Rosi in New York, and Emil and Rosl in Toledo were trying to figure out which forms would get Frida and the Mosbachers out of Holland.

acquisition of the coffee machine from which we gathered that your tastes haven't changed. May you always enjoy it in moderation so that you can continue to use the noble beverage.

Since the beginning of this week we have been living in our own room at 102 Rijnstraat, first floor, c/o Sabel,[119] and since the day before yesterday Ari and Trude are also in the same house, but on the third floor. Despite this, it should be assumed that our incoming mail will continue to be delivered to Knollers'. I just telephoned to Apeldoorn to inquire about the condition of Franz's mother. Her depression, unfortunately, is exactly as it was, and I regret that I can't report any improvement. The written discussions continue with him [Franz]. At times his nauseating pedantry makes me want to vomit, and sometimes when he refuses to understand me I make myself very clear indeed. Of course he is greatly to be pitied, but he likes to play the role of the strong man, upset by nothing; then he suddenly changes to the opposite extreme.

He who does not manage his own affairs and thus makes himself dependent on the Committee will come to know the disadvantages. I could imagine that, if a favorable decision by the consulate were to be achieved today, we might hear about it in a week. If it were unfavorable, nothing would be said about it. In other words, it would be hushed up to keep us in a good mood. That's just an assumption on my part. I want to make the point that we are left hanging in the air, and that departure can be announced at any time. God grant that it happens in such a surprising way.

Clara Fenigstein would like to hear from me, through you, about the nature of dear Ludwig's illness. I hope that meanwhile you can give us some good news about his condition. Of course we send our regards to the entire

---

[119]The family Sabel does not have any known connection to the "Sabel portfolio" that Hugo mentions in his June 5, 1939, letter.

family. The news from Erna[120] is very sad; they are probably going to a *camp* again. With financial assistance their situation could be alleviated or at least improved. Unfortunately it's not possible for us to transfer funds from here. The cold season has begun very early here; the raw wind is especially unpleasant. Sleep is most restful in the afternoon; during the night it varies, as it has done for years. Dear Rosi, I hope you are well and contented and also not in straitened circumstances materially. And, if you can answer that in the affirmative, then I hope you will not hesitate to follow the path that stands open to you. With affectionate kisses and regards from your father who loves you.

---

[120]Alfred, Erna's husband, had been arrested by the Belgian authorities shortly after the German invasion of Belgium on May 10, 1940, and deported to the Saint Cyprien detention camp in southern France. The Belgians arrested and deported more than 8,000 men, mainly Jewish refugees, as "enemy aliens." Erna and her daughter Marion left Belgium, Alfred somehow escaped the camp, and the three were living in Vichy France. The details of this new deportation danger are not known.

$1,000,000
RESCUE THRU EMIGRATION
HIAS Campaign

HEBREW SHELTERING AND IMMIGRANT AID SOCIETY
425 LAFAYETTE STREET — ALgonquin 4-2900 — NEW YORK

CAMPAIGN OFFICERS
HON. MITCHELL MAY, *Chairman*
MAURICE LEVIN
ALBERT ROSENBLATT
MAX J. SCHNEIDER, *Co-Chairmen*
JOHN L. BERNSTEIN
MORRIS FEINSTONE
ABRAHAM HERMAN, *Vice-Chairmen*
HARRY FISCHEL, *Treasurer*
NATHAN SCHOENFELD, *Associate Treasurer*
ISAAC L. ASOFSKY, *Secretary*

PLAN and SCOPE COMMITTEE
SAMUEL A. TELSEY, *Chairman*
JACOB MASSEL
HON. JONAH J. GOLDSTEIN
SAMUEL GOLDSTEIN
S. DINGOL
MURRAY I. GURFEIN
REUBEN GUSKIN
BENJAMIN J. WEINBERG
and Campaign Officers
ALBERT A. PETERS, *Campaign Director*

October 31, 1940

Dr. Emil Mosbacher
2134 Perth Street
Toledo, Ohio

Re: Hugo Mosbacher & wife
Aribert Knoller, 72 Beethovenstraat

Dear Dr. Mosbacher:

We have received the following report from our Amsterdam Committee:

"the visas of the above named are already expired. However, the so-called "Ausreisegenehmigung" had been applied for an we hope that should the departure be granted this family will get new visas.

Mr. Mosbacher is in constant touch with us and we do our best to advise Mr. Mosbacher and his family as far as possible."

Very sincerely yours,

for Isaac L. Asofsky,
EXECUTIVE DIRECTOR

An October 31, 1941, letter from HIAS to Emil that he forwarded to Rosi.

[2899-2161]
[Undated letter, probably just after November 3, 1940.][121]

My dear Rosi!

Your detailed, lovely letter gave us great pleasure. It came Saturday morning. I had just finished reading it when Father came from the synagogue, and then we read it together with great interest. We found the pictures of the Doktors delightful; Rosl looks especially beautiful. I thought that sending pictures was forbidden, but, since that isn't the case, I would like to ask you, dear Rosi, to send us some photos of you as quickly as possible. I know that taking pictures isn't your forte, but just for our sake you need to bite into the sour apple. It has been one and a half years since we last saw you, a long time.[122] We hope our visa issue will finally be resolved—and we hardly dare to hope. Meanwhile we are so thankful if we keep our health, and we wish the same for you, my dear Rosi. I was happy that you mentioned Carla and Ruth; Aunt Trude was very much waiting for that.

My time is very full right now. Today I started a sewing course, and next week we'll start English lessons. Life has completely changed now that we're on our own. I'm able to fix proper meals for Father, something that never got done right at the Knollers' and that Father badly needs. A gentle query, dear Rosi: Are you getting good nutrition? Just make sure that you always take plenty of vitamins. What's your job at the factory? Do you sew complete gloves there or just single parts? You've described everything so nicely for us. We heard from Aunt Mela that Hertha was ready to depart and now has no possibility of

---

[121]This letter has six lipstick marks on the back. Either Clemy sent kisses to Rosi or Rosi reacted to her mother's letter with kisses.

[122]Hugo and Clemy had last seen Rosi at the beginning of June 1939, and Clemy said here it had been "one and a half years since we have seen you," thus supporting the early November dating. Her references to being on their own now, Heddy's upcoming November 22 birthday, Els' recent letter, and Rosi's new job corroborate the early November dating.

traveling. We would be very interested in knowing if Aunt Lily got away. We worry so much about every single person, and we usually have so much to do on our own account. Our nerves could, of course, use a respite, but when, God willing, we are together, then all will be well again. Lenchen is our constant guest on Sundays. We feel deeply sorry for her because her children show so little concern for her, as Elschen wrote so coldly. She is exactly like her father. Have you heard anything from Fredl/Luise [Lusi]; has Luise started her new job? Rosl's friend Irma was lucky to get Luise's apartment. Franz writes every two weeks. He has constant worry with his mother; unfortunately she is in a bad way. We've also had news from Aunt Dina, very bad this time; she was cursing the entire family. Heddy's birthday is November 22. Even though we didn't send congratulations, we still think about her a lot. She wrote us such a nice letter at *Rosh Hashanah*, and I miss her very much. And now, my good little Rosi: Stay well, keep on writing, and accept many greetings and kisses from your mother. Many greetings to Ludwig's family.

November 7, 1940

Dear Rosi!

This morning we received the enclosed telegram.[123] I have already written to [Pauline] Rubens about renewing the affidavit and sending it to your address. As vexatious as all these stipulations by the consul seem, I am still hopeful because I assume that our loved ones have gotten the exit permit and that the consul is trying every possible trick before issuing the visa. Today I tried to find out what Form 575 is—whether successfully or not I don't know. Insofar as I understand this telegram, I have to submit this form and an affidavit. You have to do the same. You and me and an affidavit—that's a joke. I'm writing to Fritz by the same mail. I assume that you and Fritz are in

---

[123]The telegram was not preserved.

agreement and will retain Paul Neurath as an expert adviser. In any case, you should inform me at once as to what I should do, even if I have already done it. All the documents should be sent to you, and you should expedite them after obtaining exact information as to the best and most secure way to send them.

I'm in a great hurry to get this all done as quickly and exactly as possible. Fritz Roederer's address: 609 West 173 Street.

Kisses from Rosl and Emil.

[1958-1266a]
November 10, 1940

My dear good Rosi!

The cable to Toledo was followed by a letter to the Doktors that is also meant for you and that will have reached you some days before this letter does. I believe that in that other letter I explained that it's not as if the consul told me, "Mr. Mosbacher, you still have to bring me these and those papers," but rather the gentleman at the Committee, who is negotiating with the consulate, has received his instructions, and then he advises the emigrants who are waiting for their visas to provide themselves with the necessary documents. This gentleman told me that the affidavit of a man who has an income of 20,000 dollars at his disposal was found insufficient, probably because there was no family relationship or the relationship was not considered close enough. I know myself from my first interview with the consul that the information that my brother was establishing his medical practice was very important. I wasn't able at that time to refer to my daughter because we didn't know then that your own departure was possible. At this time it's impossible for us to deal directly from here with the consulate in Rotterdam. We probably would not be able to go there in person without a summons, for example if Washington would instruct the consul in Rotterdam to complete the process for Hugo and Clemy and Aunt Frida. We were told, of course, that the consul has the final authority to make decisions within his consular district; it is up to him to act upon suggestions. It's also possible that, after a ruling has been made, the requirements will be eased, and the consulates will receive directives that will favor our prompt departure. At this point we just need to be thankful that no further difficulties have arisen and hope and trust that none will. In addition to the tickets, there will be all kinds of errands for you and Uncle Emil and also Mrs. Rubens to attend to, and, if everything goes well, then it will turn out that the one thing or the other wasn't really necessary. I would be happy if, after the submission of all the papers, the consulate would be satisfied and not bring up something new. As our Lina used to say, "I only believe what I see and sometimes not even that."

Franz, by the way, frequently mentioned Lina, but not, apparently, in recent months. We have heard nothing from her, but this is typical of her and we find it quite understandable and approve of it. We're convinced that her relatives have been told all the more about us and have had plenty to listen to. Dear Mother has arranged a very cozy home for me, and I am very grateful to her. The little room requires strict orderliness in order to be nice-looking and livable. I can rely on Mother in this respect, and I'm also well and plentifully fed. I'm happy that I now have to get by with smaller amounts of potatoes, of which I consumed too much in previous months. As long as we're on this subject, I assume, dear Rosi, that you, too, will maintain a regular, sufficient, and healthy nutritional intake, and that you will also be reasonable in this respect. Always dress according to the weather and eat fruit, and you'll stay well! With many hearty kisses from your father who loves you, and many regards to the Ludwigs.

My dearest Rosi!

We hope that something from you will arrive in the next few days. Your last letter, which made us very happy, was dated October 20. I hope that you, dear Rosi, are now free of toothache, and I'm sorry that you had to suffer from it so persistently. For about the last fourteen days I've been busy with housework again, but it's my own housework; we possess a room and a foldout bed and a sofa bed, and also hot and cold running water in the room, and we're entitled to kitchen privileges. The room is of course very small for two persons, but it's mine, and that is an advantage that cannot be valued highly enough. Our landlords are very good people. Perhaps their only flaw is that they want too much to include us in their family circle. But since they are good, hardworking people, we can put up with it. Of course, with the housework I will get less sewing done, but I am going to begin learning English again in a serious way.

If you were thinking that we would arrive anytime soon, then it will have been disappointing for you to hear from Toledo that our supporting documents have to be submitted all over again. We were not, of course, all that optimistic, but, after the consul, some months back, had explicitly not required any papers from us, we had felt ourselves justified in drawing the conclusion that we had dealt with that particular matter. But now the procedure is starting all over again. The expenses will begin again, and even your meager savings will be called upon, but the essential point is that the papers that Father is required to submit must be sent here as soon as possible. Perhaps for once the saying "First come, first served" will prove true.

Aunt Lenchen was very pleased with your report; this Sunday evening we will have the pleasure of her company again. You write, dear Rosi, that winter has showed itself over there, and here we too have felt the cold very much. Do you have all your baggage with you where you're living or is some of it in storage with the relatives? Have Hertha and Aunt Lily and her husband arrived? And, if they have, did they really come by ship? In the meantime we have heard nothing more about Paul's efforts in W[ashington]. If such things are really so successful, they could be very helpful to us right now. We would like to hear from you whether, in your opinion, Paul and his friends can do something for us. Father always takes a skeptical attitude at the outset in this regard and says that every case is special.

Do you get together often with the Fleischmanns and the Rosenstocks? Did you speak to Fredl-Lusi again? We had a very satisfactory letter from Heddy. She misses your letters and does not have your address. Dear Rosi, are you in contact with Pauline? Has Albrecht changed much in the picture?[124] I am curious whether he decides to follow you soon. Is his brother still in the same place? Have you heard anything from Fellheimer in the meantime? Has Franz written?

Now, my dear Rosi, I've asked you enough questions and am looking forward happily to your response. I also hope we will hear soon that Ludwig's family is doing better. I send them my regards, and I send you, my dear Rosi, the most affectionate greetings and kisses from your mother.

---

[124] Clemy referred to a recent photograph of Albrecht that Rosi has evidently mentioned in a letter.

> Oakland, Cal. 10. November 1940
>
> Liebe Doktors :
>
> Ich habe eben einen ausführlichen Brief an Fritz von Stapel gelassen und ihn mit seinen Aufgaben vertraut gemacht, die aus dem von Euch empfangenen Telegram für ihn erwachsen.
>
> Das Telegram glaube ich folgendermassen richtig gedeutet zu haben :
>
> Der Consul in Rotterdam verlangt für die Anerung der Visen for Mosbacher und Roederer form 575 von Euch (Emil Bosbachers) und Rsi (d.h. Ihr und Rosi müsst form 575 for Mosbachers ausfüllen) ebenfalls form 633 für den Sohn Fritz (dies ist für Mutter und nicht richtig : Fritz muss ebenfalls form 575 ausfüllen, und Florence als Amerikanerin form 633). Weiter 4 Affidavits müssen neu ausgestellt werden von Euch, Rosi und Rubens für Mosbachers, und von Fritz für Frida Roederer. Diese letzteren Papiere sind schleunigst an die Antragsteller zu senden.
>
> Ich habe dementsprechend an Fritz geschrieben, und da er sehr eigenartig ist, ihm na gelegt evtl. seine Papiere an den Consul direkt zu schicken.
>
> Wir haben dieser Tage die Bestätigung (return receipt for registered mail) unsrer Affidavits von Rotterdam bekommen, das wir am 15. August abgesandt hatten und das vom 20. September bestätigt war. Wir hatten es Clipper, Registered, Return Receipt requested, Special Delivery geschickt. Wie Du richtig sagst, haben wir im Augenblick nichts weiter zu tun.
>
> Ich will die Briefe zur Post bringen und schliesse daher kurz, mit vielen Dank für Eure prompte Berichterstattung und ziemlich hoffnungsvoll
>
> Euer
> Philips

Philip White signed "Your Philips" to indicate Anna and himself

A translation of Philip White's letter:

Dear Doktors:

I just sent a detailed letter to Fritz and informed him of the tasks that he has to carry out, according to the telegram that I just received from you.

I believe I have understood the telegram correctly as follows:

In order to renew the visas for Mosbacher and Roederer, the consul in Rotterdam requires you and Rosi to fill out form 575 for the Mosbachers and likewise form 633 for the son Fritz. (This is for Mother, and incorrect: Fritz also has to fill out form 575, and Florence, as an American, has to fill out form 633.) Also: Renewed affidavits must be supplied by you, Rosi, and Rubens for the Mosbachers and by Fritz for Frida Roederer. These last papers must be sent to the applicant as soon as possible.

I have written to Fritz and explained this, and, since he is very peculiar, I suggested that he might want to send his papers directly to the consul.

We recently received confirmation of our affidavit from Rotterdam (*return receipt for registered mail*). We sent it on August 15 and its receipt was confirmed on September 20. We sent it Clipper Registered, *Return Receipt Requested, Special Delivery*. As you said, correctly, for the moment there is nothing more for us to do.

I want to bring these letters to the post office so I'm going to close now, with many thanks for informing me so promptly. I remain, somewhat hopefully,

Your
Philips

[2899-292]
November 18, 1940

My dear Rosi!

On November 16 we received your letter of October 27 and that of the dear Doktors of October 25, which I will confirm separately. On November 17 we received your cable that we weren't expecting at all, but for which we are very thankful. We were quite especially happy with your letter and with the cable: "*Affidavits Rubens, Doctors, Rosi airmailed, forms 575 filed.*" We concluded from this that our cable had been correctly understood, and that everything had, God willing, been carried out correctly. We know that these things not only take up a lot of time; they also cost a lot of money—a lot, at least, for someone who isn't earning very much, and we hope that there is someone to advance you the money for these extra expenses. In any case, dear Rosi, we thank you warmly for all the effort, no matter how obvious that may be. I hope our letter has also arrived, which we told you was underway but that hadn't reached you yet. Was Paul N[eurath] able to accomplish something for us in Washington or was he unable to undertake anything? Your letter gave us much pleasure. Since it doesn't say anything about Ludwig M[osbacher]., we conclude that he is back to normal. Much of what you had to say was very amusing, and all the readers and listeners enjoyed it. Perhaps in the new country, Mirko[125] will learn the meaning of "work" and become more reasonable.

So Mrs. Vieyra is your boss in the afternoon, and the blonde lady whose hair is so heavily dyed and who thinks so highly of her youthful appearance is the glove madam. I might perhaps also know the baker's wife from Bavaria

---

[125]Mirko Engelsrath was one of Albert Engelsrath's sons from his first marriage. He emigrated from Yugoslavia to the United States in August 1940. Hugo may have referred to Mirko's devotion to religious study rather than to earning a living.

if I had more personal details. In any case, it's nice that you get such good treatment at good prices.

Some days ago Lenchen, for the first time, got a handwritten letter from her Els, posted in Lisbon,[126] which is where she also wants to have letters sent to her in the future; probably a relative of theirs lives in Lisbon. I'm sorry to hear that Uncle Emil[127] had such heavy losses. As a consequence we will also lose the share that he promised us once. I imagine that our business will proceed as follows: After the arrival of the affidavits, they will be accepted by the Committee and taken to Rotterdam. I don't know whether another medical examination will follow, and we also do not know today whether, if everything is really ready and in order, the possibility of travel will then exist, just as we also do not know today what will happen in two weeks nor what will happen in four weeks. The main thing is to keep our health, and that, too, is not within our power; we need protection wherever we go, and we pray for it anew daily. This afternoon dear Mother began attending a sewing course. Perhaps that and the advance payment of costs means that we will be leaving soon. In Nuremberg, after all, when Mother had begun a similar course and had paid a fifty mark deposit, we departed immediately. I hope that Fritz Roederer works as quickly for his mother as the Doktors and you do, and we hope that we are right in assuming that Fritz has already become a citizen by virtue of his marriage and that Aunt Frida will thus be placed in a preferred category.

Last Friday evening we were invited to the Knollers, together with Aunt Lenchen, and yesterday, Saturday evening, Lenchen came to eat with us. She appreciates both quantity and quality, and with Mother she gets both

---

[126] Apparently this was the first communication from Els since she fled Holland on August 30, 1940. Clemy's earlier remark, "as Elschen wrote so coldly," probably refers to this same letter.
[127] Hugo's cousin Emil in England.

and is full of praise. The unpleasant thing is just that she likes to come about four in the afternoon and to stay until eleven in the evening. Our nerves can no longer endure this. Four hours of continuous conversation in one little room are more than enough, and, starting now, we are going to stipulate just when it is that we will receive company. Aside from this, going out in the evening, in general, involves a certain risk. One stays at home as a matter of principle; the other isn't afraid to go out, but runs the danger of having to remain somewhere, and that can also become quite unpleasant for the one who is being visited.

Was it a mistake for the Doktors to leave New York? It looks as though he would have been able to build up his practice quicker there, but, after all, one must do what seems best. It's interesting to hear that people with expert knowledge in metals are in demand, but I believe that it is younger personnel who are being sought, and, dear Rosi, that is probably your opinion, too. Our landlord's family is extremely nice and likeable, altogether too much so, but better that way than the opposite. Because we are very fond of our peace and quiet, whenever of an evening things are about to become a bit loud, they are right there at our door, inviting us to join them. One needs a community today. Dear Rosi, please always be very careful so that we won't have to worry about anything in that respect. Stay well and be most warmly greeted and kissed by your father who loves you.

Many greetings to Ludwig's family and the Fleischmanns, etc.

ISIDORE VIEYRA
INDUSTRIAL DIAMONDS
580 FIFTH AVENUE
NEW YORK

TELEPHONE
LONGACRE 3-1820

CABLE ADDRESS
ISIDECES NEW YORK

To whom it may concern.

I, Isidore Vieyra, residing at 50 West 72nd. Street, declare that Miss Rosi Mosbacher, residing at 101 West 93rd. Street, is doing parttime work in my household.

Her salary amounts to $ 6.00 weekly, and Mrs. Vieyra, who is very satisfied with her work, intends to maintain Miss Mosbacher in her service.

New York, November 12, 1940

Isidore Vieyra

Subscribed to before me
this 12th day of November 1940
Max Kahn

NOTARY PUBLIC, New York County
Clerk's No. 16, Register's No. 7-K-18
Commission Expires March 30, 1942

Rosi's employment contract with Mr. Vieyra.

November 18, 1940

My Dear Ones,

On November 16 we received your letter of October 25, together with Rosi's letter from New York. All of us here were made enormously happy by your letters, dear Rosl and dear Emil. Seeing new photos of you gave us all great pleasure. You, dear Rosl, were especially admired by everyone who saw your picture. We hope Lore, or Marianne, is quite well again. Seeing her face once more was also very nice. The word "*charmant*" fits her very well, and it is easy to imagine her personality. Stephen's reports are also a source of entertainment and pleasure, and it appears that the outdoor life will be an excellent school for him. We're sorry to hear that the practice is still doing poorly, but perhaps you should wait a bit before you make any changes and proceed very cautiously, since relocating would involve a lot of work and expense. Perhaps Cincinnati would be the right place? I probably mention this only because I formed a good opinion of Cincinnati after learning something about it, while I knew nothing at all about Toledo. Many thanks for your quick work in regard to the affidavits and related matters. Rosi's telegram informed us that the affidavits are on their way to us by air mail and that Form 575 has been cabled to Rotterdam. I am very pleased that you understood our telegrams to you and took the correct action on them.

Walter F[full name unknown]: Did you have the impression that you had to help him out of a momentary difficulty? He would not, of course, have given any indication of his chronic poverty. When one remembers his father it is easy to believe in the reliability of the son, and I can only hope that events will justify that belief. Do you hear anything from Ullis? While we were still at home we used to hear about the exams that Späth had passed, and the story would not be totally uninteresting for later times were it not for all the stupid nonsense that has been uttered in recent years. The Bonnlander D[full name unknown]. won't have done it [passed his exams?] yet, either.

We had news from Dina again. As long as she is writing about others, it's often quite amusing, but, when she writes about those with whom she talks and about herself, she becomes unbearably sarcastic. Also, she is stupid when she does this, because, as she admits, she believes she can allow herself some latitude in her written accounts because the object of her ridicule is far away. I am in ongoing correspondence with Franz. Unfortunately I'm unable to answer his many questions, all of which have to do with the treatment of his mother, etc., etc. That is because no one tells us anything. She is not in Bayreuth, but in a large facility with an enormous number of patients in the third class. When I called the doctor a few weeks ago, he told me that her depression had not changed. I think it is not at all impossible that her condition will not change. I have never exchanged a word with Dina about this matter, and I know nothing of what Franz has told her about it. It's incomprehensible that Alfons is still concerned with utopias; earlier reports about them [Alfons and Irma] indicate, I'm pleased to note, that they are doing very well. One may dismiss Irma's usual complaining—she is certainly quite robust. Lenchen has received the first handwritten letter from her daughter Els. The letter was mailed in Lisbon, and of course it evoked great joy while the reading of its few sentences made me ice cold. She [Lenchen] was our guest yesterday, Saturday evening. She places great importance on her visits, and Clemy satisfies her in every direction: *Chosvenu-Chosmenu*.[128]

We are staying with very nice, cultivated, younger people with a strong rural accent from the Fulda area who have been here for some time. Wedding songs, family

---

[128] Hugo used the Hebrew from the High Holiday liturgy meaning, "written and sealed," referring to inscription in the book of life for the coming year. His meaning seems to be that neither Helene nor Clemy will ever change.

poems, and bar mitzvah verses are shared with us and cards are read aloud. Sent by the mother years ago, they contain the news that she is having a new foulard dress made, etc., etc. We are astounded at the naiveté and the optimism that these good people still have. When the weather outside is stormy it's pleasant, sometimes, to hold a conversation à la 1890, but our nerves can no longer endure the trivial and the insignificant. We are no longer accustomed to pleasantness. Still, it's very agreeable to dwell under one roof with good and decent people. It's also still more important that this same roof never be attacked because in that case the good and decent people would not be able to help. What counts, as the Lower Franconians put it, is different: It's not a matter of affidavits or of the visa or the departure, but things much greater. First, it's a matter of staying healthy and then of being able to leave without great risk.

Dear Mother [Jettchen], I send you my warmest greetings. I'm very glad that you will have a pleasant time during the holidays and I send you my best wishes. To you, my dear ones, I send my warmest greetings and love. Your Hugo.

November 19, 1940

My Dear Ones,[129]

Hugo sends the mail on so quickly that I often don't have a chance to read it to my satisfaction, but I do have a share in everything he writes. Your pictures gave us great joy. I'm quite satisfied with the photographs, but, despite that, I long to be with the originals. Whenever I think about the trouble and work we have already put you to, it seems that success should have been achieved long ago. Instead, difficulties always arise that only serve to drag the matter out. We now hear from Rosi that old

---

[129]Clemy usually addressed Emil and Rosl as "My Dear Ones." Emil and Rosl passed the letter on to Rosi.

Cousin Emil, who always used to be much too slow with his payments, has lost a large part of his capital. I see how much work my one small room with kitchen causes for me, and I often think of you, dear Rosl, and the amount of work you have to get through every day. At least I can devote myself to all my other chores after eleven a.m., and I'm happy to be alone and free from other people's noise. We agreed with Henriette that we will visit each other on alternate Wednesdays. She was happy to accept the suggestion. Trude and Henriette don't understand each other so well, but outwardly they are as sweet as sugar to each other and kisses are always exchanged. Lenchen, for whose sake I'm glad to do something extra and who really is very much to be pitied, has the unfortunate habit of stretching her visits out much too long. If I invite her to supper she would prefer to come at four in the afternoon and stay until eleven. I can't, of course, endure that, and Hugo even less; he always says that his nerves are worn out after so much long-winded prattle. As I said, after nine months a change would be more than welcome, but everything is so uncertain that one can't count on anything. In five weeks Sigmund will be with you again; he will be very happy to see you, and we will write to him in the next few days. Hertha Engelsrath had everything ready to go, but now it isn't possible. We think that things will work out for Lily and Albert. Erna and Alfred, fortunately, did not go to a camp. Lore pleases me very well, and you, dear Mother, will be happy with the granddaughter and the children.

Many greetings and kisses to all my loved ones from your Clemy.

[3958-3051]
November 27, 1940

My dear Rosi!

This letter would have been sent several days ago, but we believed that we could wait for an answer from you. It seems, though, that the mail is delayed again. We are well, thank God, despite the bad weather. In the meantime, nothing has happened in respect to our concerns since, until we have the papers in hand that are now on their way from you, everything is at a standstill. And, when they have arrived, we still won't know whether all the conditions have been fulfilled. Because we have no direct contact with the consulate, we are entirely dependent on the information we receive from the Committee. We act according to it; we can't do anything else.

Unfortunately we are unable to report to you much from here that's of interest. You're in a much better position to be able to entertain us than we are to entertain you with our letters. With us one day is like the next: We speak to the Knollers daily, several times a week to Lenchen, once a week to Henriette. Several times we have had the opportunity to look up earlier acquaintances, but mostly we avoid such obligations because there is very little interest. We finally got more reassuring news from Alfred and Erna; they have found better living quarters where they hope they will be able to remain. It appears that Alfred, who was having liver problems, was in need of an extended period of recovery.[130] Yesterday another card came from Fellh[eimer]; among other things he writes that he heard that Rosi is engaged,[131] and he asks us to write him

---

[130] Alfred was very ill at Saint Cyprien. The Falcks moved from Reveille to Beaulieu-sur-Dordogne, presumably a safer place. An evacuation center for Jewish refugee children was located in this village.

[131] Rosi met Alexander Baczewski in October 1940, not long after her arrival in the United States. It's unlikely that they were already engaged, so perhaps Hugo's friend Fellheimer was joking. Rosi had probably written to Hugo and Clemy about Alexander, but this is Hugo's first reference to their relationship.

about it. It appears that he wants to draw his own conclusions from our failure to report this to him. Otherwise he told us about people who have departed from there and, like the Herzsteins, have gotten stuck in Japan because in the meantime their American visas had expired—now renewed—and about persons who have died. I can imagine that in the meantime you have formed many new relationships with former old acquaintances. There are so infinitely many of them there, together with you on the same soil. A young Carlebach from Leipzig is supposed to be here. Do you have any idea where the Sichels might be?

We are daily thankful, dear Rosi, that you are where you are, and we are very aware of the increased anxiety that we would have every day if things were different. If our current sojourn cannot be called ideal, still it is so in comparison to your former situation.[132] We haven't kept up most of our correspondence from here; I'm thinking specifically of the Hammelburgers who are surely still in W[ürzburg]. Cousin Ida Rau writes often; Dina shows her maliciousness on paper; the correspondence with Franz has become somewhat calmer now that there is no longer so much to write about. Yesterday I was able for the first time to report a little improvement since the physician told me on the telephone that his mother is receiving injections and that some improvement can be observed. Will it continue? I am pleased that after such a long time I am finally able to give Franz a more positive report. If I had gotten the kind of letters from my mother that he was already actually getting during the time when we were all at home together, I would have known exactly what was going on. I've already gathered enough from the letters they showed me. At that time, full and total attention and care on the part of the son was lacking.

We are obliged to go out every day because we con-

---

[132] Perhaps Hugo thought they were relatively safe since there was no active war or bombing in Holland, unlike in England. At this point Nazis had not begun deportations of Jews, and things may have seemed quiet to him.

tinue to report to the authority to which you first wrote. This takes up time every day, which matters less than the expense of carfare. We do not have to report on Saturday; on Sunday we start all over again. I applied to Clara Fenigstein on behalf of Erna, in order to get the Baums, who are living in Zurich, to do something for Alfred and Erna. Those who are not in need of assistance themselves can make some sacrifices. Have you seen Frida Maier again and gotten to know her daughter? Do you remember Louis Mosb[acher], the father of the affluent son, who visited us many years ago? Where is Alfred M[osbacher][133] working now, and how are Ludwig's family and all the dear ones? I'm telling myself that, as soon as I have mailed this, your letter is going to arrive promptly, so I'm in a great hurry, and I greet and kiss you, Rosi, often and warmly. With love, your father.

My dear Rosi!

This time it seems like we haven't heard from you for a long time; I have no doubt that a letter from you is on its way. I hope we will soon have the papers in hand—we hope and hope and sadly we don't get any further. We are lucky in that we always have work to do and that keeps us from thinking too much. Father stays busy helping me. Rosi, you would be amazed what good coffee Father can make; we take one beer glass of coffee and one beer glass of coffee substitute, and it tastes much, much better than malt. I like the tailoring course very much, and I hope to gain a lot of new skills. At the moment I'm putting together a dark blue knitted suit. My sisters-in-law are coming this afternoon; Trude, obviously, will be among them. I certainly prefer her coming to visit us, rather than the other way round. Trude is terribly pettyminded. Our cooking is complicated; we have to be inventive, but that poses no problem for the two of us. It's real-

---

[133] Alfred Mosbacher was Ludwig's eldest son. Louis Mosbacher was Hugo's second cousin and the Baums were distant cousins on the Mosbacher side.

ly cold here now. In particular, the wind is biting. Do you have any news from Albrecht? How are your hands, dear Rosi? Are they still getting cramps so often? Just stay well and always take care of yourself. My dearest Rosi, accept many warm greetings and kisses from your mother.

[2236]
December 6, 1940

My Dear Ones!

In a letter to Rosi, just now completed, I expressed my great appreciation for your prompt and completely outstanding achievement, and I will not err if I state that everything could go smoothly if the local agency would only work with the same promptness, the same dedication, and the same conscientiousness. Unfortunately, however, much is lacking in that respect. When we got your cable a few days ago saying that Washington had approved and requested the issuance of the three visas, I went immediately to the Committee,[134] with that cable and the one that had come earlier from Rosi saying that the documents were in the mail, to deliver that information and, primarily, to speak with the gentleman who is handling our application. This gentleman had the cables brought to him and sent word to me that I will have a decision by the end of the next week. As it happens, the gentleman will be traveling to Rotterdam with a stack of files, and mine will be among them. It's too bad that I can't represent myself. When I was at the consulate in April and spoke with them, everything went very quickly. The self-importance of these gentlemen is very unfair and very ugly. This same man would only need to say, "Mr.

---

[134] It is not clear which committee Hugo was dealing with at this point. Perhaps the Committee for Jewish Refugees was still operating. In December 1940, the Amsterdam Jewish community established a Jewish Coordinating Committee as a defensive measure against the Nazis, but the Nazis replaced it with their own Judenrat (de Joodse Raad) in February 1941.

Mosbacher, I only have five minutes," and I would be able to tell him everything in those five minutes. But, if I complain, I run the danger of being treated even worse. In fairness to these people, I must admit that they are often held up by those who never finish making their applications and who show up every day with new requests. I, on the other hand, come with nothing and demand nothing. So the registered, special delivery letter with the affidavits from you, Rosi, and Rubens, came today. We are absolutely satisfied with what you have done. Many thanks, too, for your cable that we hope will not fail to have its effect.

We hope that you are all well and provided with good reports from Sigmund, who will surely be with you by the time our letter arrives and to whom we send our warmest regards. For the last week, Clemy has had the same stomach or gallbladder pains that she had at home. Any kind of exertion tires her; she suffers from hunger pangs, an upset stomach after eating, and back pain. We haven't gone to the doctor yet because we know that bed rest and diet are the best medicine. I recently suffered a recurrence of those bouts of nighttime coughing that used to bother me so much. I was able to treat it with codeine and a cough syrup. Every day I want to know if all my nearest and dearest are well: whether my dear Rosl is free of migraine and whether you, dear Emil, place your hand on your heart and calm yourself. You won't yet, unfortunately, have had business problems to upset you. But perhaps things have improved in the meantime. We haven't had news from you for a long while. Lenchen is coming to the Knollers this evening, Friday, and Ari has invited her to come there regularly in the future. Sunday evening she is our guest. Fortunately she is fully mobile and goes out when it is completely dark and does not need to be accompanied. In this respect she is bolder than Frida, who, we hope, will also soon get her papers from Fritz. So far she has heard nothing from him about the matter.

It's very good to hear that Jacques is satisfied. Are you still getting reports from Mohr?[135]

Dear Mother [Jettchen], we hope you are still able to get around. We often speak of W[ürzburg], especially when Ida Rau writes to us; she is deprived of almost everything and never complains. To make herself useful she takes care of sick people and ninety-year-olds. The Knollers send you many warm regards. Trude was here just now visiting Clemy. Living together in one house is very convenient for us, especially in the evening; otherwise we would have no possibility, since we don't leave the house. We hope to hear from you soon, and something good. My dears, receive many, many greetings and kisses from your Hugo.

Letters from January 1941 through December 1941

The Mosbacher Family in 1941:

Rosi Mosbacher was living and working in New York City.

Dr. Emil Mosbacher, his wife Rosl, their daughter Marianne, and Rosl's mother, Jettchen Neumann, were living in Toledo, Ohio, where Emil was establishing a medical practice.

Hugo and Clemy Mosbacher, Frida Mosbacher Roederer, Lenchen Mosbacher van Gelder, Henriette Mosbacher and her son Bruno Mosbacher, and the Knollers (Ari, Trude, Ruth, and Carla) remained trapped in German-occupied Amsterdam.

Jewish Life under German Occupation—The Netherlands, 1941[136]

January 10, 1941—All Jews were required to register with the Town Registrar.

---

[135]Perhaps a relative of Heddy Fleischmann née Mohr who was passing on reports from Heddy in Chile to Emil and Rosl.

[136]This is only a small sampling of the restrictions that the Nazis imposed on Jews in the Netherlands. Nazi laws from 1940 through 1942 gradually deprived Jews of economic, civil, and cultural life.

February 13, 1941—Nazis established a Judenrat (Jewish Council) to administer Jewish affairs for the city of Amsterdam.

February 22-23, 1941—*Razzias* (random raids) were carried out against Jews on the city streets. About 400 Jews, mostly young men, were sent to Mauthausen and not heard from again

April 11, 1941—The *Jewish Weekly* newspaper produced by the Jewish Council under the direction of the Nazis became the only newspaper Jews were permitted to read.

September 1, 1941—Jewish children were barred from public schools and required to attend Jewish schools.

September 15, 1941—Signs reading *"Verboden voor Joden"* ("Prohibited for Jews") appeared in all public places.

November 7, 1941—Jews were required to obtain permits to travel.

Sign ("Jewish Quarter") in German and Dutch at border of the Nazi-imposed Jewish District of Amsterdam, 1941.

"Verboden voor Joden" ("Prohibited for Jews") signs appeared throughout Amsterdam after September 15, 1941.

[274-21]
January 30, 1941

My dear good Rosi!

Your letter gave us the same great joy as always, even without a date. The postmark isn't clear; presumably it was sent on December 13 and arrived on January 27. Another one came a few days ago from Toledo, which I answered today. We are always happy when we get something from you and know that you are well and able to do what you need to do. We heartily thank Mrs. V[ieyra] for the invitation to the first Friday evening. In the meantime she will have heard that I promptly called upon her lady friend here. How beautiful it would be if we could enjoy that first Friday evening together! The 575 forms have finally arrived in Rotterdam, and we have inquired of the Committee in Rotterdam what the attitude there is about issuing visas to us. If we are especially lucky and obtain the visas, then other issues will arise that we will have to address. But I would still be pleased to get the visas. I regret so much that we still aren't able to tell you anything definite, but it would not be wise to awaken false hopes.

Aunt Lenchen is here with us right now, and of course she is disturbing me while I try to write. Mother and I enjoy the distinction of receiving more visitors than we would really prefer to have. You know, dear Rosi, that we don't need a lot of company. We can entertain ourselves quite well and in any case always have plenty to do. Trude has been laid up with bronchitis and a rather high fever, and Mother caught an especially strong case of the sniffles that bothers her a great deal. I still go every day to report myself while Mother has been excused on account of illness.[137] Aunt Frida continues to march on undeterred. We recently had a very reassuring letter from Heddy; she is living a life free of worry and is in very good health. Remarkably, she seems to have reconciled herself to her great loss much more rapidly than I would have believed possible.[138] The grim seriousness of the age seems to play a major role there, and people are, understandably, becoming hardened and more indifferent. We've also heard from Toledo that the Rubens are pleased with you, which didn't surprise us at all but still pleased us. There seem to be big differences between Meyers and Rubens in regard to *noblesse*, but like you, dear Rosi, we are quite satisfied with what has been done and is being done. For Uncle Emil, the assistance was of the greatest importance because without it, due to his financial problems, he would not have been able to successfully pass his examinations.[139]

I asked Franz to obtain the character affidavits that the consulate demanded from Aunt Frida. Although these affidavits were not demanded in our case, I also requested

---

[137] Hugo and Clemy were still required to report daily to the Dutch prison where they had been held in early 1940.
[138] Heddy's husband Jacob Fleishmann died in 1938 in Nuremberg. Heddy, and her younger son, Ludwig, immigrated to Chile in 1939.
[139] Probably exams required in order for Emil to practice medicine in the United States.

them. Apparently they are issued by the Jewish Council. I've always said that, as soon as you take care of one thing, something else comes up and it never ends. Still, we don't want to complain and must thank God when we hear good things from you and our dear ones and everyone remains in good health. Our pains are shared by many others. We have to keep telling ourselves that we are not the exceptions and must continue to find the patience and that we're going to do it whether we like it or not. Right now we are happy about the report that you wanted to write on a Sunday and that is on its way from you. Many greetings and sincere kisses from your father who loves you. Warm greetings to Ludwig's family; special greetings to you, dear Rosi, from the Knollers, [Henriette] Dittus,[140] Aunt Lenchen, Frida, etc.

Friday early, January 31, 1941, 9 a.m.

My dear good Rosi!

Actually, I wanted to write yesterday evening, but, due to the extended stay of Aunt Lenchen, I had to postpone it until today. That my daughter has been described as "very charming" gives me, naturally, great pleasure. Uncertainty is always the worst thing. If we would only be given a definite day and year on which we can depart, we could calm down, but not knowing anything increases our nervousness. And, on top of everything else, Father got up an hour early this morning in the belief that it was seven o'clock. Of course that put an end to my own sleep. According to what you wrote about Mrs. Tuchmann's position, it seems that over there people can easily find employment after even a brief period of training. Mrs. T. is, after all, not a fully trained employee, and I am happy both for her and for myself because under

---

[140] Henriette remarried Gotthilf Dittus in 1911 after Don Mosbacher's death in 1909. Dittus committed suicide in 1938. Nothing is known of the circumstances, but Henriette was once again a widow.

those circumstances I, too, would have a chance, if we could only arrive soon.

Eight days ago, to our surprise, we got a card from [?] Goldberger,[141] who asked how we are doing. We responded promptly, and I wrote him honestly what a good account his Eva has given of herself. Eva is together with me in the sewing course, and her manner is significantly more likeable and friendly than that of my niece Ruth. Father disapproves of the attitude of both nieces—of Ruth, for the reasons I have indicated, and of Carla because, although she can be likeable and nice, she is egotistical and inconsiderate and boundlessly impudent toward her parents. If you live together with families for such a long time you form all sorts of impressions. Just as you, dear Rosi, will have seen many things that once were strange to you. Concerning Aunt Lily, we think they are on their way to Lisbon. Your picture, which will arrive soon, has already made us very happy; no matter how it turns out, it will be fine.

The winter here continues with severe cold. We are happy that so far we don't have to complain about the heating. I hope, dear Rosi, that you always put on clothing that is warm enough so that you don't catch cold. How far do you live from the Ludwigs? Have you heard anything lately from old Uncle Emil? With whom is Frida Meier staying? Have you had any letters from Albrecht in the meantime? Except for our very closest relatives and friends, we don't, as a rule, carry on a correspondence from here with anyone.

Stay well, dear Rosi, and be most warmly greeted and kissed by your mother.

---

[141] Probably the husband of Clemy's friend Ella Cohn-Goldberger and the father of Eva. It is not clear where he was writing from. In a later letter he still seemed to be in Amsterdam.

[309-1402b]
February 8, 1941, Saturday evening

My dear good Rosi!

This letter actually should already have been written on Thursday, but I put it off intentionally, and yesterday, Friday evening, your letter of December 27 reached us after forty-two days. You can imagine our joy! You mention in this letter that you had sent us pictures, and we regretted very much that they had not arrived. So how surprised we were when now, Saturday evening, the letter of December 17, posted on December 18, came with the three photos for which, of course, we are enthusiastically thankful. One of the pictures is quite splendid and can't be surpassed by the original. The family came to our room to have a look at you and to share our joy and pleasure. Simultaneously with your letter of December 18 we got one from Toledo, of January 4, 1941. The mail delivery often works in strange ways, and, if I apply this circumstance to everything else, it gives me renewed hope and allows me to say that someday our affair is going to turn out well. The Doktors write as if it were possible that their letters might not reach us and that we might already be underway. I don't know how they can be so hopeful; we are no longer so optimistic. Even if all the preparations were made, I don't believe our departure could take place immediately.

So we are enormously happy when we hear from you and hope that you were spared having to search for a job. We were astonished at all the presents you received: stockings, a jacket, a splendid blue handbag, and a chic black cap. From the Doktors the presents seem to have rained down. We couldn't decipher one of the articles (even after four readings) that you received from them: stockings, then the difficult word (perhaps "raisins"), and *stollen*. We were glad to take note of Ludwig's beautiful handkerchiefs and are pleased that he remained in his line of business, which he mastered in an admirable way within a few years, as I have often heard his competitors acknowledge. One must not think so much about the skills one used to command and that are now useless. It's interesting that the chemist[142] is also such a "Franz"; the latter owes me an answer and I don't understand him. We are waiting for the affidavits of character, which, as you know, we entrusted him to obtain for us.

The oilcloth tablecloth is very practical, especially for the vendor if, every time he sells one, he is invited to coffee. The seating problem in the room appears to be exactly the same for us. Fortunately it seems too confining to the guests so that they quickly get the feeling that they need to leave us again. I can well imagine your financial situation. Still, I'm impressed by everything you're able to pay for: food and lodging, the hairdresser, the manicurist, photographs, the dentist, and nice new shoes. You are, praise God, moving up in the world. The *Seminar*[143] earlier and the beautiful weekly Thursday evening packages that Mother would still love to arrange today and I would just as gladly bring to the post office: You may rest assured that we are not a penny richer by being relieved of that expense. Still, this time had its good side, and we are content that you have done what you wanted to do.

We also found it nice of Aunt Clara to think about you and Americanize you. The names Vieyra[144] and also Fiegafuer [?] are here well known and esteemed. You've moved from fruit juice to a taste for sherry and Malaga. That's a progression that many people would like to make, if they don't abstain from alcohol on principle. Since you haven't said anything about smoking, we assume that you have remained as moderate as ever in this regard which can only please us because the practice

---

[142] Alexander Baczewski, Rosi's fiancé, was a chemist.
[143] German term for a teacher training school. Hugo referred to the time when Rosi was in a teacher-training program in Würzburg. An awkward sentence, but Hugo's meaning seems to be that they would be happy to be doing these things for Rosi again.
[144] Vieyra was an old name in the Amsterdam Portuguese-Jewish community.

has had very bad and injurious effects on those members of our family who have overindulged in it. I have long since forgotten dear Trudl's Virginia cigars, but I like the other more usual ones better than they please Mother. But, then, I like everything else that Mother makes for us, and in saying that I'm not telling you anything new, dear Rosi.

The Knollers and we had an old report from Columbia. Irma is complaining, just as she was complaining about her previous situation. It isn't tragic; they are alive and of course they have it hard, but there are masses of people who have it much, much harder and who may be having a much worse time of it. There are many who would welcome the opportunity to be in Columbia, and sometimes we are dissatisfied with a situation that later we would be glad to return to. On Monday I will go to the Committee to find out whether the consulate has made up its mind or not. A decisive answer has to come at some point. Even if we do get a positive answer we will still be far from being ready to depart. Still we greet every visible sign of progress and find it easier to keep on hoping. Carla has done several advertising drawings and earned her first gulden, to the joy and pride of her family. Ella Cohn and her husband had to cancel their visit with us tomorrow because they have come down with the flu. Aunt Frida continues to go out with her walking stick during the cold weather; when I see her marching along I always think Mother Jettchen has turned up. She has enough to bear, and I'm not too happy about the situation of the two sisters, either. I would certainly like to make things easier for them if I had the means. Dear Rosi, receive many greetings and affectionate kisses and again many thanks for the great joy you have provided to your father who loves you.

[309-1402b]
Early Sunday morning, February 9, 1941

My dear Rosi!

    Last night, Father read me his letter to you, and I had to laugh. He certainly can't be accused of egotism, but, when it comes to responding to your letters, he doesn't leave anything for me to talk about. However, when it comes to such beautiful subjects as your pictures, then I'm happy to chew the cud and express the enormous pleasure that you have given me by sending them. I'm also thankful that they arrived at all because on Friday evening I was still skeptical about that. I find that you are very good-looking, especially in the picture where you're smiling. Your figure hasn't changed, and the coat, which is probably the blue one I was asking about, seems to fit you very well. The preparations have cost you time and money, and I thank you many times for the surprise. Uncle Emil asked in his letter, which came yesterday, whether I had received the birthday greetings they sent me, but they haven't arrived yet. Sigmund also wrote us a very nice letter, saying that he believes we will be there by the time of his next summer holidays. We'll be happy to accept that deadline, provided it's certain.

    Did you go to the Rosenstocks' *bar mitzvah*? It's good to know that the clothes that Aunt Clara sent you fit. Have you spoken again to your friend Strauss? We may be happy that, at a time in which there are shortages in every area, we are able to live by ourselves and manage our own affairs. If we had to live with relatives it would be hard for us to bear, and our nervousness would only become more intense. We would like to join you in the practice of your favorite daily custom, but these are things that no longer touch us.[145] Uncle Emil also writes that the affidavits for the Falcks have been sent. This week I want to start the

---

[145] Rosi's favorite "customs" were coffee, cigarettes, and sweets, scarce items in German-occupied Amsterdam.

English lessons again. It's good to get started because I've noticed repeatedly that people have to stop their English lessons soon after beginning them because their departure is at hand. Let's hope it works out that way.

In that spirit, your mother kisses and embraces you most affectionately.

Best regards to Ludwig's family.

[1589-]
February 14, 1941

My dear good Rosi!

Your letter of January 1 arrived on February 11, making three letters one after the other: February 7, February 8, and February 11. However, dear Rosi, our great joy can only be complete if we are certain that you have heard from us just as often as we have heard from you. We're happy to know, dear Rosi, that you celebrated the New Year both extensively and intensively, and we thank you for the good wishes that have been reaching us daily. It's also nice that there are other people there who pamper you a bit and that you received presents not just at *Hanukkah* but at New Year's as well. We read with interest that Alfred has developed so well and that little Eric[146] has remained the same dear boy that he has always been. Since our last letter, dear Rosi, nothing has happened here with us. A few days ago I went to the Committee to check on the decision by the consulate. The consulate's decision has not reached the Committee. If it hasn't arrived by February 16, then an inquiry will be made. Dear Mother is better; the swellings and itching on her body are nervous in origin, which is not surprising.

A long typewritten report came from Fellheimer; he is apparently proud of corresponding with us and sends compliments to you and Mother as always. His letter is mostly a list of people who have died, not only in the

---
[146] Alfred and Eric were Ludwig Mosbacher's sons.

homeland but also those in the U.S.A. whom he has learned about from acquaintances. Mostly his reports have to do with people we don't know: a ninety-year-old woman and a woman ninety-nine years and eight months old who passed away in a home for the aged. The most important and pleasing thing we get from his letters is the knowledge that he is well. On Wednesday afternoon Mother had her first English lesson here. Her previous knowledge, which she had partly forgotten, makes the new start easy for her. Through Fellh[eimer] we also heard of the demise of the previous tenant in our home and of my landlord Grünbaum who became such a good friend to me in recent years and who would have been so glad to have you as a daughter-in-law, a man who became very wealthy through unrelenting industry and extreme thrift. Now I would also gladly report to you the arrival of boys and girls, of which there has also been no shortage here, but we're not acquainted with the parties concerned and Fellh[eimer] hasn't informed us of any.[147]

It's urgently necessary that I start English lessons. We left everything behind because we believed we would be leaving, and I still believe we will, even though it may take a long time. The Herzsteins[148] have arrived in San Francisco, and Theilheimer and mama, with their much higher number, are said to have received a summons to Stuttgart for the middle of the month. Time passes here with such incredible speed. The months simply fly by, and, when I think about it today, I find it inconceivable that the waiting time at home lasted so long. But brooding and regret are pointless; we have to take things as they are. Dear Rosi, be greeted many times and affectionately kissed by your father who loves you.

---

[147]Apparently Fellheimer also reported on births in Fürth/Nuremberg.
[148]Friends who had escaped to Japan, mentioned in November 27, 1940, letter.

My dearest Rosi!

Once again our joy was great when we received your letter that cheered us so much. I follow everything with great interest. I now look at you every day, dear Rosi. You look especially nice in the laughing picture. I enjoy your writing about your personal appearance, clothing, hairstyle, etc. Just make yourself beautiful every day, dear Rosi. It always gives me a jolt when I hear how the people at home are leaving.[149] We're still sitting right here. The one thing that somewhat consoles me is that I'm putting my time to good use and learning a lot. I really enjoy the sewing. Always take care of your health, dear Rosi, and eat well and properly. I hope we will soon hear from the Committee; our impatience is understandable. A thousand kisses from your mother.

[2838-3051]
January 20, 1941 [Misdated by Hugo; probably February 20, 1941.]

My dear good Rosi!

Shabbos came to a wonderful close on February 15 with the arrival of your letter of January 19,[150] together with a letter from Toledo of January 15. Our life, which goes along so monotonously, is only enlivened by the mail we get from you and the dear ones I just mentioned. That's why we always report the same things and repeat ourselves: Nothing else of significance happens with us. And that, too, is good!

Our pleasure did not end with the mail delivery on Saturday. On Tuesday, February 18, there came your extra long report of December 1, so the letter written earlier

---

[149]German Jews who obtained immigration visas were allowed to leave Germany up until October 1941. If Clemy and Hugo had waited to complete their immigration visas in Stuttgart, they would probably have arrived in the United States in 1940.

[150]Rosi's letters were taking at least two weeks to arrive so Hugo's letter cannot have been written on January 20.

arrived later. Now our joy was truly complete, and we can't thank you enough for having written so faithfully. The typewritten report of December 12 is not only thorough, but it's also a brilliant stylistic achievement that was admired on all sides. And it was so good for the dear Knollers that you referred to them several times. Everyone who was mentioned feels exalted, and we might feel that way, too, if we weren't the direct recipients of the letter. Recognition makes people feel so good, and, if it is not extended to them, they sense enmity or at least indifference, which is just as hurtful.

Goldschmidts' and Schucos' visits to Ludwig reminded me of old acquaintances, and we were also pleased to hear the names of Rudi Späth and Lotte Blümlein again. Are Lotte's parents still not with her? That she does not wish to be disturbed in her happiness shows her to be crassly egotistical. In the meantime you will have landed at Staudingers'. Does Else[151] visit Ludwig M[osbacher] often?

If piecework is decently paid, then it's not to be despised; you can be certain that you're getting the full value of your labor. Hichenberg always said jokingly—I don't remember his exact words—that his good income represented only a fraction of the value of what he did and that he was never paid what he had really earned. With all due respect for his abilities, my opinion differed from his on that point.

It was, of course, also greatly appreciated that you remembered the various birthdays. In a time like the present, everything relating to love and affection is valued more than it is in a time in which everyone has too much of everything. It's a Dutch custom to congratulate the children on their parents' birthdays. On every occasion and especially on anniversaries, one receives a handshake and the wish of "many more years." But it's still much nicer if, as you do, dear Rosi, one can celebrate other people's pay raises in a ceremonious and enjoyable way.

---

[151] Else Staudinger was the daughter of Frida Maier. The Goldschmidts were cousins on the Mosbacher side.

Meanwhile you've answered all our questions completely and to our satisfaction. As far as I'm concerned there is nothing outstanding. It's possible that dear Mother may still be awaiting your answer to some question. This afternoon we are going to call on Henriette. During the past year we only went to eat with her once. You can understand from that how important our visit is to her. If she didn't have so extraordinarily many discussions with Mother about questions of clothing and if Mother didn't please her with all sorts of sewing and alterations that Henriette wants to have done, then her interest in us would probably be several degrees less.

Bruno is completely uninterested—interested only during his stay with us, and that is very unusual. I wrote to you, or to Toledo, at one point that my affection for him is not diminished by this because I see in him my brother's son. Bruno, for his part, has only the most superficial impression that I am the brother of his father, and that's understandable.[152]

Your neighbor's saying, "*What do I care when I pay? There's a lot of time till next Xmas*" was amusing. Did she mean that she has credit until Christmas? That would be something. However, the saying of your countrymen, calling you a ray of sunshine in an old folks' home, was no less amusing. When you write that you already miss the parental spats, I have to think of the story that our beloved mother often enjoyed telling: A girl, who had a hard time finding a husband but who finally got engaged, began to express all kinds of misgivings about her betrothed to her mother, to which her mother responded, "I wish he was already beating you!" Forgive me if I bring up this old joke again that you may already have heard many times before, but you provoked me into it.

Today I've omitted saying anything about our departure, etc., because we have heard nothing more about it, not from the Committee nor from the consulate nor from

---

[152] Bruno was only three years old when Don Mosbacher died.

Franz whom I trusted to procure documents for us. My greetings to all those who take an interest in us—above all, Ludwig's family—and for you, dear Rosi, many greetings and affectionate kisses from your father who loves you.

My good Rosi!

Like Father, I was enormously pleased by your especially lovely letters that diverted me and put me in a different mood at once. As always, including the last time, Father has already responded to most of what you wrote, but he left a few things open for me that belong more in my domain, such as (1) your fashion report (2) the fur from Grandpa and (3) eggnog.

I passed your fashion report around in my sewing class. I found it very interesting, as did all the other participants. My teacher asked me to inquire if it would be possible for you to send some pictures of your dresses and coats. She would be very interested in learning something about American taste. Perhaps Mrs. V[ieyra] has a book of fashion illustrations from which you could send some excerpts. You needn't go to any special trouble with this; it's not such an important matter. It seems that you've followed some good advice in not sitting down on the coat.

That Lorenz Kleid is still alive is wonderful news. I'll send the eggnog recipe with the next letter. When no progress is being made, the yearning becomes even greater, and you may well believe, dear Rosi, that I am even more disconsolate here than I was at home. We heard today from Aunt Mela that Lily and Albert haven't been able to leave yet. Some time ago, Ari applied to Fredl concerning an affidavit for Carla. So far there hasn't been an answer. Perhaps you might find an opportunity to ask him about it. Frida, after a long pause, has finally heard from the Whites. Paul and Vally,[153] who are going

---

[153]Paul and Vally Engelsrath left Vienna in 1939 and lived in New York City and Seattle before settling in Los Angeles.

to live in Los Angeles, interrupted their journey there to spend some very pleasant days with Philip and Anna. Uncle Emil wrote that he successfully performed a major operation. It appears that in time he will establish himself. Rosl has a lot to do; her commitments are very great and the addition of the mother is quite a burden for Rosl since the woman is very spoilt. I miss Rosl very much. I had to laugh when you reminded me of Lina and the way she always called in sick at the same time. We have heard nothing else from her. That Franz has still not let anyone hear from him leaves us dumbfounded. I wish that we could report some progress to you in our next letter. With that thought I'll close for today. With the warmest hugs and kisses—your mother.

[3390-]
February 28, 1941

My dearest good Rosi!

Your detailed letter of the twenty-sixth reached us yesterday and as always it brought happiness to the entire house. Today I want for once to begin the reply. We here, praise God, are all well; you know our pains and pressures yourself. Yesterday I was with the doctor once again on account of the intense itching all over my body. He told me that it is entirely harmless. I got an injection that may have to be repeated several times. It is no wonder that our nerves, about which we have written you so often, have been affected, since we, too, believed that we would get our visas much more quickly, and we still don't have them.

The enclosed letter from Sigmund gave us great pleasure; his lines express his love and his attachment to us.

Dear Rosi, I can well imagine that you are tired out at eight o'clock after a strenuous workday, but that you still want to go out in pursuit of a little pleasure and amusement; after all, our cares are the same as yours. I think it's splendid that you were invited to a private concert and that you have such a nice circle of acquaintants with whom you can pass the time so well. In regard to your room and your landlord, you refer to exactly the same kind of thing that we also praise on the one hand and regret on the other hand. I sometimes enjoy cleaning up, too, and our landlady goes to a lot more trouble for us than we like or than we need. We often think of Lina and what she told us when she said, "Mrs. M., you will still think of me often." We especially miss her letters because it was such fun to read what she had written. There is surely no malicious reason for Lina's silence, and I feel certain that she still talks about us much more than her people care to hear. We still have no news from Franz. Father has now written to Dina by way of Trudl to ask why she and also Franz have been silent. Interruptions like this make us nervous, and, besides that, we've been waiting for many weeks for the papers that we requested from home. A very dear letter came today from the Doktors. It's sad that it's so difficult to build up the practice, and Rosl admits that the location was a mistake. We're going to the photographer next week so that we can return the compliment. Henriette and Bruno left on a trip yesterday. Now and then people make the same kind of little excursions that we used to do. They are going to visit her sister who recently married. All the relatives here feel themselves especially honored when they find themselves mentioned in your letters, and they send their warmest greetings to you, dear Rosi. Aunt Frida talks about you, not just a little, and she would be happy to bake anything for you that your heart desires. And so would I, and I wouldn't complain, not even if the whole pantry had to be restocked. You know yourself, dear Rosi, how I've always wanted everything for you, and how happy I would be if I could do it all over again very soon.

In this hope, my dear Rosi, I embrace you and give you a big kiss—your mother, who loves you.

My dear good Rosi!

Today dear Mother will deliver the main report, and I'm providing a little postscript, basically in order to repeat everything that Mother has already talked about. The main thing is the assurance that we and all our loved ones are in the best of health. "Best" is of course something of an exaggeration, but I call it that if nothing else is amiss. Mother continues to overexert herself. She demands too much of herself, more than she can cope with. I can't change her, so may she keep on until she's 120. I, on the other hand, know the limits of my abilities and rest before I'm completely tired out. After reading these lines, a stranger might believe that we were running a big boarding house or some other large concern, but we are still, unfortunately, not liable for income taxes, albeit not unoccupied for all of that.

Your letter, which arrived yesterday, gave us much pleasure. It's nice that people are taking such an interest in you and are trying to arrange a more suitable position for you. God willing, you'll get the right job soon. As pleased as I am that you have your dear mother's talents, I do not wish that you adopt her attitude toward hard work. One should not exaggerate in anything, but practice moderation in all things. Now we are already in *Adar*. I believed it to be a settled fact that we would be sitting together with you at the table by the time of the next *Pesach*. I believe now that, even if the most favorable surprises were to occur, we would still not be able to be with you on April 14. But we don't want to grumble about it. *Pesach* will come again, and we are already happy about that and about the one that we will celebrate together with you and the dear Doktors.

There isn't any point in talking about past mistakes since our trip had already been so beautifully and perfectly planned, and it would have been carried out if nothing had intervened. We're not the only ones to be affected in this way. Let us rather be happy for those who did not miss their connection and who, far away, feel for us and work for us and do what is in their power to do. The Knollers did not apply to Uncle Emil for help with Carla because they do not want to place an undue burden upon him. They believed that Fredl and Alfons could accomplish something. Of course the Trudari[154] are happy if Uncle Emil helps because, if Carla can come, then later it will be easier for her parents. And now, dear Rosi, keep on doing well for yourself and doing the right thing. Stay well and be careful—the same wishes as those you expressed in English—and be warmly greeted and kissed by your father who loves you. Greetings to Ludwig's family.

[2946]
March 7, 1941

My dear Rosi!

Father has already acknowledged your dear letter, and my joy was as always very great. I am happy when I hear from you, my dear Rosi, that you are well and contented. I can understand that you are very tired in the evenings. I'm sure that the housework is much more demanding than working in the factory. I always read your letters a number of times, and we always feel, when you recall memories, dear Rosi, that you are wholly with us.

My gallbladder, thank God, is in order again. Now if only the itching would stop; I often wake up in the morning with my face completely swollen. It goes down again in the course of the day, but I am disfigured, and it makes me quite nervous. The doctor assures me that this is not important. At the moment I am getting calcium injections, but they haven't helped so far. When I am once again with you, dear Rosi, I am convinced that all will be well.

We got a card from Lily/Albert from Lisbon, and now we're waiting for news about their good arrival. Henriette

---

[154] Trude and Ari Knoller were "the Trudari."

and for the first time Bruno were with us yesterday afternoon; he mostly talked to Father. I find it hard to establish contact with him. But he listened with great attention to your letter, which Father read aloud. The word "*Funsen*"[155] is unfortunately unknown to me from my native dialect, and its meaning would interest me. It's also a special coincidence that your friend Walter Neumann was together with Alfred. It's quite regrettable, Rosi, that you hear so little from Albrecht, but I don't think that he is the guilty party. Aunt Frida has still not had an answer from Senta[156] and her relatives to her repeated inquiries.

Father has already wished you *gut yontif.* I don't even want to think about it, and I'll wait with my wishes until my next letter. Below you'll find the recipe for eggnog[157] that you asked for. Enjoy it, and be hugged and most affectionately kissed by your mother.

My dear good Rosi!

We have the great and indescribable pleasure of being able to answer your letter of Saturday, February 4, which arrived on March 4. A letter arrived today from Toledo, and Uncle Emil writes that, unusually, he sent our letter to Columbia and then on to you, although always he sends our letters directly to you. That's the explanation because Uncle Emil promised me, as a general rule, to forward our letters only to you because that's what we're comfortable with since what Mother and I write to the Doktors is not what we write to Irma and readers for whom the letters are not explicitly intended and who are inclined to misinterpret some things. Thus it might occur, dear Rosi, that a remark that I might make about you and Rubens would not be understood by them in the completely well-mean-

---

[155]Possibly Viennese slang for a "not very intelligent woman."
[156]Senta was probably Centa Seligsberger, Philip White's mother. Although Centa had converted to Judaism, she was born a German Catholic. She remained in Germany and died a natural death in 1946. We don't know why Frida was writing to Centa, but it's possible that Frida left property or business matters with Centa or had asked her for a character affidavit.
[157]Clemy's eggnog recipe has been lost.

ing way in which it was made. I can't remember the relevant passage in my letter any more, but I was probably, for example, thinking about how, when Rubens happens to speak with you about religion—her hobbyhorse—she may encounter a certain, not unjustified, resistance. She doesn't have that experience with me because I'm older and more hardened. She can talk as long as she wants and say all she wants and then I do whatever I think is right. And now this question is well and truly resolved.

It's a shame, dear Rosi, that you're so often left without mail and so much more poorly served in this respect than we are when recently we've been so well provided for. We really aren't to blame. We write diligently, and, dear Rosi, you will be able to ascertain this to our exoneration, delayed though it may be. I'm just concerned that, due to the length of our stay, we may run out of material to write about to you and the Doktors since our experiences are either absolutely nil or identical with those we've already had to the point of satiety and no longer worth communicating. You have work to do, and you have a social life, and we have neither; the former is impossible, and the latter, here, we find totally uninteresting.

Uncle Emil complains about the Committee's treatment, and he is quite right to do so. Nevertheless I believe and hope that one day, when we least expect it, it will all come to pass. Henriette called us day before yesterday to say that she had heard that sixty passengers, who had booked on the *Veendam* as we had and who like us were ready to sail, had received their visas. I felt not a single spark of envy on receiving this communication. I told myself, well, we have a chance at being among the next sixty. I went to the Committee, where I enjoy at least as much respect as anyone else, and in response to my question I was told that Henriette's report didn't have a word of truth in it. Not just sixty *Veendam* passengers, but probably hundreds of passengers have their visas and are unable to meet the new, more stringent conditions imposed at Rotterdam because, if you don't have a child over there, it appears to be a lot harder. Dear Rosi, do we not have every reason to be inexpressibly happy with you, our only one? It's a shame that I can no longer remember why, such an infinitely long time ago, you got a quarrel from me on account of Ludwig M[osbacher]. Still, it really must have made an impression, if you can still recall it.

That you are now the owner of a wireless—I believe that's the expression—makes us happy, too, because, in addition to the enjoyment you will have from it, the purchase itself is a sign of prosperity. I was recently studying an English conversation about a wireless apparatus: "*Have you the newest model with a loud speaker and fitted with all the latest improvements?*" In the conversation, unfortunately, I'm not able to produce a single sentence, and, if I dared to try, no one would understand a word. "*It is nice to be able to listen to a foreign station when an interesting lecture or speech is to be heard.*" I recently wrote that in my notebook, but will I retain it?

Your extended working hours on Friday evening, at V., are somewhat premature. There would have been time for that once we are there and they invite us over. To demand extended work time on account of this invitation yet to come is not entirely appropriate, but what lengths will some people not go to keep other people from seeing through their little games? We feel sorry for Aunt Frida. At the Knollers' she is a kind of superior cook with a certain claim to family status; at six o'clock in the evening she appears at our home for a more plentiful midday or evening repast and pours out her heart. The niece should always be much more respectful to her and in any case should offer her something of every bite that she takes into her mouth so often in front of her aunt's very eyes. But she does this seldom and not at all gladly. Mother always compensates her when she spends time with us, and this always puts Frida in a good mood and makes her amenable to reason. On the other hand, it's good that she is kept so busy because that provides material for conversation and discussion. It's not a tragic matter, but she deserves better, and one apple, which is what we talked about yesterday, is not going to strain the budget in any way. Mother would like most of all to give her a part of our supplies; Mother is so utterly different from her supercilious, sarcastic, and selfish sister. Nevertheless, we like her, too, and as a niece and sister we treat her well. People can't always help the way they turn out, and they can't change their skins. When I write "skin" I think about the wretched itching that afflicts Mother. The doctor says it is harmless, thank God, but the patient doesn't feel that way about it and suffers from this harmlessness, which makes her more nervous.

Now, dear Rosi, all good wishes as ever. We hope that in the meantime letters from us and other wished-for letters will have reached you. Warm and heartfelt kisses from your father who loves you.

Today I already wished the Doktors *gut yontif*. As a precaution I want to do the same for you and also pleasant *seder* evenings. The death of Dr. Klein, fortunately, is not true! He is said to be in good health.

[3207-]
March 14, 1941

My dear Rosi!

It is so splendid, dear Rosi, that you write us every week. Today I can confirm your letter of February 18, which was underway for a total of fourteen days; this was a very quick delivery. I hope you got over your attack of catarrh quickly. One must be very cautious in this uncertain weather, and I am sure you are, dear Rosi. The climate here is not easy to bear, either; most people have problems with rheumatism due to the damp air. In respect to my health I feel better, thank God. This week I had three injections, including one of my own blood. I hope I will soon be free of this itching.

Dear Rosi, your last letter gave us much, much joy. You write so interestingly and so beautifully. I really enjoyed your report about your toilette. Surely the blue hat has been purchased by now. We heard yesterday from Aunt Mela about the safe arrival of Lily and Albert and breathed a sigh of relief. Perhaps in your next report you will be able to write to us about the dear ones. Aunt Lily will certainly be more than a little pleased with you; after all, you haven't seen her since you were a child.

In regard to our problem here, nothing has changed. I don't want to make you downhearted, but we have heard nothing, either from the Committee or the consulate. We know, however, that only a very few people have been able to leave. The waiting, the uncertainty, and so much else makes one very nervous. For that reason I am most contented when I am able to work and don't have time to think about things. I have made good progress with the sewing.

Henriette, who after all is rather spoiled, is pleased when I work for her and grateful for every little thing. Yesterday afternoon at her place was very pleasant; that is the only afternoon when I take time off. Frida's only pleasure is in the reports from her children. Anna writes so nicely about her boys; the little one must be a real darling. They got a lot of enjoyment from the visit of Paul and Vally, who are now living in Los Angeles. Fritzerl[158] is very industrious at the Knollers and is busy from early morning

---

[158] Clemy has clearly written "fritzerl" but seems to have meant Frida. The next sentence refers to the same person and uses "she." We know that Frida was helping out at the Knollers during the day and often eating dinner with Hugo and Clemy. Perhaps "fritzerl" was a nickname for Frida that Rosi would have understood.

to evening. She relaxes when she comes to dine with us in the evening. What do you think about Franz not writing any longer? We hear from Dina that he is at home. We had been worried; he is after all an unpredictable, peculiar person. We didn't pay any attention to *Purim* except for Father's going to synagogue. Now, my dear Rosi, keep on writing to us so diligently, and receive many warm greetings and kisses from your mother.

Many greetings to Ludwig's family.

[1635]
[Undated, but probably late March, as Lily and Albert have arrived in the United States.]

My dear Rosi!

I assume that Father has already written everything about the delivery of your letters so I'm just going to express the happiness that they bring me. Whether they are recent or of an earlier date, the joy is always the same. Not a day passes when we don't think very intensely about you, and it is high time for your daily dream to be realized. At the moment we are quite *down*. There is no prospect whatever for our departure, and you can imagine what that does to our spirits. That said, we can bear many things much more easily now that we are alone together and can express ourselves freely. If I had known my brother-in-law as I do today, then we certainly would never have come here. His interest has never been great, and the same is true for Trude. We would have behaved quite differently in such a case. God willing, the time will come when we can speak openly about this. I admit freely that we are somewhat agitated and, as a result, are perhaps too severe in our judgments. If Father wants you to pass his letter on to the Doktors then, of course, he doesn't intend to include my words, like these, that are meant only for you, dear Rosi.

In the meantime, you will have spoken with Aunt Lily. We are honestly delighted but also shocked to know that she is there, of all places. When I was with her about four years ago and mentioned the idea of the U.S.A. for her sons, I saw a look of astonishment on her face, and she pinched me under the table to let me know that I should drop the subject. She and dear Albert, who never thought of doing such a thing, have jumped ahead of all of us. We were only late sending in our pictures because during these last weeks we simply had no desire to do so, but we have made an appointment with the photographer for the coming Sunday.

Now I'll come back to your letter. In regard to landladies, curiosity, and the need for conversation, we have exactly the same complaints as you do, dear Rosi. We are entirely too well liked. It's very pleasant to know that you usually have port wine on Fridays. I have a taste for that wine myself. I'm glad to hear that you like it at Mirko's. Aunt Lily has some choice about where she wants to settle down.

We were also very pleased to learn that Albrecht has written to you and reports good news. We intentionally did not continue our correspondence with N[uremberg?] and for that reason his parents have not heard from us.

Dear Rosi, if soon you could tell us in person "Be careful" how beautiful everything would be.

My dear Rosi, receive many greetings and affectionate kisses from your mother who loves you.

[2707/1+^BrW]
Friday, March 28, 1941

My dear good Rosi!

I hope your parents will find applause from their daughter for the accompanying enclosure. My only complaint is that the picture turned out too heavy and was not printed on overseas paper as had been agreed to. I really don't look that plump; people are saying that my face has become thinner.

Now to you, dear Rosi, to your letter of February 23, which reached us on March 24 and gave us renewed joy. What kind of acquaintances are you making there, probably in a cafeteria frequented by Austrian chemists? The painter Stössel[159] is indeed an old friend of all the Adlers, who resembles Richard Wagner and is also an admirer of that composer, according to Mother. And even learning to make curtain lace[160] will come in handy. I never could keep up when it came to bock beer. As you know, I'm more a friend of pale beer. I seldom get it here, but I don't miss it. And, while we're on the subject of drinking, I want to move on to eating and ask you whether your attitude has changed in this respect as well, and whether, for example, you continue to take the same rejectionist stance in the matter of cheese. We would be glad to consume your share of it here.

There is something that, unfortunately, we didn't understand. You write that in regard to Hans,[161] the "*pros*" are certainly exceeded by the "*cons.*" Not even the lexicon could enlighten me about *pros* and *cons*. We had to laugh, too, at the telegram that was sent to Mrs. V[ieyra] in response to her inquiry. We recently read, in their letter that got here yesterday, that the dear Doktors would be very pleased by your visit. Of course it's up to you to choose the most appropriate time, and you are quite right to arrange the trip so that you don't miss out on a job on your return. Although Dina wrote me that Franz has now

---

[159] Likely Oskar Stössel (1879–1964) who was born in Graz and fled Austria after the Anschluss in 1938. He was living and working in New York City at the time of this letter. A self-portrait available online does show some resemblance to Wagner.

[160] "*Raschileruen*," apparently referring to Raschel lace—the most common type of machine-made lace. Hugo might have been responding to something Rosi has communicated about her work in the factory or perhaps making a joke of some sort.

[161] Possibly Hans Neurath, Lily's other son, who was also living in New York City.

written, nothing has come from him so far. I don't mean to reflect on our long-standing friendly correspondence. All I want now is that he finally sends us the papers that we have to submit to the consulate in the proper form. If this happens, we will be a step closer to the visas, but as long as these papers aren't here nothing will happen. I've written to you so often about this Franz, to whom we were so friendly and who is now behaving so oddly, to put it mildly. I've traveled for many hours to visit his mother, and sacrificed time and money, and this is my thanks. Nevertheless, I don't want to speak the last word and pass judgment on him and will wait a few more days until we get an explanation from him about this matter. In any case, he absolutely should have written us a card and not have left us dangling like this.

The Committee has already received Uncle Emil's affidavit for Carla, and the Knollers were informed both by the Committee and by a letter from Toledo to us. The papers are still not complete, and the Committee has written once again to New York. The Knollers, of course, are very pleased at the prompt handling of the matter and very thankful for it. A few days ago a friend of Ruth's, Judith Wolf, left for over there with a children's transport by way of Berlin; she has your address. Her parents are already there, and she is following them—a reversal. People are saying that an agency is going to be established and opened here very soon that will expedite emigration and concern itself particularly with those who have been prepared to leave for a long time. Now that we have heard this information from several sources, it appears that it may, unusually, be true. Let's hope for the best! Otherwise we will continue to believe only what we see.

I don't want, today, to weigh the letter down with an appendix, and so I'm going to yield the floor to dear Mother somewhat earlier than usual so that she can fill out the page. With sincere love and many kisses from your father who loves you.

My dear Rosi,

Many thanks for your dear letter. Your encounter with Stössel interested me very much, and of course I send him my greetings. When you heard the name perhaps you thought first of my relative of the same name. When the picture was taken, I made an effort to look friendly, and, although that succeeded, I find that a lot of other things didn't. But *never mind.*

In the meantime you will already have spoken a number of times with Aunt Lily, and I'm already very keen to see what you have to say. We always send Aunt Lily and Uncle Albert our regards, even if it isn't in the letter; let that be said once and for all. Friday evening after supper we always go to the Knollers. Ruth has accepted an external position with a large company and will start work after Easter. Carla is very pleased with the affidavit; I find her very sympathetic and always nice.

Dear Rosi, I advise you to put all your winter things in mothballs. I saw Ruth take out a dress that was completely eaten up, and she was very upset. Stay well, always be careful, and be most affectionately kissed by your mother.

The photograph taken March 23, 1941, that Hugo and Clemy included in their March 28, 1941, letter to Rosi.

[1623-2889]
Sunday, March 30, 1941

My Dear Ones!
    On March 27 we received your letter of February 20. We heartily thank you and Uncle Emil, dear Rosl. As always you have delighted and entertained us with your words. You should never imagine that something might not interest us. Everything that you communicate to us is received with interest and understood as you intend it.
    Dear Rosl, we hope you're rid of your gallstones again; if Lina [full name unknown] invites you to dine very often, you can always get them back. Dear Mother hopes you are in good health. You should be enjoying spring now. The name Friedsam is known to me, but I can't remember anything in connection with it, only that in the Mid [?] family they were always making witty remarks and the amusing things that Carl Ullmann always said about Mid.

The Knollers, in the same mail delivery with your above-mentioned letter, received word from the Committee that the affidavit for Carla had arrived here. Something had been left out of the form so that the Committee had to write once again to New York. The Knollers, obviously, are very happy to have the matter taken care of and are grateful—I personally vouch for that with these words—but I think it would be more correct if the very indolent Ari and the even more indolent Trude would sit down at once and without delay to render their thanks to you. Perhaps they will do so yet. You, and we, are satisfied whether they do so or not, and I wouldn't mention something like this if they themselves didn't know what correct behavior was. This kind of thing goes against my grain, if they believe that everything is taken care of by my letter. It always makes me angry whenever I see that people are so reluctant to take a stand on the helpful side of life and are only anxiously concerned about their own physical well-being. I take great satisfaction in going well out of my way for someone else if I know I can be helpful and useful, and I know, my dears, that that is precisely your attitude as well. Here I see none of that: no empathy, no serious reflection, uneducated, lazy, and greedy. Those are just my impressions that I am passing on to you, but not to Columbia, and I also don't want any reprisals if the Knollers need help from you. My express wish is that you will do whatever you can. When Trude stuffs herself full of candy—I mentioned this once already—and then behaves in such a stinkingly stingy way to Frida and Clemy, then I feel sorry for her on account of her disposition. She makes an effort to be very nice to me, and, besides, I am neither petty nor stingy. After this backward glance, I no longer regard the *seder* evenings with so much pleasure. I would much rather have passed them in my room, albeit with less ceremony, but of course we have to accept these courtesies.

Seidenberger's visit will have brought you great pleasure.

Is he already done with his examinations and ready to establish himself? Leo can learn from your experience in this area, dear Emil. If, after the passage of another year, you should see that mere waiting has not brought you that which you are expecting, then your friends and benefactors will be open to reason and approve of the decision that you are forced to make. Since we seldom hear anything from Columbia, I had to learn about Clara's illness from your letter—the latest letter from Irma and Alfons doesn't mention the mother at all—we would like to hear again soon how Clara is doing now. Lenchen has done the only correct thing and separated from her ex-husband (as she always calls him); he insisted on imposing such mean conditions on her in return for their living together that refusal was her only option. His letter could have had no other purpose, and it almost seems to me that things were not as Lenchen says they were and that the suggestion did not come from him but from her. People of a nervous disposition such as Lenchen are often mistaken in their perception of reality.

Rosl, was our former residence a metropolis compared to where you are now or about the same?

Rosi also wrote that she would like to come to see you and how happy a reunion would make her. However, she would like to wait until things have settled down so that she would not be putting her jobs at risk.

Rosi has already spoken to Aunt Lily and Uncle Albert. Lily in New York—who would have believed that just a few years ago? If the Committee sends Form 6, which has to do with the affidavit of character, etc., then it must be considered a sign of progress, because it is an indication that the consulate acknowledges that all the other documents for the visa are in order. So I think, as I was saying, that after the character affidavits have been submitted we shall receive the visas. But even then we still won't be gone! However, people are saying that an official agency is being opened that will take care of the emigrants and facilitate their departure. The consul also probably sees no point in issuing visas that always expire after a while if the departure is not guaranteed, and I firmly believe that this is the reason why no progress is being made here. Both the visa and the other thing are required.

If you read our letters, I mean our letters to Rosi, then you have to hear everything two and three times over, and I pity you! This Franz is a real problem for me. Nordschild junior, since deceased, whose father always used to say that about him (you always used to talk about that, dear Emil), was nothing by comparison. So many things, mostly unimportant and trivial, remain firmly stuck in my memory—why is it so hard to get English into my skull? If I could only retain that better. And then there is my Bavarian accent.

It's too late for holiday wishes, but perhaps this letter will arrive before they are quite over. Many, many greetings for Sigmund and greetings and kisses to all of you from your Hugo.

[1398a]
Friday, April 4, 1941

My dear good Rosi!

On March 29 we received your letter of March 6, for which we heartily thank you. We have to admit that we are well satisfied here with the mail delivery from over there and wish only that nothing changes in that respect. We wrote you a week ago and enclosed our picture, and we hope that that important enclosure reaches you before today's letter does.

I can only be pleased that you've retained some contacts with your "comrades," such as trips, etc. Such excursions can only be good for you physically, and, particularly in troubled times, communion with nature is very peaceful and consoling. We are also pleased to see the attachment and sincerity of your former employers [the

Vieyras] and that you take the same attitude toward them. I'm happy that you've gotten acquainted with circles like these and know how to appreciate them, because only in this way does one learn about life's possibilities and acquire the proper attitude to one's fellow human beings. Anyone who, as so many do, only and frequently associates with the Hammelburgers and people of that sort will not acquire the views and the perceptions that are needed in real life. It's certainly unpleasant that the firm had a big order returned, but the return of a draft is far, far worse—that is, a signed promise to pay by a certain date that the debtor does not honor and that is returned unpaid. Please forgive these explanations that probably aren't very interesting for you; perhaps you remember this kind of thing from your work at the shoe factory.

Little Bär may also be there in your city. My friend Metall [?] "Strauss"[162] and his son-in-law Levy [?] would certainly be very happy to see you, although I certainly don't intend to give you the least encouragement to seek them out. I am in no doubt whatever that there is more worthwhile and more pleasant society for you than those two. Dreyfuss with Else and their brother and mother may turn up there soon, as Fellheimer recently reported.

Mother's condition has improved. Unfortunately she makes the mistake of working too intensively. She usually returns exhausted from the three-hour sewing course. Cooking poses the same tasks for her as before, for which her previous knowledge is entirely adequate. If we wanted to, we could be rather proud of the fact that the family especially likes to spend time with us, although, as I've already written you so often, it's so terribly cramped here, and, due to me, so smoky, but all that doesn't hinder them. If, on the other hand, we, in consideration of the approaching *yontif,* cancel a visit to Henriette planned for next Thursday, as we did yesterday when she was with us, she accepts most readily.

---

[162] Why Hugo put "Strauss" in quotation marks is a mystery.

I have to laugh at myself for telling you about such trifling matters and writing about them, but, if we are going to have conversations with you, then after all it ought to be the same as it was at home. I'm also not telling you anything new or nice by continually repeating that the documents requested from Franz and the visas have not yet arrived here. Eight days from today, when we are sitting at the *seder* table, we will think often of you and of the dear ones in Toledo and about why things can't work out better. But all these reproaches are useless—just a few days later and everything would have gone according to plan, and we still can't get past it, and we start all over again.

In the meanwhile, apparently, Fips has bought a small house, and Anna has given her mother a precise description of it, and it is fervently to be desired that Aunt Frida might move into it soon. We are concerned about her appearance although she doesn't complain about any ailments, but her stay here is not a refreshing moment, neither for her nor for us.

We are happy that Aunt Lily and Uncle Albert have reached their goal, and I send warmest greetings to them and to Ludwig's family. Dear Rosi, I continue to wish you a very pleasant and successful time, both at and after work, with affectionate greetings and kisses from your father who loves you.

My dearest Rosi!

Father really has a special gift for writing so beautifully; whenever I tell him this, he quickly wipes my mouth. You know how modest he is. Except for our nervousness, we are, God willing, well. I'm feeling better again, thank God. If only our most passionate wish might be fulfilled soon! Today Aunt Frida had a letter from Anna; we usually can also expect some mail from her. We always think of you, but eight days from today our thoughts will be intently with you and the Doktors and how nice it must be. In your last report, your first meeting with Aunt Lily and Albert interested me especially, and I hope that we will soon hear directly from them as well. We were glad for the news we got from Fredl and Lusi's letter, that came by way of the Doktors. You certainly have no lack of family there either. Have you made your trip to Toledo in the meanwhile? My dear Rosi, stay well and be affectionately kissed by your mother.

[3576-1yc9]
Wednesday, April 30, 1941

My dear good Rosi!

There's been a delay of a few days, but it doesn't matter; as a result we have before us your well-written and amusing letter of March 23 and 24 (postmarked March 25), together with the no-less-detailed letter of the dear Doktors. As it is, we already got your letter of March 31, without an enclosure, on April 21, while we only received the earlier letters of March 25 today. And from Toledo, on April 25, we received a letter of April 6, while the one dated earlier arrived today. In any case, we owe you as well as the dear ones in Toledo our great appreciation for being so attentive because we can see that your letters and those of the dear ones are written with the intention of entertaining us and making us happy. And, even without that intention, the letters succeed in doing this every time, and the days on which they arrive are days of joy. To complete the postal discussion, it has also happened that first the package of cookies without a word of greeting and then the letter from Gertrud [full name unknown] arrived. Our first news of Albrecht's illness came from you; until now I didn't know that such a young person could have kidney stones. But the main thing is that he is rid of them and healthy again.

There can be no doubt that Cousin Ludwig is genuinely fond of you, but his innate jealousy can also lash out at those whom he loves. He grew up in very modest, unhappy circumstances; his father didn't earn much, and his mother was always eyeing those who were rich or who had a good position. Ludwig's mother hammered it into him, first during his school years and then later in his professional life, that he had to attain the highest goals possible in both material and social respects. So, when he was at home with his parents and they were drinking their morning coffee, he could tell them that at a meeting of the businessmen's club the evening before he had gotten up to speak right after Mr. H[full name unknown] the bank director, and his parents could experience a feeling of exaltation and didn't notice the wretched taste of the cheap, low-grade coffee they were drinking. The parental home was in a state of severe decline, both within and without, and the flames of the son's ambition were fanned to a point that was more than he could stand. And his envy has its origin in this upbringing. He is just barely able to endure those who are his equals and whose knowledge and abilities are no greater than his own. But his envy and his criticism come into play as soon as it is a matter of those who know more than he does, that is, have attained higher levels of education and better positions than he has. He secretly begrudges you your modest income; he says it jokingly, but it's still serious. And therein lies a profound difference between us and our cousin, and we must be grateful that we have neither inherited such an unpleasant tendency nor acquired it through our upbringing. It must be admitted that he has attained his almost undeservedly important position as a director solely and exclusively through careerism and bootlicking.

Floral displays are unnecessary here; among the street vendors and in the show windows you can see the most marvelous flowers and plants; so far there's no shortage. The kind of tunes that you get to hear on the radio have long since become strange to our ears. It's regrettable that piecework is paid at a worse rate, and I am eager to know what sort of job you will be able to take up when you come back again from your trip and what sort of job it was that you gave up so willingly. Franz has finally written now, after many months, and promised that the character affidavits will soon arrive. He acts as though he has behaved quite correctly. Yesterday a letter from Fellheimer arrived; he was very pleased to get your card, the reception of which we are meanwhile supposed to confirm. As always, he gave me an extract from the obituaries, but this time I can check his errors: He does not list Aunt Anna B[full name unknown]. The joke you told about Mr. Porlak provoked amusement, dear Rosi, but not the loss of your fountain pen, which you perhaps lent out and this time didn't see again. So, my dear Rosi, carry on as before; yesterday was the seventeenth day;[163] another thirty-two days and it will already be *Shavuot.* Be heartily greeted and kissed, dear Rosi, by your father who loves you, and sincere greetings to Uncle Albert, Aunt Lily.

My dearest, good Rosi!

I see that Father has responded so thoroughly to your letters that there is little left for me to discuss. My pleasure in reading your letters was great, very great. You are brilliant, dear Rosi, at redirecting our thoughts, and that is such a comfort at a time like this. I was so sorry to hear about Albrecht's sickness. The main thing is that he makes a good recovery and gets back to his job. I found your drawing amusing and perfectly rendered. I passed on your little fashion report, and it is attracting great interest and attention. Right now I am making a blue wool dress for Frida; she has hardly anything to put on and this way it won't cost much. We are hoping that our luggage is still waiting in Rotterdam. When Father gets permission he will go there. Tomorrow is Carla's and Rosl's birthday. What a

---

[163] Hugo was counting the Omer. Shavuot was on June 1 in 1941.

beautiful day that used to be, when we would have the birthday coffee in the afternoon at the Doktors'. When people are separated, the memories stand out with special clarity. Meanwhile, I am sure you have been to see Aunt Lily a number of times. We are so endlessly happy that the dear ones reached their goal so well. How beautiful everything will be again when, God willing, we are reunited once more. We leave that entirely to the good Father. Dear Rosi, stay well and give our greetings to all the dear ones. With best wishes and kisses from your mother. Write us often; it's the only thing we have. The Doktors' letter did us good. It was very nice of Lusi to send you the things.

[839-2114,1+jfoto]
May 15, 1941

My dear good Rosi!

It looks as if you already knew that I have been doing a little research on the travel time of your letters. Since I know that you write every week, I carry a piece of paper around with me on which I note the approximate dates, such as April 16, April 23, April 30. Now, when your letter of April 23 arrives on May 12, then we know that we can expect an earlier letter, and—presto!—the next day, on May 13, your letter of April 16 arrived. Our joy was once again indescribably great, and we are extraordinarily thankful to you for your efforts to entertain us really well. You provide us with excellent information and report on events of daily life that interest us very much. On May 13 a letter from the dear Doktors arrived, and our happiness was more than complete, although Uncle Emil did not write about what he will decide to do now that Chicago[164] does not agree to the starting of a practice. From our letters, dear Rosi, you will have observed that you felt exactly the same way as we did before the *seder*

---

[164]Meyer and Mayer relatives in Chicago had advised Emil to open his practice in Toledo. When Emil wanted to relocate once again, they were unable to provide financial assistance.

evenings, but that the end result in both cases turned out quite well. We are glad to know that you enjoyed getting our picture. After we sent you the first one, we got a second photo, which, in the meantime, went to the Doktors on Rosl's birthday. It's not very different from the first, and, because we don't want to withhold anything from you, we're enclosing another picture today.

We were glad to hear that you've gotten over the pains of giving notice;[165] being able to give notice is in any case better, or more respectable, than being discharged. "*Kündigen*" means "*to give notice*" in English, but, if you're suddenly discharged, then I have to translate: "*She got sacked.*" Is that right? Mother and I each take a one hour lesson per week, separately, but I haven't yet gotten to the point where I understand the teacher or can even form and pronounce a sentence independently. The teacher places great importance on grammar and says that those who haven't mastered grammar can't form sentences. Unfortunately the teacher isn't a teacher at all but just someone who knows English well, and there is no method whatever. If I come to her and casually say something about "*floor*," she uses up part of the hour with "*floor*," "*ground*," "*soil*," "*bottom*," and then she says, "Do you know what dirty laundry is called? '*Soiled linen*,' and when it's being washed the laundry is called '*washing*.'" The instructress is the same age as I am, and unfortunately she never knows what she has already said several times and what we have gone over together. But the worst thing is that she has such a good opinion of herself and only wants to reap praise. When Mother comes home from her lesson, I hear the same story on Friday that I heard on Monday. Still, all in all, it's better to take something in and retain it, rather than absolutely nothing.

I was just thinking that someone like Alexander would know more about our tradition. Mother, in the meantime,

---

[165]Rosi had stopped working for the Vieyras. She remained on good terms with them.

has had to make a few concessions in regard to *Pesach* and the utensils, but on the whole the Knollers supplied our needs quite well.

In contrast to you, we haven't had a warm day right down to today, and I am still wearing my winter overcoat. Because of the unpleasant cold in the room, Mother has just plugged in the electric heater that Henriette lent us. Your decision not to apply for the private secretary's job is to my taste. I've always regarded the persons holding such positions with a degree of skepticism, unfairly perhaps but consistently.

If I did not turn also to Kolb, about whom I assume that he has already long since departed, I nevertheless did the same thing when I wrote at that time to Franz in such a way that he could forward my letter to Parnes Katzenberger. That was done, but in the meantime I heard that L. K. [?] unfortunately is no longer at home. Nevertheless Franz still must take some responsibility; at the least he needs to let us hear something from him.[166] We recently had a card from his mother from which we learned that she is getting better. From Dina we got a long and amusing letter; she appeals, in everything, to her age and her ignorance. To those who don't know her—for example, Ari—she seems especially interesting. Give our regards to Uncle Albert, Aunt Lily, the Ludwigs, and all those who ask about us. My dear good Rosi, accept my heartiest greetings and affectionate kisses from your father, who loves you.

My dear good Rosi!

I shall have to write first next time so that I, too, shall have something to communicate. We are delighted by your letters. I'm pleased that you're enjoying yourself, and

---

[166]In his April 30, 1941, letter, Hugo indicated that they had finally heard from Franz after many months, but that they were waiting for him to send the character affidavits that they needed for a new round of visa applications. Hugo's comments about Kolb and Parnes Katzenberger are obscure, but seem to refer to previous requests for character affidavits.

it would not be clever to economize precisely in that area. I wish I could provide you with a few bottles of Kobes. Do you remember getting a bottle on your birthday? When Trude read your letter, where you began by talking about what you ought to do with your dresses, she said that they would be suitable for her daughter. If it doesn't cost you too much in postage, can you send them to the Knollers as cast-off clothing? As of now, Carla has no prospect of going over there. If things are busy at the factory, your trip to Toledo may have to be postponed. I assume that you left the employ of the Vieyras sometime between May 5 and May 10. Are you working more hours at the factory now? In any case, it's better in summer not to have to stand in the kitchen and to enjoy the evening. By the time this letter reaches you, *Shavuot* will already be over. Perhaps you will be there for Uncle Emil's birthday on June 7. Dear Rosi, receive many heartfelt greetings and kisses from your mother.

May 25, 1941

My dear good Rosi!

I know my habits and so I begin as always first by confirming the arrival of your letter of May 2 and then by noting its travel time of twenty-one days. I'm in the same situation as you, dear Rosi, in that I should have written a few days earlier, but the mood wasn't right. Now, after the receipt of your letter, it's much better, and when I communicate with you, dear Rosi, I prefer if possible to be in a good mood, and, even if my mood isn't perfect, I can still work myself up into a good one. Man is simply ungrateful and considers far too little how thankful he ought to be if his health is good.

Last week Hans Bachmann came to see Aunt Frida in order to inform her of his engagement to a Miss Rosenfeld from Cologne, who has also been here for some time and is a self-employed seamstress. Last Thursday evening we were at his place for tea, our first evening out, and got to know his *fiancée*, whom we liked. At the same time his brother Paul, whose *fiancée* is well known to you, got engaged. He is a physician and works as an assistant to two doctors. Father Bachmann celebrated his seventieth birthday.[167] I'm not saying this to be critical, but simply to characterize the Bachmann attitude, if I further report about the evening that, after the tea, he also somewhat redundantly served up a dish of stewed rhubarb. People like us would either have omitted this course or would have served a different fruit, but he is certainly very frugal when it comes to himself so he was staying within his limits, and I found this amusing.

I have observed, with regret, that our joy in the seventh day has noticeably diminished, due to nightfall coming so late. Last night it was 10:45 p.m. before I could light my first cigar, and then I wanted a second one right afterwards. The longest day will come in the middle of June, but so far we have noticed very little summer. From your letter, dear Rosi, I was interested to infer that the *Aguda*[168] can make an effort for us or has made an effort for us. The contributions that I was able to make to it at home were not entirely in vain. I am obtaining here the papers that are lacking because I don't want to wait any longer for those that were requested from Franz. He wrote in a letter in April that they would be sent off in that same month. I'm less irritated by their not arriving than by the fact that he has left me dangling like this and cares too little to send me a card and inform me that he is still unable to send me the desired items. And most of all I am annoyed at his notion that he is still behaving correctly toward me. We received another long letter from his mother. She still needs injections, but her overall health is

---

[167]Hans and Paul were the sons of Julius Bachmann, who was the business partner of Gustav Roederer (Frida's late husband) in Seidenhaus Gebrüder Bachmann (Bachmann Brothers House of Silk).

[168]"Aguda" is the nickname of Agudat Israel, an international Orthodox Jewish political/social organization that was started in the late 1800s. Aguda was very active during/after World War II in saving Jews.

much better. You had better postpone your trip to Toledo until a time when things have settled down at work. Stay well, be careful, and be warmly greeted and affectionately kissed by your father who loves you, and best regards to Uncle Albert and Lily and Ludwig.

[2020-1300]
May 25, 1941

My dearest Rosi!

We were rather skeptical about getting a letter from you this week, but behold—it came Friday evening and we were enormously pleased with your dear lines. According to the written record that Father always carries with him, we write to each other weekly; that's almost accurate. We entirely agree with you, dear Rosi, about quitting your housekeeper's position. The daily washing-up and everything that goes with it is so distasteful, but I at least get some help from Father. Unfortunately, I can't get much sewing done in the mornings so I make up for it afternoons and evenings. The dress for Aunt Frida promises to turn out very nicely. The whole family could keep me busy, but I only want to learn and, God willing, I'll be able to do something with it. Dear Rosi, I imagine your little hat is very nice, but I can't quite picture you in it because I'm only accustomed to your more severe fashions. Little Rosi, if you can do it without extra expense, send us another picture of you in your American clothes and hat. Aunt Clara has written, by the way, that she has some more clothing for you. When you are cleaning out your closet, if the things are still halfway good, you can send them all over here for the daughters. There is a hat for you among my things that you certainly wouldn't wear now. In your next letter you might tell me something about your new room. I hope you find a nice room and a nice landlady; that's also very important.

Right now I take a sleeping tablet every evening,

mainly on account of the mice that have made their nest in my room. After the mousetraps turned out to be useless, we put out poison yesterday, and this morning it was all gone. I hope we will have some peace now. This would not be grounds for breaking the lease here. They're in almost all the houses. Our nieces Carla and Ruth came to see us yesterday afternoon. It's especially nice when the parents aren't here as well. Today, Monday the twenty-sixth, we got your letter of May 9, which pleased us greatly and which we will answer in the next few days.

Stay well, and, dear Rosi, receive many warm greetings and kisses from your mother. Many greetings to all the loved ones. The letter is only for you.

[1823/2889]
[Undated letter, probably written at end of May or early June.]

My Dear Ones!

On several occasions, recently, Hugo has sent you letters to which I did not add anything. I hope you won't think ill of me on that account, because in my present frame of mind I often simply don't feel like it. I would have gotten through the past year much better if someone had told me it was going to last another fifteen months[169] until we could depart and if we now finally knew a date. But we have to be thankful if we and our neighbors remain well. By now Rosi already may have been with you or is about to come to you. Although we're at home in our room every evening, we still always go to bed very late. We are spared the invitations that come too plentifully to you. We are also glad to dispense with them because, first, things often get too noisy and, second, because, as you know, dear Rosl, a few intimate friends are quite enough for me. In recent days we have often thought of Ernst and Mela and are happy to know they are well. Is it true that Alfons and Irma intend to leave Columbia? This

---

[169]Fifteen months places this letter in either late May or early June 1941, as they had left Germany in February 1940.

evening, as always on Saturday, Lenchen is coming to dinner with us, and then you, dear Emil, will be quoted often by Hugo, both before the arrival and after the departure. Hugo always says that you, dear Emil, always warned against speaking about clothes in front of her or showing them off because that's her sore spot. Right now I'm working on a vest to go with the dress that Lenchen was given by you. Dear Mother, do you often use your Wiegner hat, and do you still like it? We often speak of you and of our visits in Sofienstraße. I wish you all good things for the future, and many greetings and kisses from your Clemy. Extra greetings for Sigmund and Lore.

June 6, 1941

My dear good Rosi!

Your letter, addressed to us on May 14 at 5:30 a.m., reached us on May 30 and thus before the beginning of *Shavuot* so that your good wishes for the feast arrived precisely on time. We thank you most warmly and hope most keenly that we continue to receive our mail as hitherto. We haven't heard anything from Toledo in a long time, since dear Rosl's birthday on May 1. That is, we haven't heard how things went, by which I want to express that we are lacking information about her. Tomorrow Uncle Emil celebrates his fifty-fifth birthday. In my last letter to you and the Doktors I discussed the matter of the ship passage and repeated word for word the text of the telegram that the American Express wanted to send to its New York office if I agreed to it, and first I have to explain why I did not let this telegram be sent. You wired us that you could book. However, that did not absolutely mean that you could book in the same place where you booked for us the first time. It could after all be possible that you had booked with some other line, and that the money, which had been on deposit elsewhere, would be withdrawn in order to pay for the passage that was being booked later. Anyway, after receipt of my letter with the text of the telegram in question, you will know what needs to be done, with the difference that you will be informed about it somewhat later. Dr. Moser, who is active with the Committee and also a *Veendam* passenger, told me several weeks ago, when I spoke to him about the difficulty of getting ship passage, that he was optimistic in that respect if one just has the exit permit. Once one has gotten that far then the ship passage will soon follow. I think, though, that once the exit permits begin to be granted here the demand will be very great. We still have heard absolutely nothing about the exit permits. We keep on hoping that we will be surprised suddenly and soon by hearing that they have been approved.

Aunt Lenchen is looking for a room once again. She is made extremely nervous by things that are completely harmless and then does us the honor of sharing her feelings with us. I am always happy when the evening passes without any special conflicts arising. A pitiably nervous person without a direction or a goal. Some woman says something to her in the street, and she takes it as a rule by which to govern her life. Dear Mother tries to give her some suggestions as to how she can earn a little extra on the side, but I think it's all pointless because I don't think she has the ability to complete any job whatever. Last Sunday evening we were invited to the Knollers. An invitation to dinner in times like these is, of course, extremely rare and for that reason especially pleasant.

Summer has finally arrived here, thank God, and we had several quite warm days that pleased us very much. Otherwise we've seen nothing of spring here. In such a gloomy time as this one rejoices at the sight of the sun. In normal times, as I went about my daily business, the weather was no problem. But when one has to pass one's time in other conditions, when one's days and nights are passed in one room, many things become problematic that were never problematic before.

Aunt Frida is expecting a letter from Oakland. Anna is

usually very punctual. A letter from Franz Dietrich arrived early today, but the papers that I'm waiting for still haven't arrived, and I'm now at the point of procuring them here. I should have done that at the beginning and saved myself a lot of aggravation. He would not and will not admit when he has made a mistake and doesn't want anyone to tell him anything, although he is still much too young to have such a wealth of experience that no one needs to tell him anything. Dear good Rosi, it always does me good to chat with you. Be careful, stay well, and receive many greetings and affectionate kisses from your father.

My dear Rosi!

I just read your last letter again which, as always, gave me great joy. Here, too, the young ladies wear their hair rather long. I believe that could suit you, dear Rosi. A nicely styled hairdo does a lot to enhance one's outfit. Although Father inquired about our things by telephone, we still don't know if our luggage is all together, the way it arrived in Rotterdam. I'm very pleased about the clothing that Aunt Clara sent you; that can save you a lot of money. We're very concerned about your income. We think that if you had a better-paying job you could quickly make up the loss caused by the interruption.[170] Aside from that, the most important thing is that you manage your life so that you make ends meet. There are, after all, a lot of people who earn much more and who still never have enough. At the end of your last letter, dear Rosi, you write, "I live in my nylons, which dry out very quickly." Please write and tell us what you mean by "nylons." Dear Rosi, just be careful when you cut.[171] I think it's lovely that you now spend Friday evenings with the family. Give my greetings to the whole family. My good one, receive many greetings and my kisses from your mother.

---

[170]Rosi had taken time off from work to visit Emil and Rosl in Toledo.
[171]Clemy used the verb "*schnitzen*" which means "to carve" or "to cut." She may have been worried about Rosi's work in the factory.

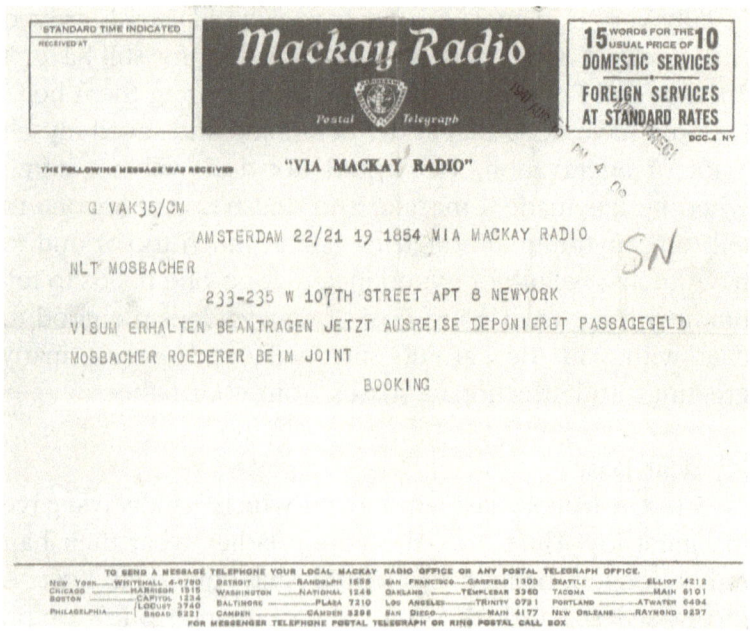

"Departure time for family Mosbacher uncertain. Nevertheless they would welcome August or September booking."

In Hugo's letter of June 16, he told Rosi that he sent this telegram on May 28, 1941.

June 16, 1941

My dear good Rosi!

Early today, after a rather long pause, we received your letter of May 22 and some days ago the long-awaited one of May 17 from Toledo. So once again we are greatly pleased and reassured. So much has happened with you in the meantime; you were with the dear ones in Toledo and have been home for the last week. Finally you were able to speak to each other face to face. How you must have chatted and discussed. What mutual enjoyment there must have been in finally seeing each other again. We are able to empathize and thus to feel a portion of the joy you experienced. And you were there for the dear uncle's birthday, and we are now especially eager to have your forthcoming report. We have your letters of the first, fourteenth, and second of May, but we are lacking one from about the eighth or ninth of May, which may still arrive.

Our telegram of May 28 may have reached you before you left on your trip. We will surely hear further details about tickets from you. In the meantime you will also have gotten our letter informing you as to what the American Express here wanted to wire. In general, exit permits don't exist yet here. In a few cases out of the many hundreds pending, exit permits for North and South America have been issued, but the general exit permit that people are waiting for is not yet issued, and, as long as it is not there, one also cannot say that it certainly will come. Today I was once more at the Committee in order to hear whether in the meantime anything has changed. Unfortunately I heard that so far nothing has gotten better. Still, I have to be concerned with the tickets because, when permission to depart is finally granted, the consulate will only issue visas to those who are ready to travel. There are those who continue to insist that it is sufficient to show proof of payment for tickets, but we have to hold ourselves to what the Committee is saying. There are also supposed to be shipping lines that extend the life of the tickets for a small surcharge if the confirmed bookings cannot be used. I hope, dear Rosi, that it is possible for you and the dear Doktors to work together to make the necessary preparations for us so that, at the moment we receive our exit permits, we can show that we are ready and able to travel. The main thing is that we get the exit permits and that nothing interferes with our departure.

Is the Dr. Held you name from our hometown? Is Anneliese Ehrenb[full name unknown]. also there? We are enormously pleased with everything that you have written us, and the Knollers have expressly instructed me to send you their greetings. Where is Mirko working? We sympathize with Ludwig M[osbacher].; it is not so easy for him to forget what once was and what he himself once was. A fully healthy and fully occupied person would find it easier to get over it. It appears that you aren't able to speak to Uncle Albert and Aunt Lily as often as they would like. Have you seen Freidl Rau[172] yet? It's regrettable to hear from Toledo that such a good little mother doesn't understand how to be peaceful and contented and adjust to living in the home, making concessions when necessary and speaking with restraint while considering time and circumstances. These criticisms come only from me. The dear ones wrote in general terms that life together is not proceeding so harmoniously. On the other hand, there are today many old gentlemen and ladies who once lived in more comfortable circumstances than the mother and who were just as pampered and who have adjusted very well, and many of them are by far not in such a good situation as the mother is in Toledo. It's also equally true that children are not perfect, but some allowances simply must be made for those who get things done and who work and who provide care. Lenchen was very happy with her children's letter that came from Toledo and we had again through that pleasure of something from Rosl and Uncle Emil to read. Lenchen's plan of living together with a woman friend came to nothing, naturally. The friend reconsidered in time. My nerves couldn't stand the sisters' babbling all evening. Friday evenings at the Knollers' and Sunday evenings from six to eleven at our place is already enough to strain my patience to the breaking point, besides which Mother has all the work. Dear Rosi, be most warmly greeted and affectionately kissed by your father who loves you.

My dearest Rosi!

Dear Rosi, you have compensated us richly for the long wait and with each of your letters the sun, so often absent here, comes into the house. Despite the difference in temperature, we still experience much that used to be

---

[172]Probably another Mosbacher cousin. We know Ida Rau in Würzburg was Hugo's cousin.

customary for us. We also found your excursions with Alexander noteworthy. Father wants to know if he is Alexander the Great? In any case, his comparison of Ludwig to a swallowed walking stick pleased us very much, and he grasped his character at once. I find it nice, too, that Aunt Clara has been so thoughtful. We thought the trip to the Doktors would be shorter; in any case I'm very eager to see your report. On this occasion you will also once more have taken another sort of suppository with you. Don't forget to send us a little picture of yourself in your new outfit very soon. We hope you can start work again after your return. Aunt Frida's suit from my atelier turned out to the satisfaction of the spoiled customer. Also, my course has now ended. I hope I can begin another one. Always be careful, my good Rosi. Greet Lily and Albert, etc., etc., for me, and be warmly kissed by your mother.

[^288-2√3429/2]
June 24, 1941

My dear good Rosi!

I have your letter of June 6 before me, which we received yesterday and in which you give your "official" report on your visit to the dear Doktors. We are enormously pleased with the joint letter from all of you and are proud to see that Uncle Emil and Aunt Rosl, who are always rather critical in their judgments, have written with such enthusiasm about their niece. The homelike atmosphere must have done you such good, dear Rosi. We felt ourselves quite transported into the warm, congenial milieu, and now we are looking forward so expectantly to the next installment because the encounter with dear Sigmund and the birthday were surely another such experience for you. I was not surprised to learn that Lore has developed so splendidly. After all, as a small child she was already beloved. I wonder what you may have found to say to dear Sigmund; he has surely become a perfect American. I thought it was terribly thoughtful that they bestowed such fine gifts upon you. Dear Rosi, I hope your return trip went well and that you found everything in order when you got back.

The heat is dreadful at the moment, but we don't want to grumble because we waited almost three quarters of a year for the weather to get warm. I'm certain it's much hotter in New York than it is here. My dear Rosi, be especially cautious now. I would absolutely give away the old clothes—they will just attract moths—everything you don't need, dear Rosi. I've learned through my own experience how unencumbered one feels when one is traveling light. Of course I would like to take our baggage, which is still in transit, when we go, but what do we know today? Unfortunately everything about our situation is unclear. As long as we don't have the exit permit we can't decide anything. I really often feel like crying, but we must endure our fate. This week, the children of Henriette's best woman friend are leaving; there are always exceptions. We have one single wish—that, God willing, we see each other again and in good health. Perhaps that will come sooner than we think. Tomorrow, Father will go to the Committee again to see what he can do. Frida had news from Fritz and Anna during the last few days; Anna always writes in an especially affectionate way.

Last night Father and I went for a stroll about 9:30. During the day it is too hot right now, and I hadn't been out of doors for two days. I almost never get out on a Saturday because that's when Lenchen shows up and makes her visit last almost until midnight. I am usually completely worn out because the chatter is dreadful. Every other statement she makes is "and Henriette says so, too," and, as you know, dear Rosi, I can't stand people who are unable to form their own opinions. From time to time your father passes his hand forcefully across her mouth because she is very nasty and especially rude to

Frida. The nicest thing is when I am alone with our good father; we are never bored.

And now to the main purpose of my letter. I know my daughter and know that she prefers that congratulations be kept brief, and you know your mother and know how much she loves you and what you mean to her—everything! And so I wish you, dear Rosi, health and good fortune on all your paths. Although since your birth you have not lived in the best of times, you have always understood how to be happy and contented, and, in the serious times that you now must live through, you shall always, God willing, find contentment despite all the hardships. That this may always come to pass is my fervent birthday wish for you. Pass the day after Saturday as if you were together with us, hope for the best with us, and receive a ceremonious and affectionate birthday kiss from your mother who loves you.

[^288-3429]
June 24, 1941

My dear good Rosi!

In Loni's[173] time we always used to start your birthday, or rather the celebration of it, several days ahead of time, and we continued to celebrate it for several days afterwards, and Loni could never reconcile herself to the father celebrating his little daughterkin this way, and the whole thing was harmless and inexpensive and was a lot more fun for the father than for the child. I'm thinking about this now because I'm hoping that, if our birthday letter arrives too early, it will be part of the pre-celebration, but if, contrary to expectation, it reaches you late, then it will have to be applied to the post-celebration of the fourteenth of July. Unfortunately we aren't able to cable our wishes to you—we would have liked very much to do that also, but

---

[173]Loni was the Mosbacher's maid when Rosi was a child. Rosi was very fond of her.

at this time it isn't possible to send such messages. For us here it would have been of some importance to do that because then, dear Rosi, we could have known with certainty that you had received our birthday wishes. On the other hand, we also know that you don't need any proofs of love from us, and, even if this letter were to be lost, you would still know that we are with you, as we always are, and that we wish you the very best.

We are truly thankful, dear Rosi, that our wishes for you continue to come true. We are happy that you are ours, and I wish only that you stay just as you are, a cheerful, conscientious, caring person, content with your lot and kind and considerate toward everyone else. That doesn't mean being self-satisfied, because every day one can observe shortcomings in oneself, and it is precisely in your young years that you have the possibility and the ability to correct yourself, to make good your deficits, and to work on yourself. It would have been so wonderful for us to be with you on your birthday, but on this day we aren't going to complain about it, but rather be happy that you are a pioneer and thank you sincerely for all your efforts and for all the paths you've been down. These paths, dear Rosi, are a lot more pleasant for you than the ones you had to travel for me, personally, years ago.[174]

Yesterday your second letter from Toledo arrived, and we are highly satisfied with your beautiful reports and very pleased by the harmonious encounter of niece and uncle and aunt and the sincere mutual happiness and respect. This letter from Toledo of June 6 came especially quickly, and we hope to hear from you again soon. Although I can no longer visualize Ilse Hemlinger, your stories about her are a vivid memory, and now I would also like to know how Ilse comes to be a member of the family. It is, after all, a very different matter if one has

---

[174]In her autobiographical notes, Rosi recounted having to bring family possessions to the Nazis after Kristallnacht. Perhaps Hugo was referring to these episodes.

become acquainted with the locale and dwelling, etc., of the dear ones. One feels anew that one is connected to them; one gets to know the environment and everything pertaining to it.

We will, of course, give you adequate notice concerning the tickets. Given the current situation, we rather believe they will not be used—first, because nothing is being done about the exit permit and, second, because after July 15 there will no longer be anyone to issue a visa, assuming that the door stays open even that long, something that, of course, I can't know. An early peace would be a blessing for all of humanity, and, God willing, the fourteenth of July 1942 will be a pure birthday of peace. We, however, have the urgent wish that we may arrive there many months before that. I know, dear Rosi, that you are glad to defer to your parents and that it would be acceptable to you if this were the only one of your birthday wishes to be fulfilled because we know how keenly you yearn for the same thing that we want. My dear Rosi, be happy, stay well and be careful, and think about your parents when you have decisions to make. That has been my practice, and it has always had a certain calming effect. And now accept a hearty and affectionate birthday kiss from your father who loves you.

Many greetings to the entire family (Ludwigs, Alberts, etc.)

[2545-685]
Friday, June 27, 1941

My Dear Ones!

Some days ago I already confirmed to Rosi your detailed letter of May 30 and June 6, and we thank you many, many times for your loving acceptance of Rosi and for your words of appreciation. Parents are always very pleased to hear compliments about their children, and we are no exception in this respect. We are glad and happy that Rosi was together with you and that you all had the opportunity to discuss everything. These days have meant a great deal to Rosi. I can read in her report how at home she felt with you and how much good this vacation did her. My dears, from here we thank you most affectionately for your loving kindness.

In my letters to Rosi I had already expressed doubt that our application would ever be considered by the American Consulate. The matter was finally cleared up on June 23 when the Committee informed us that the consulate is no longer taking applications and that no visas are being issued. So our ship's tickets are now invalid, and I hope the monetary loss will remain within narrow limits when the cancellation occurs under such circumstances. Now that the U.S.A. is out of the question, the Committee is talking to us about Cuba, and I wouldn't consider it if the Falcks[175] had not gotten their visa for there with such amazing speed—and apparently the cost is also not so unaffordable if the Falcks could come up with it. To be sure, the sums that were quoted to me at the Committee are high enough: (1) $2,000 US per person, nonrefundable for six months, paid at the Havana branch of the National City Bank of New York; (2) $500 US per person landing deposit; (3) $200 US per person other costs. $2,700 US per person, therefore, besides the trip.

If we knew when peace, for which we long, was going to come, and especially if it were to come soon, we would not need to discuss new problems, but, since we know absolutely nothing, we are always clinging to new projects. Aside from the fact that we don't know whether you could make such a request on our behalf to Rubens, and whether she would agree to it, and whether you can also find someone for Frida if the children aren't diligent, we still have absolutely no idea whether the occupying power

---

[175] The Falcks were living in southern France. Presumably they had applied for their visas at the Cuban Consulate in Marseilles, but the details are not known.

will allow us to leave. It could happen that you have secured the visas for us—or the money to pay for them—and that we are not allowed to leave. The difference in the situation is simply that the consulate for Cuba in Rotterdam continues to operate while the U.S.A. Consulate no longer functions or, more accurately, no longer processes anything.[176] You've had the opportunity over there to take counsel and to inform yourselves. The same reasons that caused us at the time to leave the Fürther Straße[177] would also now cause us to depart from here. Forgive me for bothering you so much, but I know that I don't need to excuse myself, and you won't think I'm being presumptuous. I'm not making any demands and am only repeating everything so that you'll be informed. Maybe we can reach you sooner if we consider Cuba first. The entire question depends on whether we are permitted to depart, and no one knows the answer to that. During recent months exit permits have been issued here, but not to all those who were waiting for them. On the other hand, the consulate has not in any way expedited the granting of visas. The reasons for this are unknown to us. The Falcks got their visas in the amazingly quick time of fourteen days. They have been invited to pick up their visas at the Cuban Consulate. Dr. Sondheimer in New York would be able to give the necessary information.

In the meantime, Sigmund's visit will have given you great pleasure. I'm rather nervous today, and as a result my writing is confused. Dear Rosl, you presented Rosi with such a beautiful dress. Accept our sincerest thanks. It is not a conventional friendly thanks for being considerate. We feel your love all the way over here, and it is so good for us, and that is all that counts. In the next letter, Clemy will put her thanks in writing. She was just as happy as I

---

[176] The US Consulate in Rotterdam was closing, so it was no longer possible for them to renew their American visas.
[177] Hugo implied that Nazi persecution of the Jews in Amsterdam had reached the same level as that which drove them from Nuremberg in 1940.

am about everything Rosi has told us about you and everything you have told us about Rosi. I greet the dear mother most sincerely, and may you, my dear ones, be most affectionately kissed, together with her, by your Hugo.

[3541-1300]
June 30, 1941

My dear good Rosi!

You will have arrived home on Monday, June 9, and, if you wrote to us shortly afterwards, we should get something from you again within the next couple of days. Last Friday, June 27, I sent a letter to the Doktors about which you will certainly have been informed. It would be nicer if the many anxieties that are being expressed would not confirm themselves so promptly. The emigration permit has not come, the consulate is no longer functioning and has stopped issuing visas, and as a consequence the tickets, insofar as any have been given out, are cancelled. The prompt response that you wished for, dear Rosi, can unfortunately take place only too quickly. I made a suggestion to Toledo about Cuba, with the observation that this consulate in Rotterdam is functioning, but that even today we are not able to say whether we will obtain the exit permit for which we have been waiting so long and whether we will be able to make use of a Cuban visa even if it can be managed financially. Today I spoke with Mrs. Laninger née Brüll (who used to spend a lot of time with Emmy Tuchmann and Kahn's Hallerstraße).[178] She told me that she wanted nothing to do with Cuba, because (1) emigration from Cuba to the U.S.A. is closed and (2) the cost of living in Cuba is very high. Over there you can certainly obtain all the necessary information about that. The second point, the cost of living, ought not to be such a hindrance if someone wants to leave his current place of residence for important reasons. And it would be even

---

[178]Hallerstraße was the Mosbachers' street in Nuremberg until April 1, 1939.

more important if the entire human race were soon to be blessed by peace[179] since people would then probably have an opportunity to leave.

Up until this point I wrote yesterday evening; then the Knollers came down, and I had to stop. The second half of 1941 begins today, and how soon *Rosh Hashanah* and *Yom Kippur* will be upon us, and we are still sitting here where we do not wish to be. But I've already written so often and so much about this that I need to break the habit once and for all of always starting the same old song all over again. One has to take the situation as it is and come to terms with it. Many people who find themselves worse off than we are would be satisfied with our situation, and we, perforce, must be satisfied, too, especially as long as our health is good. To be sure, one of my front teeth is loose, and the dentist wants to wait until its neighbor also becomes loose so that he can do the whole job at one go, both front and back. My mouth so far has remained free of dentures, but that has to happen sometime and there's no need to get excited about it.

This afternoon Mother is attending a coffee klatch that the sewing teacher is giving for the students in her course to celebrate the vacation. The teacher is an especially nice woman. Mrs. Ella Cohn-Goldberger is there, too. It's something special for Mother when she must decide to take a few hours off, and I'm happy when she has to leave the worktable. Tomorrow afternoon there is a reception between four and five at Hans Bachmann's on the occasion of his wedding. It will only be a civil ceremony. He has had, praise God, good news concerning his parents.[180] His father Julius would certainly have liked to be a witness

---

[179]"In early 1941 Germany tried to negotiate peace with Britain through diplomatic communications via Sweden."
See http://www.wiki30.com/wa?s=Rudolf_Hess) These efforts were murky and ineffective. Moreover, it's unlikely that Hugo would have heard of them; more probably his hopes for an early peace were, in fact, hopes.
[180]Hugo may have meant that the older Bachmanns had left Germany and reached a safe country. Julius Bachmann does not appear on the list of Shoah victims from Nuremberg; Hans does.

at the wedding, but nothing is perfect and everywhere something gets left out and there is cause for complaint.

Have you perhaps heard at the Doktors', by chance, what Mr. Kahn is doing with our house there in Hallerstraße? My asking is not at all important, but when I was speaking with Mrs. Laninger yesterday I did not, for politeness' sake, ask about the Kahns, but it did cause me to think about Kahn. The supporting documents about which I wrote you so often and which Franz was supposed to supply have been obtained in the meantime from acquaintances who live here. Franz had been entrusted with this task since January, but so far he hasn't written that he is unable to send them. Now the documents that I obtained here previously have to be renewed, and who knows what new regulations, what new conditions, will now be in place? Usually they do not become easier, but harder. Still, I would be happy to be occupied with these matters again.

What is Ludwig Mosbacher doing? Frida Maier? Give them all our greetings and also Uncle Albert and Aunt Lily. Perhaps she knows Ludwig's family. If not, then perhaps you, dear Rosi, can establish the connection, if that seems desirable. I can very well imagine a satisfying conversation between Lily and Ludwig. When Mother comes home, she will at the very least add her own greetings in her own handwriting, so I need to leave space for her and stop. Let's hope that our contact doesn't suffer an interruption, and let's be thankful for that which brings us joy. In that spirit, and with many greetings and affectionate kisses, your loving father.

My dearest good Rosi!

Your most recent pictures make me so happy! I look at them often, and, whether my mood is good or bad, they always make it better. We are now once more waiting intently for the mail. I don't want to say anything more about our story. Father has already talked enough about it. The main thing is that everyone stays well and that the news from you and the Doktors continues to be positive. My afternoon with the ladies today was very nice. Unfortunately my mind is always elsewhere. My good Rosi, please accept my heartfelt greetings and kisses. Best regards to all the loved ones—your mother.

[2882-/1266c]
July 21, 1941

My dear good Rosi!

On Friday, July 18, to my great joy, we received your letter of July 1, mailed on July 2. The mail service from you to us is significantly better than from us to you since our letter of May 30 did not reach you until July 1. We are well, praise God, except for a few minor matters, such as toothache that I am going to take care of within the next hour because, as a matter of principle, I don't allow these things to torture me any longer than necessary.

So that I don't forget, I want to pass on these lines that Miss Hammelburger added to a card from Ida Rau: "I am so very happy that I can get news about you; may it only be much happier. I'm always asking about you. My mother has been in Z[urich?] with my sister for the last four weeks. We have achieved that happy outcome, but, as you may well believe, it wasn't easy. I would have been able to leave in fourteen days, and I went to Stuttgart, but visas were no longer being issued. And now, here I stand. I don't want to give up hope completely, but it's hard." Fanny wanted to go there [the U.S.A.]. How much this separation must have meant to both of them. I conclude from this that perhaps Dr. H[full name unknown]. is also already in America. Every family has the same difficulties and the same worries. I wrote to Toledo on June 27 concerning Cuba. The letter may be there already. By the time you have considered it and passed it on to Pauline and decided either for or against it, in the best case another four weeks will go by before we hear from you about it. I believe I told you in our last letter that the Committee now considers the prospects for leaving the country to be somewhat improved. We don't know, of course, what might intervene; we can only hope for the best.

We have changed our Sunday visit from Aunt Lenchen to a weekday. It had become too stressful for Mother to do all that cooking on a Sunday and to have the house full—or the room, rather. Personally speaking, I find the peace and quiet does me a lot of good. Instead of being invited and relieved of the burden—although we ourselves honestly prefer to decline invitations—we must observe all the niceties with punctilio if Frida is to hold sway. This little change almost caused a scandal. Anna wrote enthusiastically about the house she has bought, and we are pleased to learn of such progress. Fip's income has certainly risen in the meantime. Strangely, one never hears a word about this, and it is precisely what would interest me. If I hear about the big incomes of strangers, then certainly I am going to be interested in the incomes of those who are closer to me. But this, too, even though I am writing about it, is absolutely unimportant. My interests, as you can understand, lie in a completely different area. It is a shame that once again the passage you booked for us came to nothing, and money was lost. It should have been clear, at the time the booking was made, that it couldn't be done.

You did not, intentionally, describe Paul Neurath's illness as being as bad as it really was and I hope it no longer is. On such sad occasions, when people's nerves are on edge, it is easy for conflicts to arise between mother-in-law and daughter-in-law, even though that sort of thing may not have happened before when the mood was better. Had Paul had these gastrointestinal complaints before? That you were able to help Lotte Roederer by accident, as it were, is truly delightful. Did she really pay no attention to her cousin Fritz? What, pray tell, does the patriarch Ludwig have against Mr. Alex? Does the latter not defer to him in everything, does he answer him back, or is Alex at least as well educated as he is? He was almost always very satisfied with me. Once I spoke bluntly to him, and then all communication between us was broken off for a long time. I feel sorry for such vain people; others, as far back as twenty years ago, were calling him "the peacock." Still, may he stay well or get well—that's my sincere wish. I hope, dear Rosi, that in the meantime you've gotten the mail. It's just as important to us for you to hear from us as for us to hear from you. Please be careful. When it's very hot you must pay particular attention to what you eat and drink. With many greetings and affectionate kisses from your father who loves you.

My dear good Rosi!
    Father just left to go to his English lesson, while I want to talk to you. Unfortunately I don't have the last letter you wrote at hand; Father always carries it around with him. In the meantime, dear Rosi, you will have heard from us and discussed the subject of Cuba with dear Uncle Emil. Is it feasible? We no longer dare to hope. I assume, my good Rosi, that you have your health back and are feeling quite well again. You will be enjoying the weather. We are very concerned about the illness of Lily's Paul; he should, God willing, be on the road to recovery. Still, he seems to have been very seriously ill. We had a letter from Lily that depressed me very much because she wrote in such a troubled way. An enclosed photo of little Ruth[181] pleased us all. Trudl transmitted all the previous letters to Zagreb. We have heard nothing more from Mela for several months. Perhaps in your next letter we will hear something about how you passed your birthday. Dear Rosi, you always describe so many events—the free concert, etc. I'm sure the *Eroica* was splendid. I would so much like to hear a concert, too; we are cut off from

---

[181] Paul Neurath's baby daughter, Lily's grandchild.

everything. Erna wrote that they are in possession of the Cuban visa and now they need the ship tickets. The procurement will not be easy, but they are very confident and, God willing, it will work out for them. We are happy about every one who gets away. I'm sure the dress from Toledo looks very nice on you. Send us a little picture of yourself wearing it. Greet all the loved ones for me and, my dear Rosi, receive many greetings and affectionate kisses from your mother.

[3065-2632]
Sunday, July 27, 1941

My dear good Rosi!

Your letter of July 10 reached us on Friday, July 25, and it was once again a very satisfactory introduction to Saturday. Our current address for you will no longer be valid, and you, dear Rosi, will already be living in a suitable room with kitchen privileges. In any case we wish you all the best with your new room. We keep our fingers crossed for you every day. In addition to the fact that we speak of you every day, it never happens that I don't talk to you before I fall asleep. At the end of the day, usually between 11 and 11:30, when I wish your dear mother a good night, it's your turn, dear Rosi. Even though a so-called estrangement between us would be out of the question, and even if our separation were to last twice as long as it has, I still feel that I always need to do something myself to maintain a feeling of vibrancy and vividness, even though in the present case it's not at all necessary.

I believe I've already told you many times how I behaved when I was a young fellow and found myself in an especially lively group and had permitted myself certain enjoyments that were perhaps more than my body or my wallet could sustain. My head was throbbing from a moral hangover, and I left the company for a few minutes and thought about my unassuming parents and my other dear ones who were sitting at home, making no demands. And it was this memory that gave me support and direction and warned me to put on the brakes while there was still time. If one often hears about young people who, when far from home, separate themselves from their relatives at home by sending no news of themselves, then the reason is often simply that they have let their feelings become dulled. It begins as laziness and neglectfulness, and then it turns into indifference. It's so odd that in my later years I like so much to think back to that time that lies so far, far in the past, for example, when my parents went on summer vacation and departed early in the morning, between four and five, for Gastein. I would accompany them to the train station and ride with them as far as Nuremberg. The beautiful home of the Holzinger family was right next to the station, and today I can still hear my unpropertied but deeply contented and happy father talk, as he always did before these trips, about the wealth and inherited property of this family. From the perspective of a simple teacher it was stupendous. Still, my parents always started out on their vacations with more pleasure and fewer worries than many other people did, and, for me, seeing them off was always a special experience and source of pleasure. I'm filling up my letter with explanations like these and with stories that, first, are very old, and, second, cannot possibly interest you. Nevertheless, I tell myself that, just as I had the Holzinger saga told to me once a year, so too may you have something served up to you by your father. In the meantime, fortunately, many things have changed. My father had a certain respect for riches; today it's no longer possible to understand how the little people, even those who were quite independent, would doff their hats when they encountered such exalted personages. Also, Holzinger senior was counted among Hannah's family, and, if Ludwig tells you a story twenty times over, then it's not so bad if I repeat myself five times.

Together with your letter, one arrived from the Doktors in Chicago, which gave us great pleasure, because of the enthusiasm with which Rosl writes about Sigmund and his good behavior. If he were our own son we couldn't be happier. Mother and I have done our best to fill the vacancy that was left for so many years after the loss of his mother, and we did our best with great love. You write, dear Rosi, about new forms from Washington. Are these necessary if the affidavit from Rubens expires again and has to be renewed, or is there a possibility that, despite the consulate being closed, we will still be able to get there by way of Washington? Despite dismal experiences, we are easily inclined to believe what we like to hear. Last Friday, day before yesterday, I went to Hoymann and Schurmann travel agency, paid thirty-five guilders, and sent a telegram to Toledo: "Departure possible if Mosbacher and Roederer tourist visas for Cuba secured. Wire Havana Consulate Rotterdam when completed." So the prospects for our departure suddenly look better. I telegraphed (1) after I had heard that a lot of people had already gotten Cuban visas and (2) so that we will get our turn as quickly as possible. Of course we will write to Toledo today or tomorrow. In any case the Doktors have not had our letter about Cuba for very long and the matter is still being processed so that our telegram and the letter will have arrived pretty much together. Then the Toledo people will first have to correspond with the Whites and Fritz [Roederer]. Although Cuba causes all kinds of expense, I have still not heard of anyone rejecting it on those grounds, but, whatever the decision, we accept it in the expectation that everything will turn out for the best.

Dear Rosi, when you write that Paul N[eurath]. is unfortunately still sick, we are still relatively contented with this information because we know then that he is still among the living. Do visit Aunt Lily as often as you can. In her present situation she needs to be pampered a little bit. Ludwig M[osbacher] cannot stand to have anyone around him except the most attentive listeners and admirers and 70 percent senile bank directors à la Sturmband, whom I just happened to think of. It's pleasantly cool today after being hot or warm for several days—just the weather we want for next Sunday. Now Mother wants to add something, and I have to close. Stay well, and be careful always, and be warmly greeted and heartily kissed by your father who loves you. Many greetings to Lily, Albert, Paul and his wife, to Mirko's wife, and Ludwig's family.

My dearest Rosi,

I was just telling Father that the letter he wrote today would better be sent to Uncle Emil because what does our Rosi know about Holzinger in F[ürth]? Father thought it over and said he agreed with me, but nevertheless such stories would do no harm. Your last letter gave us much pleasure. Now we are awaiting the report on July 14. I can picture your new skirt very well. I'm glad to see that you're now willing to consider flared skirts; you used to not like them at all. We were of course very interested in your nice weekend. You reported the same kind of weather as the Doktors did for Chicago. The weather here has changed. I'm pleased with the coolness, but I'd rather not think about the cold. I'm hoping that when winter comes we'll be in a better climate. Rosi, how happy we would be to be warm just for once. God willing, Paul is doing better. I have to think so often about him and about Albert's family. Is Alexander working as a chemist? A teacher recently told us that her married daughter in New York is earning $125 a month as a beginning seamstress. I'll believe something like that when I see it. And now, good Rosi, it's time for my usual wish: Stay well and accept, together with all the loved ones, many greetings. Your mother kisses you tenderly.

[493-1388]
Sunday, August 10, 1941

My dear good Rosi!

We received your letter of July 18 four days ago and once again our joy was great, knowing that you are well and have work. Now we are partly satisfied. I congratulate you on moving into your new room and hope that meanwhile you have made yourself comfortable and feel good about living there. As of today you will have already slept there two dozen nights and will have drawn your conclusions about the quality of the bed, the hygienic conditions, etc. Although Aunt Frida got her birthday greetings to you in the mail later than we and Trudl did, you did not, unfortunately, receive our congratulations punctually, which we rather regret, for we believed that they would be too early rather than too late, especially when we were at such pains to send them early enough. We are pleased to learn of the presents that were so richly bestowed upon you, both by the dear ones in Carolina and those in Toledo, and we found your report especially desirable. Alex has almost surpassed us (I'm referring to the times at home). In any case, we have learned that he is one of those people who like making other people happy, a character trait that we find very sympathetic because we ourselves like to promote it in every walk of life.

Before your letter reached us, I had expressed myself in written form concerning the putative urgency of our case. It would of course be most gratifying if people in W[ashington?] would concur with Uncle Emil's opinion and deal with our case accordingly. That would be to prefer Cuba, and I think that we will hear from Toledo during the next few days whether that is a possibility. If the efforts there are in vain, I leave it to Toledo to decide whether to apply to Heddy on our behalf. Perhaps she can prevail upon her brother-in-law Zollfrei to make the sacrifice. We haven't written directly to Heddy because we see how endlessly slow the postal service is here; it has been months since we heard anything from her.[182] Before I hear anything about Cuba in respect to Aunt Frida, I want to say in advance that, if you all think it is desirable to secure this visa, then the three children must or should secure it. Fips and Fritz can be sure of Ludwig's[183] agreement. Ludwig's friend Dr. Erlanger brought his Uncle Max to Montevideo, and Ludwig could have made the necessary sacrifices and done that for his mother. Unfortunately they were only interested in the U.S.A., and besides Ludwig, understandably, did not encourage Frida to take up this suggestion. She could have made a nice trip with Uncle Max, and she certainly could have come to you from Montevideo. But what good does it do to talk about things that are over and done with? I only mention it in connection with the request that I am making to Aunt Frida's children on her behalf, a view of the matter that I feel sure you will share.

Yesterday afternoon—*Shabbos Nachamu*—we strolled in Dina's tracks[184] and invited the Knollers in and commemorated the birthday of our dear departed grandfather that has always been celebrated on this day. We have never yet encountered such a man who, every day until he went to sleep, did nothing but strive, think, and work; who had such undeniable qualities as he had; and who could be counted among the best of men. In a time like the present, when everyone is full of his own sorrows and other thoughts, it is especially fitting to arrange such memorials. It was our dear Mother who arranged this one.

Although it was possible for us to send a letter to Mela, we have heard nothing from that quarter and hope that all is well and in order with them and also with Erwin and with Lily and Albert's children. And how is Paul today?

---

[182]Details of this plan are not known. Perhaps Hugo was considering asking Heddy or Zollfrei for help obtaining visas to Chile.
[183]Ludwig Neuburger, half-brother of Fritz Roederer, was Frida's other stepson. He was living in Montevideo, Uruguay.
[184]Hugo meant that they had received a detailed, newsy letter from Dina.

We think of him every day. After he had gotten over his fever, at the time you went to see him, we naturally hoped that his condition had materially improved. How fortunate that one is permitted to hope, although recently a verse from a poem of our great poet, which I had to memorize in school, has caused our hope and our affirmation of life to dissolve, every day and most unpleasantly. The verse states, "E'en now, mayhap, whilst hope we cherish, / Calamity doth make us perish."[185] In fact, this passage from the poem does not represent an enrichment of our knowledge or an alleviation of our conscience, and it would have been better to let people have their hope in its pure form. One inclines to skepticism in a given matter only when one must rely upon hope or is compelled to hope, and it simply becomes too much, and one recalls the words of the poet.

My correspondence with Franz Schweizer has sharply declined. He hears the truth from me, and his splendid dialectics can't impress me. He can't stand it when he has to accept being corrected. He was recently complaining that he has not received a single line from the U.S.A. from you. He has his facts straight there, and I assume that you suppressed the impulse to send written greetings reluctantly and only because you didn't want to conjure up any new relationships and obligations to write. If my assumption is wrong, then I beg you, dear Rosi, to correct me, because I want to be corrected, and I can stand it quite well when it's appropriate. The Falcks have not left yet; we learned from a long letter that arrived yesterday that the problem with the tickets has not yet been cleared up. The tickets on which payments were already made have been cancelled. Klara Klein[186] from Miltenberg has been in Oakland for several days visiting her son, her brother, and her niece and her niece's family. She also made a side trip to Los Angeles

---

[185] "Ach, vielleicht indem wir hoffen, hat uns Unheil schon betroffen." From "The Song of the Bell" by Friedrich Schiller, published in 1799.
[186] Klara Klein was Hugo's first cousin.

to the Eschauers, although her relationship with the Strausses was very troubled when she departed because Herrmann had behaved very unfairly toward her cousin.

I've just now noticed that once again I've reported something that doesn't interest you at all. Please excuse these unnecessary familial digressions. For the last several days I've carried your graduation certificate from the *Seminar* in my coat pocket. Now and then I like to have something I love to read besides the pack of letters. If you need a photocopy I'll be happy to have one made. In the certificate, the commentary about you says, "Her ethical, serious view of life, pleasing personality, and lively pursuit of knowledge deserve acknowledgment. Her very laudable industriousness has enabled her to achieve good results." Whenever I read this assessment it gives me joy. Also it's extremely well formulated, and Stoll was an outstanding educator, although in your day that was no longer the case. Now, dear Rosi, you're thinking, how does he get from Cuba to Stoll? In any event, it would be good if you would stay in touch with the Committee there so that you can be informed immediately about any possibilities that arise. I always say that everything has a beginning and an end, and this will turn out well for us. And in this sense, dear Rosi, be greeted and kissed many times by your father who loves you.

My dear Rosi!

I was already happy at home, when my dear Rosi unusually became somewhat more tender, exactly as I am now when I hear the word "*Mütterle*"[187] from a great distance. Rosi, it touched my heart, and I'm giving you a hearty kiss right now. I know that you mean it just as well without having to be unusually tender, but sometimes it does me a lot of good and is especially welcome. Quite apart from the separation, which is painful and which will continue to exist in Cuba, we're in favor of this move

---

[187]"*Mütterle*" means "Little Mother" and indicates affection.

since we believe that it's for the better, but whether it's really the right thing is still a question mark. I sometimes feel myself in a mood similar to the one I was in when we were waiting for Father.[188]

All your friends made an appearance on your birthday; even Fellh[eimer] did not forget you. I found it terribly considerate of Aunt Clara to give you such lovely stationery, and you certainly didn't expect that our dear Doktors would make such generous arrangements—the dress itself was already a birthday present. Everything over there seems to be very practical (pertaining to celebrations). Alexander represented Father very well. We wrote to Aunt Lily; the first letter seems not to have arrived. We hope that Paul is on the road to recovery. Visit Aunt Lily when you can. That's very important to her. We hope you're comfortably settled into your room. I would so like to see what you've done with it! Yesterday I was in the synagogue in honor of Papa's birthday; it's only a few minutes' distance from us. If only the mail will keep on arriving so punctually! My good Rosi, accept affectionate greetings and kisses from your mother.

[161-1906]
August 17, 1941

My dear good Rosi!

It was a happy surprise for us to receive your telegram of August 11 telling us that we have received our visas for Cuba and that Aunt Frida's visa will follow. That last piece of information was very important for us and was an especially good reason for sending the telegram because, if we hadn't gotten that news from you and had only received the written communication of the Cuban consulate on the following day, then we would have been unnecessarily worried about Aunt Frida. In the meantime we already

---

[188] Probably a reference to 1938 when Clemy waited over a month for Hugo to be released from Dachau where he was imprisoned after Kristallnacht.

have the Cuban visas in our passports—arranged by Bruno in Rotterdam—and yesterday Frida got her notification from the consulate. So things couldn't have gone quicker. Now we have to fill out the forms for the agency that issues the exit permits and, God willing, this time nothing will interfere and everything will go as it should. No one can tell us how long it's going to take. I'm thinking two or three months maximum. Of course there is always the possibility that it will go much quicker.

It cannot have been easy for the dear ones in Toledo to convince our benefactors, that is, their friends and Pauline, of the necessity of the sacrifices that had to be made, and I give the dear ones my deepest thanks for their great work and trouble, and you, dear Rosi, not less for all the roads you traveled and all the efforts you made on our behalf, and not least those who made the great sacrifice and helped us to obtain the visas. Even though these visas are now pouring in from all sides, I still don't fail to recognize the great willingness to help. I have to take into consideration that they had to step into the breach for us so many times and that our constant living expenses never stop.[189] We're happy, of course, that we've finally gotten this far and we hope that it's finally going to work and that we will finally and definitely be able to depart. When once we get to Cuba there will be another solution.

We thank you many times and extra for the telegram because, without it, as already mentioned, we would have been only partially satisfied and would have been worrying about the visa for Aunt Frida up until yesterday. It's so easy for me to write of our sincere and honest gratitude, but I am deeply moved when I do so, and I know only too well what you, my dear ones, had to do and how hard it is to have to keep making the same request over and over again. I mention all this so that you will know that

---

[189]Hugo and Clemy depended on money that relatives in the US were able to send them, though the method of transmittal is not clear. Rosi and others seem to have been able to send them clothes and food packages before the United States entered the war.

we aren't lacking in appreciation and that we know that the visas didn't fall into our laps and that it took all kinds of diplomacy and skill to make something like this happen. But, since we're convinced that you have done your best for us and never grown tired of the effort, we also know that our very best thanks will be enough and that what has been accomplished makes you as happy as it does us.

On August 14 we got your letter of July 24–25, which confirmed for us that our birthday letter had finally arrived after a long delay for which we, however, weren't to blame. We've never received a telegram from Lisbon, probably because it was already known there at the time that travel was no longer possible. An important point in your letter was the improvement in Paul's condition, which has been and is one of our constant concerns. We were amused that Aunt Lily provided you with a nutpick, which you used in such a practical way. When you write about your evenings out and excursions, going to concerts, etc., you usually write in the plural, without naming your companion. However, it's not hard for us to figure out whom you're going with, and we know quite well that, for example, you went to dinner with the Mirkos without your companion, because he wasn't invited, either by them or by Ludwig's family, and I believe and hope that the parties named will gradually become more amiable.

Aunt Lenchen is coming to have lunch with us today at noon. This is an extra invitation because she was busy helping a niece in Hilversum for two weeks and returned yesterday afternoon. The two-week interruption amounted to a vacation for us. It is sad that we have to make this admission, but unfortunately we can't get around it. Whether we set out a platter with twelve sweetmeats or with twenty-four it matters not at all. By the time she leaves us, the platter is empty without any intervention whatever on our part. We know that her enjoyment is sincere, and our pleasure in her enjoyment is equally sincere, and in this greed I see a fault that pains me. Henriette is better able to disguise her nature through her attractive appearance and her charm, but she too is sufficiently spiteful, envious, and embittered. Of course I am not going to thank her for the fact that I encouraged Pauline to become acquainted with Henny, and that the dear ones in Toledo, through their sympathy, helped to foster the relationship. Nevertheless, a few days ago in conversation Henriette expressed the opinion that it should be clear to all of us that it was only due to her friendship that everything had worked out. I was on the point of saying that, if we had had to involve her in such matters, it would have been a total fiasco. I was recently afraid that she had done something wrong, but I don't want to make false accusations. Her envy and jealousy do not speak well of her, and that's sad.

This afternoon at 1:50, dear Rosi, we got your second telegram, concerning Aunt Frida. Even though we already had the news, we rejoiced all over again with the sender "Rosi," and Frida was no less pleased by your attentiveness. I hope to be able very soon to answer by telegram your further question as to the earliest possible passage. First I will have to go to the Committee or to the Jewish Council because all Jewish emigration now proceeds through these agencies that have to negotiate with the authority.[190] A travel agency can't do anything nor can the individual represent himself. The Committee, which wants to be especially cautious with its information, is only willing to say at this point that it can't determine when the authority will grant the exit permits. You'll want to have the desired information from us so that the tickets can be ordered in time. If the Cuban consulate over there lets the visa number continue to run in the same sequence, then 248 visas will have been issued between the Mosbacher and the Roederer visas. We are paying 20 *gulden* per visa here. I have the feeling that everything is going to work

---

[190] The "authority" is a reference to the German occupation force.

out and that, when exit permits are issued, ours will be among them. I estimate that the time required for processing will be at most six weeks, and I can't permit myself to telegraph this deadline to you because it's only a guess on my part. In any case I hope to be able to send you a timely answer. Next *Shabbos* we will be in *Elul* and the *shofar* will be heard again.[191] With best wishes for you, my dear Rosi, and for the dear ones in Toledo, with warmest greetings and the most affectionate kisses from your father who loves you.

My dear Rosi,

Father writes about everything in such detail that, with the best intentions, I'm unable to figure out what there might be left to communicate. So the only thing left for me to do is to thank the dear Doktors and you for all your love and kindness. You have accomplished something great, and, God willing, this time it will work—Hold the cannons.[192] We breathed a sigh of relief when we heard of dear Paul's recovery. Is it true that Roserl, Milan, and Hertha[193] are on their way there? We haven't heard anything directly from Mela. Erna sent us this last news and also that Mela's son-in-law is not at home but writes faithfully. I assume that Aunt Clara is perhaps now staying in Toledo or will be there soon. After your letter has reached the Doktors safely, give them and Aunt Clara my warmest regards. Since we were already on the first departure list, the number we had at that time will also be valid for the current departure. Your last letter made me very happy. Just stay nice and well, and, God willing, there will be a

---

[191] During Elul, the last month of the Jewish year, there are a number of rituals leading up to the High Holy Days. It is customary to blow the *shofar* every morning (except on the Sabbath) as a call to repentance.

[192] Clemy seems to have meant "Don't celebrate yet," since they had endured so many disappointments.

[193] Hertha Engelsrath escaped to Italy from Yugoslavia in late 1941. Roserl Neurath and her husband Milan Engelsrath had also been living in Yugoslavia but were in a refugee camp in Italy by this point. Apparently they hoped to travel to the United States together.

reunion soon. Weilheimer told Father that his ship will stop at New York for two days. My dear Rosi, receive many greetings and kisses from your mother.

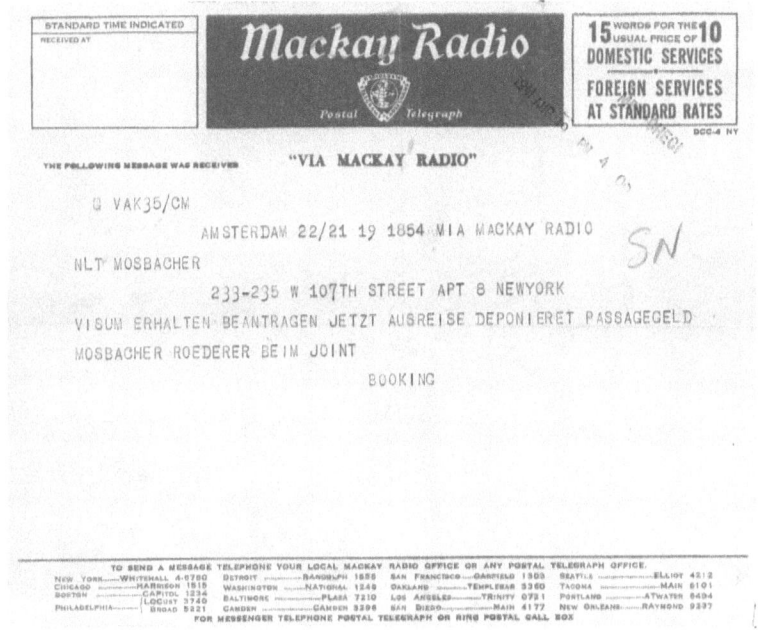

Hugo's August 19, 1941, telegram.
"Obtained visa, now applying for departure. Deposit passage money for Mosbacher, Roederer with the Joint."

ADDRESS OFFICIAL COMMUNICATIONS TO
THE SECRETARY OF STATE
WASHINGTON, D.C.

DEPARTMENT OF STATE
WASHINGTON

In reply refer to
VD 811.111 Mosbacher, Hugo

AUGUST 29, 1941

Miss Rosi Mosbacher,
101 West 93rd Street,
New York, New York.

Madam:

    With reference to your letter of July 9, 1941 requesting necessary forms to sponsor your parents, Hugo and Clementine Mosbacher,

now residing in Amsterdam Zuid Holland
I have to inform you that no action may be taken in this case at present because there are no American consular offices operating in the district under reference.

    In the event the alien or aliens in whom you are interested are able to proceed to a territory in which they may appear at an American Consulate, you should notify the Department immediately in order that appropriate advice may be given regarding your further procedure. Before taking action the Department should be furnished with some definite evidence that the alien or aliens concerned will be able to obtain permission to leave the country in which they are now residing and to enter some other country where the visa application will be executed. Otherwise it is not believed that any useful purpose will be served by further correspondence in this matter.

    Very truly yours,

A. M. Warren
Chief, Visa Division

Visa Form A-3

The Department of State's August 29, 1941, reply to Rosi's letter of July 9, 1941. As long as Hugo and Clemy were unable to leave Holland, there was nothing to be done.

[2507-3420]
Monday, September 15, 1941

My dear good Rosi!

Today, the second day of *Slichot*, we received your letter of August 26. To my joy, it was lying on the table when I came home, and dear Mother had had the pleasure before me. I was saying yesterday that a letter from you would arrive early this morning. We thank you warmly for your lovely letter. I simply had to read it to Trudl, who paid us a brief visit just for that purpose. As soon as word gets around the building that we have gotten mail, all the interested parties show up, especially when a cable is delivered.

We have only wired you in response to a cable from you or your office, and, because we ourselves are not permitted to send telegrams, as we've mentioned many times, we've sent our messages through the travel agency which has that authorization. Once, on the advice of the Committee, we wired you: "Deposit passage money with *Joint*."[194] In response, a telegram came back from you: "I'm booking with Atlantic Tours. Wire departure date." I took this telegram to Hoymann & Schurmann, who wanted to show me an entirely different way to do the deal. I didn't agree to it because I didn't know what funds were available to you and the agency might have asked for more than you had at your disposal. I've written about all this once already. After you didn't get a telegraphic answer from us, the Committee received information about another telegram concerning our affair, which had been sent to Hoymann & Schurmann by Tracesery: "Mosb. Roed. family passage money paid in with us. Wire if *open* deposit with Cook urgent for departure." Tracesery and the word "urgent" led to the conclusion that this telegram originated

---

[194]The American Jewish Joint Distribution Committee (often called "the Joint," or the JDC) is a worldwide Jewish relief organization established in 1914 and headquartered in New York. Hugo was asking Rosi (and probably his brother Emil) to deposit money to pay for their passage.

with Atlantic Tours. We then discussed at the Committee what reply we should make and how we should send it. Hoymann & Schurmann had no interest in sending a telegram that would help its competitor Cook. After Tracesery had suggested an *open* deposit with Cook, I went to the local Cook office, which then wired Tracesery for us that we agreed to the *open* deposit with Cook. I want to point out, however, that I only did it this way because Tracesery had suggested it, and I assume that this agency will do everything correctly. Once we have the exit permit in hand, we will send a telegram through Cook here that we have gotten that far so that the further steps can be taken. When I went to Hoymann & Schurmann with your telegram "I am booking with Atlantic Tours" and showed it to them, they did not say that they were in any kind of contact with Atlantic Tours. They advised me rather to cable you that, instead of paying a deposit to Atlantic Tours, you should open an account with Banco X [?] in Bilbao. However, I didn't do that, and you wrote that Hoymann & Schurmann here and Atlantic Tours there were working together, that the one firm represented the other.[195]

Enough of that now. It will get straightened out, and you know all the connections. When we instructed you to pay the deposit to the *Joint*, then surely you did not pay the deposit at that time because the *Joint* apprised you of another way. However, in your letter which arrived today, you wrote that, if we think it's important to pay the deposit to the *Joint*, then we should inform you at once. Our request to you at the time was made on the basis of the advice given us by the Committee. But in the final analysis it won't make any difference when the money is on *open* deposit if, at the moment when we have the exit permits, the firm that is holding the money does everything promptly and correctly.

---

[195]This discussion of money and travel arrangements is difficult to follow. It would seem that Hoymann & Schurmann was a local travel agent and Atlantic Tours and Tracesery were American travel or booking agencies.

We were most pleasantly surprised that you remembered September 3, 1911. We had believed that in such troubled times people forget such things. We thank you for your good wishes. The Knollers were especially kind. The daughters brought little presents with "30" inscribed on them, and the parents gave us a package of "coffee" decorated in the same way. Otherwise, no one knew about it, and this was entirely in accordance with our attitude and also agrees with the attitude that you expressed. Indeed, would you not be the eloquent evidence of a marriage of at least twenty-six years—measured by old, middle-class standards. Mother and I don't feel that it has been such a terribly long time since we got married. It has never become boring for us, we constantly have something to talk about, we always have concerns in common and always share our happiness, and, if one of us doesn't say something in order to avoid disagreement, then the other still knows what he is thinking and didn't want to say.

We sublet from a family which, when we moved in, presented itself to us as being totally happy and in love with one another, but how that picture changed with the course of time. Kisses are still exchanged at every coming and going. The father kisses the mother, and the son kisses the parents; the smooching never ends. But when they're at table, where we always liked so much to sit with our Rosi, and they catch me, then they implore me, "Come in, Mr. M., and sit with us while we have dinner," etc. Why? When they're alone together, every word is a reason to have a fight and for nasty disputes, but not a single sentence begins without "dear Else" or "dear Eugen."

Your use of the word "sublimate" tells me that you're going on a lot of walks with a chemist. You write that wedding day wishes and wishes for porcelain mingle and sublimate themselves. A five-hour hike is quite enough, and you don't need to be surprised if you're worn out. I think these lines will reach you during the first days of *Sukkot*; in any case, good wishes and a *gut yontif.* You have our full support in your search for a new line of work. There is a right time for everything, and we would be pleased if you succeeded in finding something related to the occupation you trained for or at least closer to it. I don't doubt that you will find something good, even if it may take a while longer. In a letter from Oakland, which came today, we read the regrettable information that Dr. Paul had to be admitted to a sanitarium for lung diseases. I believe that the condition is acute, and that, while recovery is not in doubt, the condition is nevertheless bad enough. Even though I'm opposed to too much coddling and pampering, I still want to advise you urgently against accepting a position that demands new daily physical exertion. For someone who has been in training since age twelve and has always had to work, it may not be especially challenging, but for someone who is not used to such demands it is very hard and injurious to health.

Mother is still convalescent because she is still in pain, and she really should spare herself more than she does. You know how hard it is for her to take it easy and to eat mush, every spoonful is precisely measured and choked down with loathing. I'll pass on your wishes to the family—they're sufficient. If these lines get to Toledo, I greet all the dear ones there most warmly. Despite all the separation, I feel myself very close to them. And, God willing, it will work out someday. Franz's well-written letter is enclosed so that you can hear from him, too. Now I'll close because Mother wants to chat with you also. With many greetings and affectionate kisses from your father who loves you.

My dear good Rosi!

Today is a nice day again, and if a letter is there from you we will hasten to answer it. After you neglected to make any mention of Lily's Paul, we concluded that he must be doing better. It is really especially unfortunate that both sons of my sisters are now seriously ill. I hope that we hear soon that both our nephews are better again. Always watch your health and don't overestimate your strength. Meanwhile, you'll have made your necessary purchases. When we arrive in Cuba it will be with the bare necessities. We still don't know if or when we will get our baggage. As soon as we get the exit permits we'll inform you by telegram, insofar as that's possible. The Falcks are still waiting for their tickets. By the time you get this letter the main part of the holidays will be over. This is now the third year where we have to celebrate the feast days without you. But we are connected all the more affectionately to you in spirit, my dear Rosi. And so I wish you everything good, many times over, and many, many greetings and kisses from your mother.

[3512-1398a]
October 9, 1941

My dear good Rosi!

The days of *Sukkoth* have already begun with the arrival of your letter of September 14 and of Uncle Emil's letter of September 10 to Aunt Lenchen. If on ordinary days we recall past times, how much more we do so on the high and highest holidays, and we felt exactly the same as you did, although the feeling of anticipation before the holidays meant more to you than you wrote to us. In the meantime, everything will have gone well and satisfactorily for you. I was completely satisfied with the divine service and everything pertaining to it. On *Rosh Hashanah* I was called upon, an honor which was to some extent due to old age. Uncle Emil's account of the shady sides of their philanthropic benefactor agreed completely with what I wrote in my last letter.[196] I'm happy that, despite the enormous distance and the lack of personal discussion, nothing has changed in our judgment and comprehension of things and situations.

---

[196]Hugo's reference is unclear. Perhaps a letter is missing.

Obviously we, just as much as Ludwig M[osbacher].,[197] would prefer to see you find a paying job that was closer to your knowledge and training, but I don't know that being dissatisfied for that reason is justified, as Ludwig M. is and as, thank God, you are not. I hear about women who are doing what you are doing, and there must be many others who would be glad to accept such a position if they could find one like it. I'm not encouraging you not to strive for something higher and better. I'm just trying to express that there is no reason to complain if one is earning a relatively satisfactory income and the work that one has to do for it is not excessively demanding and does not injure one's health. It's necessary to make a final break with the opinions of Philistines; it seems that I am better able to do that than is my cousin over there. During the World War, I had to correspond with a cousin of Pauline R[ubens]., a Mr. Meyer in Chicago, and the situation was such at the time that I was doing favors for them (Mr. M. and Pauline). Nevertheless, Mr. M. had the cheek to write to me that the time had come for me to start writing to him in his language. He was rather annoyed that he kept getting letters like this one, although typewritten, and the trouble that this caused him. If I had only taken his reproaches to heart then my linguistic situation today would be quite different. I considered the question at the time as a meaningless little *chutzpah*.

The story about the "powder room" and "smoking room" and "men enter the latter" in small print pleased us simply because we are happy whenever we get to hear something different from the same old thing, like Cuba, about which we know only that it is still being worked on but that there is still no fixed date. I'm satisfied if I don't hear anything negative and can keep on waiting for something positive. Mother is differently inclined. She torments

---

[197] Ludwig Mosbacher disapproved of Rosi's factory job, which he considered beneath her. He also disapproved of her dating Alexander Baczewski, who was born in Vienna but had Polish Jewish roots

herself with all sorts of doubts and would like to force the issue. She gets this from her father, and she can't help it. Sometimes the stubborn energy of dear Grandpapa was a good thing, but it wasn't appropriate in every case. Contrasts like these are fortunate and productive in marriage; it would be quite boring and probably harmful if they were absent. One partner contributes something and the other assimilates it, and a mixture is produced which is comfortable and acceptable to both parties. Precisely in these recent years, which have been so rich in disappointments, it has been necessary to reduce everything to a common denominator and not to become entangled in reproaches about why we did this and didn't do that. If today we had to justify this decision or that, it would be impossible because each one arose from the conditions of the moment that were constantly changing. Quite by accident I observed the same thing in Uncle Emil's last letter, where he writes that dear Rosl reacts to disappointments more emotionally, whereas he remains calm. That they react differently is quite natural; the pure, straightforward process of thought ought to be uniform.

After a very long time we heard a few days ago from Aunt Mela, Uncle Ernst, Rose, and Hertha. Rose's husband is absent, but is expected back soon.[198] Erwin is staying with the aforementioned, and all of them are living with Rose. Erwin has even been indulging himself with poetry. While we were worrying about him, not without justification, he was busy versifying and, with regret, has had to leave the worrying to others. They seem to have had no idea of Paul E[lgart]'s illness; we hope the two Pauls are doing better. A detailed letter also arrived from Aunt Clara Rau who appears to be, relatively, quite satisfied, while Irma, just as when she was back in Graz, would like to see a number of unalterable things changed. In Graz, she wanted to see the culture and institutions of Cologne, her earlier

---

[198] The Germans occupied Yugoslavia on April 6, 1941. Rose Engelsrath's husband Leo Weinberger was arrested almost immediately.

residence, introduced, and now she would probably like to see Graz's climate, landscape, and friendships in South Carolina. I'm constantly reminded of the telling remark of Franz Schweizer, who said to us back then that we shouldn't imagine that we were going to a paradise. [large ink blot] The ink blot tells me, that I need to stop now; otherwise there will be more. If this letter goes on to Toledo, then, dear Emil, I want to thank you very much for your letter; it gained our applause and made us genuinely happy. Franz Schw. wrote me that he had sent you a cable about Cuban visas. I assume it was in order to intercede with his uncle in Los Angeles. If I would put up with it, he would keep me busy with his mother's affairs from morning to night. The director of the Apeldoorn sanitarium will soon be sick and tired of his constant questions and know-it-all attitude. Dear Rosi, accept many warm greetings and affectionate kisses from your father who loves you, and may your dear fellow readers also be warmly greeted and kissed.

My good Rosi!

What a beautiful Saturday it was once again when we had your letter in our hands and on the same day the letter from Toledo came through Lenchen. We celebrated Aunt Frida's birthday briefly, according to our custom. We had been invited to tea first, and I provided the sandwiches. Besides us the Knollers and Aunt Lenchen were present. On next Sunday, the twelfth, the same thing will be repeated with Aunt Lenchen. So Alexander's vacation was also a vacation for you; you got to bed early and were able to rest. I'm glad to hear that the skirt is so nice; you drew a very good picture of it. Meanwhile a hat and coat will also have been found. If only I could see it all for myself—I'm already so impatient. We were very pleased by the letter from Lily and Albert, especially since we had good news about dear Paul's improvement. I'll write again soon. I have to stop now because we're going to Henriette's.

Stay well, dear Rosi, and receive many, many affectionate kisses from your mother.

In a hurry. I'll write to the Doktors next.

[27783-2632]
October 26, 1941

My Dear Ones!

I have already confirmed to New York all the letters sent by you, my dear ones, and I may well assume that you have read my responses. In the meantime, we made ourselves guilty once again of a slight oversight by overlooking the birthday of our dear Sigmund, for which we beg to be forgiven. Dear Sigmund, please accept our warm and sincere congratulations, late though they are. May you become the kind of son and brother and complete human being that we may expect you to be. Most young people only learn late in life what they neglected and failed to do when they were young—I belong in that category myself—and for that reason, dear Sigmund, I urgently advise you to follow what mature people tell you, in the firm belief that they mean well by you. How glad we would be to see you with us this Sunday afternoon for coffee with *challah* and butter as we used to do.

We assume that you are all well and have no complaints regarding your basic health. Unfortunately, Clemy has been very susceptible recently. She often has a temperature that caused us to consult a doctor a few days ago. He diagnosed an inflammation of the bladder and ordered her to take a few days' bed rest and also prescribed a powder and we have the impression that, as a trained gynecologist, the general practitioner feels very sure of this treatment. The condition is, thank God, such that Clemy would immediately get up if we were to hear that our departure would take place in the next few days. Unfortunately we haven't heard anything although now another nine weeks have passed, but despite all the silence I still firmly believe that the thing will start to move and that your efforts have not been in vain.

When Rosi's father was at Franz's a few days ago, the latter, as I was told, was again very nice and likeable, but with the very precise restriction that he could not be any more accommodating if Pauline doesn't take an interest in Henny and at the least show a somewhat positive attitude toward her. After Henny never reported any kind of accommodation, Franz drew his own conclusions and remains dismissive. In the end that's the way it always is in life. If my child, far from home, is frequently invited by relatives or good friends, then they also expect that I will show concern for their next of kin if they are sojourning among us and take an interest in them.[199]

We know, my dear ones, that letters from you are underway to us which will inform us about your plans, plans which always preoccupy us here because we know that they always involve worry and agitation and, in your case, dear Rosl, can cause migraines. I hope that you have been freed from these very unpleasant and bothersome headaches during the last weeks. On those afternoons on which we meet with Henriette, at her place or ours, Bruno is usually present. He has more time to spare and spending time with us is also much more important to him. His situation is now completely similar to our own, and everything has become more homogeneous. But, if he should ever marry, his choice will certainly not be made according to our wishes, unless he is willing to make concessions in this respect.[200] Obviously he would now have the greatest possible interest in changing his domicile, but at the moment neither he nor the Trudari have the slightest

---

[199] Hugo was apparently writing about his correspondence with Franz Schweizer. Why Franz was so concerned about Henriette is unclear. Hugo's letter of August 17, 1941, mentioned his effort to enlist Pauline Ruben's help with Henriette's immigration to the United States. Franz Schweizer was not in Amsterdam, so Hugo could not literally be visiting him. Hugo's analogy is also unclear.
[200] Bruno's girlfriend was a Gentile.

chance. In a word, there are more petitioners today than people who are able to help. Lenchen frequently gets the idea of helping out in return for a fee. This idea always remains in the planning stage, which is fortunate, because in a week it would all be over. Clemy thought she could teach her some little handicraft skills, but she has no successes to report in this area, either. Henriette and Lenchen inherited an assortment of clothing and linen from the estate of a friend. Henriette, who was closer to the lady, naturally received the nicer pieces, while Lenchen had to content herself with the more ordinary ones. Both Henny and Pauline need to consider that life today is much more demanding than it used to be.

Eight days ago I had to pay a visit to Beppele and his wife Cilli [?], who are living here with their children. Their son-in-law has been working [here] for years, quite successfully; actually it was a condolence visit, because Beppele's only son died. I think often of your prematurely deceased colleague Katz and of his successes on the stage. Unfortunately I'm not able to visit Paula Schweizer, and her son Franz has the idea that I would be able to call the physician/director and find out everything he wants to know. It is my impression that this director, with the best will in the world, would not be able to deal even in writing with all the many questions that Franz asks. I believe I've already written to you that the unpleasant thing about this correspondence is the impression that the questions are posed within a framework of medical information, which is something that these gentlemen don't like at all when they are confronted with so much knowledge. Paula writes us reports a meter long, and we can be thankful that she is still being kept there. In the present situation, releasing her would not lead to anything good.

Frida—now almost entirely gray or white—had a nice report from Anna a few days ago; Fips seems to have a somewhat better income as a salesman. Cousin Klara Klein seems to be having a hard time getting used to

Portland. Oakland, it appears, would agree with her (or her son Hugo) better than Portland (than the daughter and son-in-law). Those are merely my personal conclusions, in parentheses. If Henny's son [Bruno] learns immediately that Pauline has put in an appearance, at least to some extent and for the time being, then he'll be satisfied if he can just see that something is in fact happening on her side. Ida Rau wrote me a few days ago that your eighty-five-year-old aunt is quite well and cheerful. Ida herself writes that she has a lot of heart pains. Rosl, I'm just now thinking about the time when this Ida sat in your room with all her visitors—this face, coming from the parlor or going to it, an irreproachable, fine character, however, and often witty and pleasant in her correspondence. Clemy recently observed quite correctly that her brother Max could have sent his sister a Cuban visa. Apparently the cold Max thinks she is quite well off where she is. And now I must attend to my dear patient, who sends you her warmest greetings. Be well and most heartily greeted and kissed by your Hugo and Clemy and a special greeting to your dear mother.

[2928-1398a]
October 31, 1941

My dear good Rosi!, dear Clara, and dear Doktors!

I really should have written to you some days ago, dear Rosi, but we were hoping to hear something from you and were waiting to be able to respond to it. We wrote to you on October 16, and on October 21 we returned to your letter of September 30. But we still did not end up entirely empty-handed because yesterday, dear Rosl and dear Emil, we were made extraordinarily happy by your letter of September 9. Neither Henriette nor Lenchen will get to read it because the former would be royally pleased if she were to read that Mrs. Henny impressed Emil as being rather formal in her manner. When Henriette comes to see us, she often puts on a big display of that sort of behavior herself and praises it as an outstanding quality of the inhabitants of the country.[201] We are excluding Lenchen simply because she would take the greatest delight in passing it on to Henriette behind our backs.

When you read this rubbish, you might easily reach the conclusion that we have nothing more important to deal with right now. But it is precisely because our minds are so overburdened that we seek relief in these trifles. You probably got enough information from my last reports and have understood us. In regard to our business, everything is completely quiet. Not a single person here has received any information, and they are all hoping for a positive decision soon. Now that my prediction has come to naught, as it so often has, I am going to extend the deadline voluntarily until the end of the year.[202] Our impatience is of course very much determined by our circumstances and both are exactly as they were when we were sitting at home. We understand, dear Rosi and you, my dear ones, that you are at least as disappointed as we are. You are saying to yourselves, first we wore ourselves out running around and writing and putting everything in motion so that the matter would finally be resolved, and, now that everything has been done and all the preparations made, things are at a standstill again. But, dear good Rosi, it has to come true, and we are not giving up hope, and we continue to live in happy anticipation, even though it is often abruptly interrupted.

And now, dear Clara, we can send you once again our warmest greetings, since we know through your letter that you have arrived on the sixth or seventh of October among the dear ones. We, too, participate in the general joy and

---

[201] Henriette née van Raap, the widow of Hugo's brother Don, was a Dutch Jew.
[202] Amsterdam Jews had no way of knowing that there would be no more exit visas. Under Himmler's direction, Heinrich Müller, head of the Gestapo, issued an order on October 23, 1941, making it illegal for Jews in German-occupied lands to emigrate.

we wish you, dear Clara, and you, my dear ones, good, healthy, and pleasant days. If things had only gone reasonably well, we would now be with you or in the country.

Yesterday I read a clumsy letter from Fred Roederer[203] to his mother. He makes the observation that he is always the last one to be told about something, but, when it comes to the most important things, he shouldn't be forgotten. It appears that he often calls on Ludwig M[osbacher]. since he frequently mentions his name. Don't let it be known that I told you this. I haven't even said anything to Frida about it so far. Fred mentioned the pleasant evening, dear Rosi, which you and Lotte R[oederer]. spent with him on October 4.

Dear Clara, did you get our birthday greeting in September? It isn't at all that I'm in need of confirmation; I just want to say that we did write you punctually.

Dear Emil, we were very glad to hear that you recently had such a lot to do. If this accident, as you put it, would only repeat itself a few times a week, then the missing three-fifths would soon be covered. It will probably be your task, in the matter of a Cuban visa for Franz Dietrich [Schweizer], to alarm the uncle in California. This visa, as well as visas for Venezuela or anywhere else, is in great demand at the moment and if you can do anything for Trudari and family, in conjunction with her siblings and their friends and acquaintances who are known to Fredl, it would be extremely desirable and necessary in order to oppose measures which could place the above-named in a situation which we do not wish to see. It seems that people over there are well informed about this because visas are arriving momentarily which were neither requested nor discussed beforehand just as, three years ago, the affidavits suddenly began to arrive and to be offered. What a fiasco, when I consider that we are among those who have now been in possession of affidavits for the past three years. The number of "ifs" is infinite. I could begin

---

[203]Friedrich [Fritz] Roederer, Frida's stepson, had apparently Americanized his name to Fred.

with, if we had first gotten the [affidavit?] from Cousin Emil,[204] then we long since would have been with you. We are now as before happy that in your case, dear Rosi, things were done right. I used to complain about the lost years, which are so painful; now I'll be satisfied if everything ends well.

Dear Rosl, you expressed the opinion that your letters might perhaps not reach us, and the same wish[205] is stated by everyone else with whom we correspond. Where is Albert Baer living? Certainly a good, decent fellow. We've had no news of Dina in a long time, and we hope that everything is in good order there. Emil wrote that you, dear Rosl, create the right atmosphere at home for *Yom Kippur*. Food and drink is a part of that, along with all the rest, and we drank up the last genuine coffee bean at Trudl's, with a snack. Every morning I make up the substitute, but without the pleasure and enjoyment with which I used to make the real article. Àpropos, dear Rosi, precisely on this point, dear Rosi, we haven't heard from you in a very, very long time, but I do not assume that you enjoy drinking it less than formerly, and I believe that Alex honors both you and it. What is the degree of relationship between the Herz family over there and ourselves? *Bosor*[206] is of course also very rare, but, if we are able to get a portion once a week, we may be content. I regale myself with such pleasures, Mother somewhat less. As a patient she can't be indulged so much, and the things she particularly likes aren't available at the moment. For this week, the doctor has prescribed bed rest and keeping warm—she is following his orders, but her hands are very active and she crochets and does other work for hours at a time.

---

[204] A reference to Hugo's early 1940 concerns that Els was not writing to Cousin Emil for the supporting paperwork for Hugo and Clemy's American visas. Perhaps she had written, but Cousin Emil wasn't prompt in supplying the supporting documents. In either case, the delay in completing their visas put off their departure.
[205] The word "wish" ("*Wunsch*") seems to be the reverse of the likely intended meaning "fear."
[206] "Bosor" probably comes from Hebrew "Basar" and means "meat." In Yiddish it is pronounced "Boser" which may account for Hugo's spelling.

I wrote to you, my dear Doktors, a few days ago about Henny and Pauline, who continue to haunt my mind the longer my stay continues here. Wherever I look, there's not a penny to be seen. We can discuss our confiscated baggage in storage in Rotterdam some other time. It could probably be released and, if the money were available, shipped over there. Most of our belongings consist of clothing and linen. And I'm now beginning to notice how much I miss those things when they're both lacking. Ari's acquaintances in New York are: Jacob Weingartner, 381 4th Avenue, New York City; Alexander Fleischer, New York; Ivan Salomon—no address for the last two. Fleischer is identical with the partner of Benjamin Wolf. Ari also gave this address for a relief action: Jacob Posen, 15 Magaw Place, New York City. Emil, you can set up a little office to process all these requests. I feel I have an obligation to pass everything on and believe that it is urgently necessary to make a serious effort in the matter, and, although I know too well that I am burdening precisely those people I would like to see enjoy a bit of rest, I am forced to play the part of a petitioner, as hard as I may find it. I think and hope, dear Rosi, that, when this letter reaches you, all of yours will have arrived here with us. Mother sends her greetings. Dear Rosi, and you, all my dear ones, and dear Clara, be greeted and kissed by your loving father and your Hugo.

[127/2√ 3577-/3ikb]
November 6, 1941[207]

My dear good Rosi!!

We received your letter of October 15 the day before yesterday, which made us very happy. We only regret that we did not get the one that you sent us on approximately the eighth of October. When one realizes that a letter has gone missing, it is easy to believe that precisely that letter

---

[207] Hugo wrote "1" over a "2." The content seems to support 1941 dating.

contained something that we needed to know, by which, however, I do not mean the meeting with Fritz and Lotte Roederer on October 4, which Fritz himself told us about. We are happy to learn that you are well and occupied, and we hope that Xander, too, has once again found a satisfactory position. Trudari recently wanted to send a cable to Uncle Emil, but I told them that a telegram without an exact explanation would be rather pointless and that I thought it would be better to wait until the letter I had written about this matter arrived in Toledo, although I can't expect very much from it right away. To be sure, people are saying that it has become easier to obtain Cuban visas, and at the moment lots of them are supposedly being issued, but I believe that they are easier to get only insofar as the banks are willing to make loans for these Cuban transactions. But, if you don't have an account with a bank, you're not going to get a loan any more than you're going to get one here. Because I have an obligation to make the effort, I would once again have need of Uncle Emil because, if anyone could get anything done, it would be him rather than the brothers, Fredl and Alfons, who have still fewer contacts. And we take this job upon ourselves, or are asked to take it upon ourselves, even though we are still sitting here with our visas, unchanged as always, and, as we point out in every one of our letters, without hearing anything about the matter. In August we were hoping for October, most recently I was writing about the end of the year, and those who were able to be processed on the basis of having received a visa believed they would have an appointment in February. Now the main thing is that, if success finally comes, nothing should stand in its way when it arrives.

    This week dear Mother is confined to home rest under doctor's orders; we hope the restriction will be lifted soon. In Großweidenmühl[208] it was possible to go for a stroll inside the apartment. We wouldn't be looking backward

---

[208] The family lived on this street along the Pegnitz River in Nuremberg prior to Hallerstraße. It was Rosi's favorite family home.

this way if the other differences were equally significant and visible. If that were true, we would merely smile at what I just said. We can see by the very few pieces that we now have left how much in the way of clothing and underwear has been worn out with the passage of time. Mother is constantly patching and darning. My brother Don[209] has an especially well-situated friend, who had him to thank for the procurement of a high-class clothing line. I recently entreated this man to help me out with a suit or with anything else from his large and excellent inventory. What's more, I knew this Mr. Bonnewit himself quite well since he used to visit me sometimes, decades ago. Showing his true colors, he put me off with empty excuses. If the situation had been reversed, I could not have brought myself to let him go away empty-handed; I would have been happy that I could be of service to him. One grows steadily richer in experience, and experiences like this one would not have to be considered a minus if one could encounter them in a pleasanter way, but mostly these experiences are identical with disappointment. I always look at those who are having a hard time and think about my younger days and about my parental home to which poor people came from the east and then became regular guests. We children took the greatest delight in their company and listened raptly to the stories they told, even if they weren't quite 100 percent true. Aunt Clara, who is now living near you, had a special relationship to one of them, by which I mean she was kind and helpful toward him—we called him "the little round man." Sometimes it takes decades before one begins to understand and comprehend the significance of things.

We have still heard nothing from Aunt Mela; we hope doctors have better reports about her Paul. Dear Rosi, after you used the word "gracious" about Aunt Lily, we see that you have assessed her mentality quite correctly. Since she is so sensitive to statements of account, you, too,

---

[209] Don Mosbacher died in 1909 at the age of thirty-four.

insofar as time permits, will make allowance for her proclivities. One has obligations to one's family, but I have always found it nicer to enjoy one's share of the unpleasant part of those obligations, rather than to take the position that one doesn't need to worry about them. That's about the way Max Fleischmann deals with those who no longer interest him. The latter is now going to have *haute saison* and do outstanding work, even though his former boss is going to be his competitor, having certainly gone into this line of business only because his able former manager went into it first. Lenchen came to see us last night. It was not a pleasant evening because she is a gossip whose chatter has no interest at all for us at this time, the infantile tittle-tattle of a sixty-year-old woman which gets me upset and actually makes me blush. However, this is family at its very closest, and complaints must fall silent.

If you find Franz's lines to me funny, you're right. He likes to play the poet with me because he knows quite well that I don't take him seriously in every instance. I'm not surprised that he wrote to you in quite a different tone, at least not yet. But other motives are at work there, which even he has known to be pointless for the last year and a half.[210] How often he used to say to me, "How's Rosi doing? I've got so many important things to tell her. It's really quite urgent. There are so many things I need to ask her." That was during the time when you were staying with Cousin Emil [in London] and correspondence was impossible, and he was spending time with us every day. When I replied to him that we were in exactly the same position, that we wanted to know a lot of things, too, he got angry and insisted that the issues that he had to settle with you were far more important. And, because we never took any interest in his issues, he got angry again. I was just thinking about these episodes that I never told you

---

[210] Franz wrote many letters to Rosi while she was in England. Hugo implied here that Franz had a romantic interest in Rosi.

about because at the time they seemed too silly. But now you can be amused by them. Stay well and be careful, with the most sincere good wishes and affectionate kisses from your father who loves you.

The matter about which I recently wrote to Toledo on behalf of the Knollers also applies to Bruno. I have just been to see him, and he asks me to forward his urgent request to Uncle Emil. Is there no authority there that makes visas available in special cases and facilitates matters? Please forward Bruno's request to Toledo. Once again, a kiss—Father.

My dearest Rosi!

After Father's thorough report I want to add a few lines and to send you my heartfelt thanks, dear Rosi, for your kind account. What a shame that one of your letters has been lost. We know that you write every week, but we heard that just this week mail had been lost. Now, my dear Rosi, we are quite satisfied that you are well and getting along well. I don't find it disgraceful that you're still working in the factory. It really doesn't matter how one earns one's money, but I am convinced that in time you will acquire skill in typing and stenography and then you can always change jobs. Our nerves are being put to a hard test; we continue to hear nothing about our departure. We will probably have to move, and it won't be easy to find a room with kitchen privileges. My health, praise God, is better. I hope that by next week I can take the air again. I have really missed that. It's already very cold here now. The most important thing is warm undergarments; I often wear two pairs of underpants. I can understand that your green suit isn't usable any more. The brown one will hold up a lot longer. After all, it's tailor-made.

We haven't heard anything from Nuremberg in a long time; one begins to wonder.[211] November 22 is Heddy's

---

[211] Clemy's concerns were justified. In November 1941, Nazis began deportations of Jews from Nuremberg-Fürth region to concentration camps.

birthday, and I believe Ludwig has his *bar mitzvah* in December. Thus the time passes. It's a shame that his father did not experience it. We often speak of dear Jakob. Aunt Frida was very busy last week after she had to cook for us and for the Knollers. As always, greet the Alberts [Lily and Albert] and Mother Jettchen, and, dear Rosi, be affectionately greeted and kissed by your mother who loves you.

[127/3577-1215]
Friday, November 7, 1941

My dear good Rosi!!

Yesterday we were about to take our letter to the post office when your letter of October 7 arrived which we were longing for so much. Many, many thanks! It would have been a real shame if we had missed out on this pleasure. We are very happy to have gotten this. My calculation is also correct: I wrote about a letter of October 8 and in fact you wrote on October 7. Most sincerely, Father and Mother.

The Knollers and Bruno will be jealous of Franz Dietr[ich],[212] who got such quick service. Franz, however, clearly has good contacts.

[3525-3798]
November 18, 1941

My dear good Rosi!!

Our situation remains the same as always. We must come to terms with it and be thankful for our health. We have seen and heard nothing about the further course of events, but our friend Fellh[eimer] wrote us that he also received a visa that he is not able to use at this time. Others can draw their own conclusions from this. For days

---

[212] Apparently Franz received an immigration visa, either to the United States or to a South American country, but, after October 23, 1941, it was useless.

we have been preoccupied by this difficult situation, and our mood is correspondingly irritable. I try to struggle against this because it doesn't make things better for us. This time I am especially disappointed although I still assume that the agency that was established three months ago is supposed to concern itself exclusively with facilitating emigration. Within three months a lot of things can change; one must take that into account. In such times, I am slightly inclined to bow to circumstances, to show them that even in better times I didn't find difficulty with anything.

On November 12 we got a very nice letter from Aunt Clara, Rosl, and Uncle Emil in Toledo that had been mailed on October 25. I am sure that you wrote to us about the same time, but your letter hasn't reached us yet. Aunt Lenchen was here with us when the letter came from Toledo, and she immediately became peeved because the letter contained congratulations on her sixtieth birthday from Aunt Clara, and they had not been sent to her earlier and separately. In her wrath she was threatening retaliation, that is, that she will treat Clara the same way on the occasion of her seventieth birthday. If we had tried to defend Clara, this trifling matter could have turned into a serious quarrel, but we soothed it over, and it was avoided. If Frida had been there, she would have defended Clara, and the uproar would have been immediate. Otherwise, viewed objectively, Lenchen is quite right about this insignificant *dreck* (which is what birthday celebrations mean to me). Her complaint is justified although the reprisal, which she announced in her anger, is repugnant.

"Oh, by the way," my landlord always says when he has to report some incident, and leads off with some expressions of empathy that have nothing to do with the matter at hand. Mother in particular, unfortunately, is always filling her head with all kinds of thoughts and tormenting herself with all sorts of questions. In the last few days the question is whether she can be harmed by the fact that she saw the light of day some years after her spouse, while I am so happy that I have a younger wife. If we become somewhat more nervous and impatient it should not come as a surprise, since we have demonstrated plenty of patience already, and, despite it all, are hoping that our turn will come. Mother stays busy all day long, but, even while she's working, she keeps on reflecting and brooding, and our conversations mostly begin and end on the same theme. I have, God be praised, the ability to calm myself down or at least to pretend that I have done so. I also hope and believe that everything will still turn out favorably for our emigration. The newspaper that one is supposed to read every day recently printed a feature article that posed the question: "Who among us could endure an all-too-clearly demonstrated eternity? Is not the duration the death of all joys and the hormone of our despair?"

And now to happier things. How would it be if we could see Xander's face since it appears as though we are going to have an even longer wait until we can make his personal acquaintance? I assume, dear Rosi, that you have a photo at your disposal to which you are entitled. Has he found a satisfactory position again? Please forgive our curiosity. Actually it's not so much curiosity as just sincere interest that is surely permissible after you've sent us so many sincere reports about your friend. We're still looking for a room with kitchen privileges that isn't so easy to find. You surely know, dear Rosi, what good old Hichenberg had to say about such matters: "Those are among my lesser worries." Have you ever run across any of my former business colleagues? I'm thinking about the good Strauss and the elegant Dreyfuss with his wife and Lotte. Several days ago I spoke with a gentleman from Else Sichel's hometown who was of the opinion that Julius and his family had arrived over there long ago. If that were true, then certainly Uncle Emil would be in touch with them, and we would already have heard about it. Dear Rosi, I know you're going to say that you can see that your father is living in a small country because he worries about little things that are never even mentioned where you are. But if you would first read Aunt Dina's letters, telling us about her encounter with schoolchildren and her subsequent conversation with the school director—that is just one observation from the two large, very closely packed pages of her letters. If only we could, once again, enjoy the good incoming mail together! Greet our dear ones in Toledo and Aunt Clara. Also greet Lily and Albert and Ludwig's family, and send us some good news soon from both the Pauls. Dear Rosi, accept the most affectionate greetings and kisses from your father who loves you.

My dear little Rosi!

Father has already described my thoughts and myself, but what should I tell you? It's not a small matter, and Nature unfortunately cannot be changed. The main thing is that everything remains straightforward and that my many thoughts will prove unfounded. Your menus pleased me very much, and I would like to try them myself, if not for all the fuss and bother. We want to beg Heddy for some of your favorite beverage, since she herself doesn't seem to have thought of giving us any.[213] One urgently needs this sort of refreshment from time to time. As long as we're talking about food, I just wanted to tell you that our mealtimes consist mainly of fish, which we find quite satisfying. When you go to visit Mother Jettchen again, take her our greetings. Unfortunately we hear nothing from Mela. The joy of anticipation is always beautiful, and now we are waiting for your letter, and, when we hear from you and the Doktors, our mood will again be elevated. Father always says that our letters turn out so lacking in content because unfortunately we always have

---

[213] Heddy was in Chile, so Clemy must have meant Henny. There has been some mention of Henriette's self-absorption, as well as some tension among family members about scarce commodities.

the same things to report. I hope that someday we will send you a decisive telegram. That would be a joy for you and more so for us. With a warm hug and an affectionate kiss from your mother who loves you.

November 28, 1941

My dear good Rosi!
Yesterday, November 27, we got your letter of October 27/28, and we immediately felt a lot better, even though, the way things are going, we are still a full four weeks apart. We thank you for your nice report. We're happy that you are well occupied, have a good job, and especially happy that your letter allows us to conclude that you're well, which for us is always the essential thing and the main thing. It's also the second time that you would have been able to accept a position in an orphanage. I received the first offer of a position for you shortly before your emigration, from the Fürth orphanage. You appear to be predestined for a position of this kind, which your grandfather held for thirty-eight years, and I think that it will work the third time. We assume as a matter of course that you have applied for a position as a teacher and educator. Institutions of this kind count room and board as part of the salary, and the monetary compensation is rather low. But, as time goes by, you will achieve a better position and better pay within your profession.

It's almost astonishing that Herrlingen and even "*Mütterle*"[214] are known there, and we are happy to hear that your activity there has led to a recommendation. In that connection, an actor is living next door to us and is currently appearing in revues and shows. This led us to

---

[214] Recounting her early years, Rosi wrote, "In the summer of 1935 I went as educational and practical helper to Frau Dr. Weimersheimer's orphanage at Herrlingen, near Ulm. After the removal of the Home to Palestine, I worked until October 1936 at the Landschulheim [boarding school] in the same village (Director: Hugo Rosenthal) as helper in kitchen and house and with the children." "Mütterle" or "little mother" was probably an affectionate name for Klara Weimersheimer.

recently go to a matinée performance. Our experience on these kinds of occasions resembles yours: It is at precisely those moments when the audience laughs and applauds the most that we have to force ourselves to do both. The fellow tenant in question—a calm, quiet, refined person with a good reputation—appears onstage first as a clown and then again as something even worse. The spectators applaud, and we were almost embarrassed to look this outstanding actor, who is almost as old as I am, in the face. We were unable to digest the contrast between professional and private life so quickly.

The climatic conditions here often impinge unpleasantly upon our consciousness. I have never had rheumatism, and during the day I feel all right and, as soon as I go to bed, the pains start in my upper right arm, and Mother has them in the same place. But those are just trivial matters, and I'm reporting them because they're part of the overall picture. We are much more affected by other things about which we lack precise information: Dina's health and that of Franz and Fellh[eimer],[215] whether in the meantime Franz has gotten his visa. Paul Neurath seems to be taking a long time to regain his health, but what matters is that he regains it at all. When you write, dear Rosi, that the sixty-year-old father of your colleague is employed as a rag sorter, I think that your father can be entrusted with a similar position sorting scrap metal, but, if this goes on much longer, then even this final remnant will be lost. If only, in exchange for these years spent so uselessly and expensively here, I had been able to work as an errand boy over there! If the Almighty will only protect us here and grant us a little bit more later on, then we will be quite satisfied with the bargain.

Aunt Frida received your congratulations, which arrived late, with pleasure, and Mother and I are in com-

---

[215] Franz was deported from Nuremberg to Jungfernhof concentration camp near Riga, Latvia, on November 11, 1941, and Fellheimer on November 29, 1941. At the time of this letter, Hugo was unaware of their fate.

plete agreement with her in this point. We shudder to think of all the congratulating that will be going on in December and January,[216] dates on which we were hoping for something quite different the last time, whose local repetition[217] can only provoke agitation. But even here one has to remind oneself that there are worse things, and that celebrating a birthday in a wholesome manner is not one of them. This morning I was in the synagogue on the occasion of the anniversary of the death of my blessed mother. Today is the eighth day of *Kislev*, and *Hanukkah* begins on the twenty-fifth, and I wish, dear Rosi, that it may pass happily for you. Xander may know nothing about the *Hanukkah* lighting ritual or he may know a lot, but that's not what matters. It's inconsequential, given his character and his many distinctly positive qualities. How often have I encountered people of the most varied faiths, without any Jewish religious convictions, who have earned my highest admiration and regard through their outstanding, exemplary behavior in every possible situation of life. Dear Rosi, accept the warmest *Hanukkah* greetings and a hearty kiss from your father who loves you.

My dearest good Rosi!

For me nothing else remains but to share joy and less joy with Father.[218] And so I was enormously happy about your beautiful letter because, as soon as your letter has been read by both of us, a new and different conversation begins, in which we digest your news. Tomorrow, Saturday, you'll be at the dentist, but my wish is that, when this letter reaches you, you will no longer be in treatment. First because you will feel better and second because of the expense. I had to have some dentures made here, and it's very hard to get used to them, and I'm

---

[216]December 20 was Clemy's birthday; January 9 was Hugo's.
[217]Celebrating their birthdays in Amsterdam, not in the United States.
[218]One of the few times Clemy refers to their difficult circumstances, even obliquely.

not at all satisfied with them. Ullmann would certainly have done a better job. Dear Rosi, after you wrote that your green suit is very worn, there's no point in keeping it. Still, if I were so happy as to be able to inform you of our arrival within the next few weeks, then I would write you to lay the suit aside until I come so as to spare me the embarrassment of arriving and standing there with no work to do. It's so sad that everything, and not only our affairs, is dragged out so long. A few days ago people were saying that some special *Oseyinem*[219] will receive permits. Father was just saying that perhaps the time will come when we will be happy with the status quo. Your encounter with Rechoskar [?] amused us. After this meeting your requirements in that direction will have been met. Greetings to Lily, Albert, and all the loved ones. My dear Rosi, receive many affectionate greetings and kisses from your mother.

[356y/2824-2363]
December 21, 1941

My Dear Ones, My dear good Rosi!

On December 16 we received your letter of November 19, and on December 18 we got your letter of November 11. The receipt of these letters was a tremendous event for us. If we had received a single written line we would have been deeply grateful, but in both these letters you were very thorough and communicative, and now we have to store up a little bit to draw on in times to come. We thank you for being such an industrious writer and for your punctuality, which has now demonstrated its value in a special way. Compared to ourselves, dear Rosi, we must completely acquit you of the charge of "sloppiness" that you have brought against yourself. Naturally we felt very annoyed by the sudden change of events, and it truly

---

[219]Clearly written, likely of Hebrew origin. The sense is of the Yiddish "*macher*," meaning an ambitious person, a schemer, so here "big shots."

pains us that we now will have to do without this one weekly pleasure.[220] I still have hopes that your wishes and especially your letter for Mother's birthday, which we celebrated yesterday, will reach us. Mother herself will write about yesterday. My gifts consisted of the presentation of some gift certificates that I made myself. I wrote them with pencil on white visiting cards, and early this morning Mother erased what I had written; in her selfless way, dear Mother promptly released me from my promise. And the gifts I was promising were by no means to be despised: one pair of gloves and half a dozen handkerchiefs.

I am not at all surprised at the industry and ambition in Ludwig's family. The parents set a good example for the sons. We are expecting another letter from the Doktors telling me that my wishes in regard to Henny were being seen to. It's important that this be done soon. I brought up the matter in question with the Doktors on October 26, so it still might get done. In our correspondence itself a fundamental change will have to be made, unfortunately, and it won't be possible to discuss everything in my responses the way I did previously. We just have to lower our expectations, and the greatest and most essential goal will have been achieved if we are assured that you, my dear ones, and you, my dear Rosi, and everything pertaining to you, are in good order and well, and if you, dear Rosi, are also willing to be undemanding and contented with the restricted communication that informs you about the state of our health. While you were staying with Cousin Emil, we already had a foretaste, literally just a little hors d'oeuvre, and you, dear Rosi, saw to it that the situation worked out to our advantage. This time there won't be any turn of events that you can bring about, but with a large portion of con-

---

[220] Mail between the United States and Holland was prohibited after the United States entered the war; letters had to be sent via Clara Fenigstein in Zurich. In the following paragraph, Hugo referred to the difficulty sending mail to Rosi after the Germans occupied Holland and suspended mail service to England.

fidence and patience we will also, God willing, get through it. The duty now devolves upon us to work on ourselves and not to do anything to make our lives still more difficult. You, my dear ones, will surely all be fully occupied, and it would be so wonderful for us to have the good fortune to be with you. Dear Clara, you have already found time to communicate with us. Dear Rosi, we are at least somewhat reassured by the knowledge that you are surrounded by loyal relatives and friends. To you, dear Rosi, and you, my dear ones, I send my best wishes and warmest greetings and kisses. With love, your father, your Hugo.

Dear Rosi and all my Dear Ones!

What a great event it was for us to be able to receive both your wonderfully beautiful letters in quick succession. We have made ourselves well acquainted with the arrangement of your room and are very happy, dear Rosi, to be so agreeably instructed. We are actively interested in what you write. You must certainly be finished with the dental treatments by now, and I'm happy about that and hope that you will have no more trouble for a long time. The Karlsbader[221] also pleases us very much, but what we find still more satisfying is the immediately found job. If I missed anyone on Saturday, dear Rosi, it would have been you. All the others appeared punctually for the coffee hour, which made me quite miserable because I wasn't in the mood and didn't at all like having so many people around me and receiving so many congratulations. I hope that your letter for the twentieth of December may still reach us, and that would be the most beautiful gift of all. Perhaps the gift table will still be made larger and more beautiful by wishes from Rosl and Emil. For us, the most important thing is that we have the certainty that you constantly look after your health and are just as careful as you

---

[221] Rosi must have written about an encounter with a recent immigrant from Karlsbad; apparently, the woman found a job quickly.

are always asking us to be. Dear Rosi, you may depend on us to act exactly as you wish and feel completely reassured on our account.

During the Christmas days your dear Arnold and dear Lilly[222] will be especially busy. Many thanks to you, dear Clara, for your last letter. Have the Falcks reached their destination yet?[223] My dear ones, receive my warmest greetings and our thanks for your help, and, dear Rosi, be most ardently kissed by your mother who loves you. Many greetings for Ludwig's family, Lily, Albert, etc.

January 6, 1942

Dear Rosi,

This letter came from your parents yesterday, and since I don't know your address I'm sending it to dear Ludwig. I hope things are going as you wish in respect both to your health and to your work. Today a letter of November 22 also came from dear Ludwig. I was greatly concerned about his silence, but in these times one can't count on regular mail delivery. You can send your letters to my address, dear Rosi, and I will take care of them promptly. With sincere regards from Uncle Arnold and Lilly and Aunt Clara.[224]

---

[222]Lilly Fenigstein's name was spelled with two "l"s.
[223]The Falcks (Erna, Alfred, and Marion) finally left France for Cuba in mid-December, 1941, on one of the last freighters to leave Europe.
[224]The note was added by Clara Mosbacher Fenigstein, Hugo's cousin.

Letters from January 1942 through January 1943

Correspondence in 1942

In 1942 Rosi received just four letters from Hugo and Clemy, all written between January and May and sent first to Clara in Switzerland who added notes and sent them on to the Doktors in Toledo, who in turn sent them to Rosi in New York. Both Hugo and Clemy mentioned not being able to write as frequently and the "severe curtailment of mail delivery."

Jewish Life under the Nazis—The Netherlands, 1942–1943

Nazi anti-Jewish laws and actions intensified in 1942. The "final solution to the Jewish question" took on urgency after the Wannsee Conference on January 20, 1942.

January 17, 1942—Jews of Zaandam were ordered to relocate to Amsterdam. During the first six months of 1942, all Dutch Jews had to move to Amsterdam. All non-Dutch Jews living in the provinces were sent to Westerbork.

January 23, 1942—Jews' identity cards had to show the letter "J."

May 2, 1942—Jews were required to wear the yellow Star of David with the inscription "Jood" (Jew).

June 26, 1942—The Jewish Council was notified of forthcoming deportations to the East.

June 30, 1942—The Nazis introduced an 8:00 curfew for all Jews in the city.

July 15, 1942—Deportations from Westerbork to Auschwitz began.

September 29, 1943—Roundup of the last Jews of Amsterdam took place.

December, 1943—The Netherlands was considered Judenfrei (free of Jews).

[29309-1+2et√2408-1402y3]
January 15, 1942

My Dear Ones!
 I wrote to you last on December 22, and I assume, my dears, that you are well. Mother and I are also, praise God, in the best of health. And we hope and wish, dear Rosi, that you, too, are in your best form and that Ludwig's family and all the other dear ones are the same. Your birthday letter for dear Mother also occasioned great joy and was an extra big present for her and for us. It's too bad that my birthday, which passed peacefully and without any special fanfare—because that was my particular wish—does not fall on the same date because then I, too, would have been made happy by the note that I missed so much. We must always try to reconcile ourselves to the facts and not complain too much about things that we can't change. The most important news from the immediate family is the departure of the dear Falcks who may already long since have arrived at their destination. We want to hope that the day is also coming for us, for which you, dear Rosi, and not least we ourselves are waiting with inexpressible longing and impatience. Due to the severe curtailment of mail delivery, we also have less to report. Through your note, dear Rosi, I at least know that my important communications of October 26 have reached the Doktors. I regret that I can't supply any answer concerning Henny and Pauline, although I assume that Uncle Emil has done everything that was asked of him. At the time I wrote without delaying and assumed that the answer would arrive here in a timely way. But perhaps things will still work out and we will arrive at a resolution. Although one has to reckon with such dreadfully long waiting times, it's still necessary to put everything in order.
 I hope that you, my dear ones—dear Clara, dear Arnold, and dear Lilly—are all doing very well and are

perhaps too busy, which I can't say about myself, but nevertheless the weeks and months fly by quicker than ever, and that's just as well. Aunt Frida has still not received the long overdue letters from Anna; we are mystified as to the reason why she has had no mail for many months. We live in a time of substitutes that, although not as good as the original, can and must still give satisfaction if one is modest in one's demands. One can transfer this "substitute" principle to anything and apply it and, since I can't write as often as I used to do, I've become accustomed to having an oral conversation with you, that I begin, in order not to be interrupted, when I go to bed. I talk to you, dear Rosi, as I used to do at the breakfast table, and I arrange the scenery accordingly because bed is precisely the place in which I had the least number of conversations with you. Thank God! After my questions have been answered I am always quite content, and this is where I have to "substitute" for you, as I said above, and a weak substitute it is, but it works. We communicate, and we stay very closely and intimately connected. We hope to hear from you soon, and may you all be heartily kissed and greeted by your Hugo and your father, who loves you. Many hearty greetings for Rosl, Emil, and children. I often speak with them, too, in the manner described above.

My Dear Ones,

The nicest of my birthday gifts, dear Rosi, was your letter that arrived after the birthday. All your communications interest us greatly, and we were happy once again to have some conversational material from you that will keep us going for a while longer. We're having a severe cold spell right now. Our little room warms up very quickly, so this, too, has its advantages. We were very pleased by the news that Paul [Neurath] has been discharged from the hospital. If only we could soon pass on to Mela the same news about her Paul [Engelsrath]. Dear Rosi, all I can do is to beg you over and over again to use the same caution that you demand of us in everything you do. In that respect, we do everything we possibly can, and we have confidence that you will act wisely, and to some extent we're reassured. You'll be corresponding with the dear Doktors. Aside from that, your mail deliveries will also be rather slight. I hope, my dear ones, that you are also well. It would make us very happy if we heard that soon from you. My dear ones, receive, with dear Rosi, many warm regards and affectionate kisses from your Clemy.

[Clara's note accompanies Hugo and Clemy's letter.]
Zurich
Splügenstraße 10
January 25, 1941[225]

My Dear Ones,[226]

Since I don't have Rosi's address, I'm sending this letter to you again and ask that it be forwarded. I hope you're all well—I can report that about us. Your last letter is dated November 22. We have been without news from you since then. I've written four times since then. It just isn't regular, and we are twice as worried. Lilly's concerts have gone extraordinarily well and received really good reviews; certainly that will interest you, despite the world-shaking events. Dear Rosi, write to me. It will be answered by return mail. I'm also asking for your exact address. Yesterday I got a card from Aunt Johanna,[227] after several inquiries. She had bronchitis, but now she's doing well. She is still in a home. Another lady has been placed in the room with her.

With love from your Clara.

Arnold and Lilly are away professionally and send warmest greetings.

---

[225] Cousin Clara mistakenly wrote 1941, a common error at the beginning of a new year.
[226] Clara sent the letter to the Doktors, expecting them to forward it to Rosi. All of Hugo and Clemy's 1942/1943 letters to the United States are addressed to "My Dear Ones" to include Emil, Rosl, Aunt Clara, and Rosi, perhaps another indication of mail restrictions.
[227] Apparently an elderly aunt still in Germany.

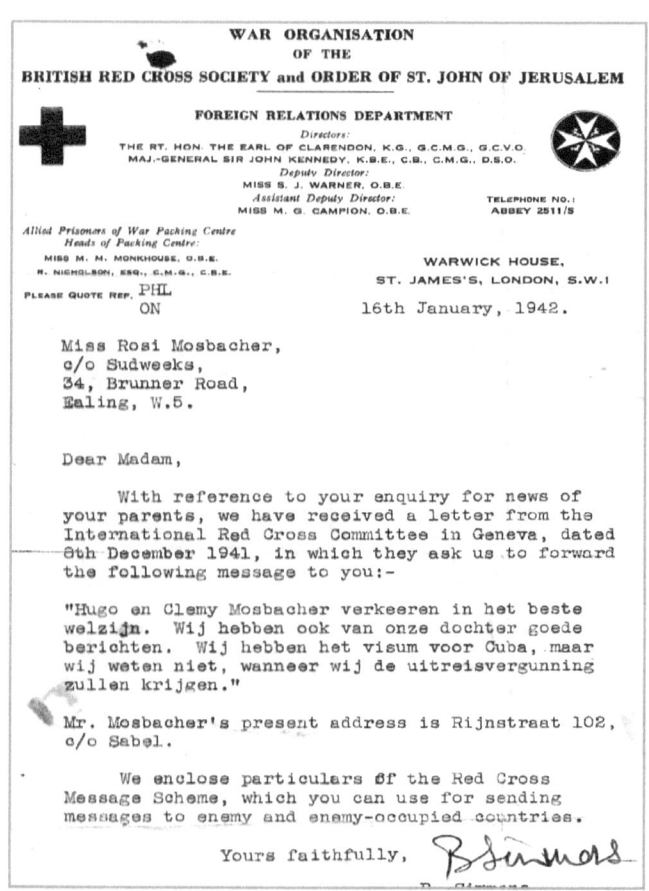

The British Red Cross relayed the following December 8, 1941, message from its Geneva office to Rosi via the Sudweeks in England.

Translation of the Mosbachers' part of the Red Cross letter (referring to themselves in the third person): "Hugo and Clemy Mosbacher are doing very well. We also have good reports from our daughter. We received the visa for Cuba, but don't know when we will be allowed to travel." Note that it took the Red Cross in England over a month to forward the message from its Geneva office. Then the Sudweeks forwarded the letter to the United States. We don't know when Rosi sent her initial inquiry, but clearly the process was slow. Rosi did not inquire through the Red Cross again.

[mp-^+3t+73314]
March 27, 1942

My Dear Ones!

This time we have let a longer pause intervene and were hoping in the meantime to receive some news from you about Ludwig's family and Rosi. However, as with so much else, this too has not gone as we wished, and we must continue to muster our patience and to wait. We are, praise God, well, and we hope that we now have the harsh winter finally behind us. I also assume that things are well with you and would be very happy, dear Clara, to hear something from you. We are convinced that you would already have written to us, long since and gladly, if the requisite documents had reached you. We have no idea whether the Doktors still have their old residence or whether they have moved. Although, dear Rosi, we earlier found it necessary to write to you about all the events of the week, both small and great, we now have to limit ourselves to the most basic necessities and are happy and thankful if we can report to you that we are well.[228] That the Falcks have arrived at their destination is extremely good news. If they had succeeded in having us join them, it would have been easy for us to be able to continue the journey much sooner than they did.[229] The news we are getting from Aunt Mela is not happy. Remarkably, we hear nothing of Rose's husband. A brief card arrives now and then from Ida Rau and we are expecting a letter from Aunt Dina, to whom we sent birthday greetings.

Dear Rosi, you can surely imagine how great and how justified our curiosity is and that we would like to know so much about you. In any case we beg you, if you have

---

[228]At the beginning of 1942 all Dutch Jews were moved into the Jewish Quarter in Amsterdam. Several roundups and deportations of "workers" (none of whom were heard from again) had occurred in early 1941, and in early 1942 "call-ups" of Jewish "workers" began again.

[229]The specifics of this plan are not known. It's possible that Hugo and Clemy hoped to join the Falcks in France and then depart for Cuba. Prior to November 1941, Hugo and Clemy had valid visas for Cuba.

arrived at any decisions, not to postpone carrying them out or to abandon them merely because we cannot be there with you. We consider that to be downright wrong, and it is our urgent wish that you do not allow anything that you think to be right and proper to depend on us. You may be certain, dear Rosi, of our agreement and satisfaction. In a time like this one cannot always afford to wait because it is impossible to determine or estimate the length of time involved, and, besides, there are affairs in which one's own ego, one's self, is permitted to play a decisive role.[230] One enjoys being surprised by good, happy things, and perhaps you would be astounded and laugh at our fantasies if you could listen to the conversations we have together before we fall asleep. Of course you are always the focal point of our discussion, which, however, is not always so richly imagined.

For the last several weeks we have had a bride in the house. Ruth has become engaged to a Mr. de Paauw, a Dutchman; in the meantime she has already become Mrs. de Paauw since the civil ceremony, at which I was present as a witness, has already taken place.[231] The thirty-four-year-old groom is a commercial employee, strictly Orthodox, and from a very good, modest family. After the wedding they will at first take a single room. Prevailing conditions don't permit occasions like this to be celebrated as joyously as they used to be. Everyone is too much burdened with his own cares, and participation in the joys and sorrows of others must be of limited extent. The reason we are still so little acquainted with our new nephew is that we aren't able to carry on a conversation in Dutch with him. In a purely external sense he is not one of the most forceful personalities. The Paauws live just opposite

---

[230]Hugo was telling Rosi not to delay her marriage to Alexander any longer. At the end of November 1941, the Nazis deprived all German Jews in Holland of their German citizenship and property. Without valid passports, Hugo and Clemy's Cuban visas were worthless and travel was impossible.
[231]The civil ceremony was performed as soon as possible so that Ruth would acquire her husband's preferential status as a Dutch Jew. The Nazis deported the "stateless" Jews (refugees from Germany, Poland, and other occupied countries) first. The Dutch Jews hoped they would be spared.

and have not been there very long. The young people knew each other from the Bund,[232] and living in close proximity intensified the relationship. If Flip—that's his first name—would only cut a somewhat more dashing figure, then his mother-in-law, such is my impression, would definitely be pleased. However, Ruth is in ecstasy, highly satisfied and happy, and that's the main thing.

I remember, dear Rosi, the letter we wrote you last year shortly before *Pesach* and how we complained about having to hold *seder* here, separated from you, for a second time. And in a few days' time it will be the third time. The first evening will be held at the Knollers' in an appropriate manner, while on the second evening I will perform the ritual myself in my room, as Hichenberg was accustomed to say. The two sisters will be on hand. It is understandable that on these evenings we will think of you and our dear ones. These hours were always especially exalting, happy, and satisfying, and, one may add, thanks to the willingness to sacrifice and the culinary and presentational competence of our dear mother, a special treat. For me personally, *seder* within the bosom of the family has always been a new experience. When the Ludwigs were staying with us during the first years of their marriage, it was very nice, and today we still sing Ludwig's melody "Ki lo Ki lo" in their honor. If only I could once more turn the second evening over to Uncle Emil. To you, my dears, I also wish pleasant *seder* evenings and good holidays. Presumably you, Arnold, and Lilly will be very much in demand during the days of Easter[233] and will have little rest. My dear ones, accept my great thanks and warmest

---

[232] Bund—Der Algemeyner Yidisher Arbeter Bund (The General Union of Jewish Workers), known simply as "the Bund"—was founded in 1897. While Zionist parties urged Jews to leave Europe and immigrate to Palestine, the Bund believed that the critical problems of Jewry needed to be resolved, not by escaping from the hard realities of everyday life, but by addressing them through an energetic political (socialist) and cultural program. Affiliated youth groups attracted young Jews all over Europe. See http://www.yivo.org

[233] Arnold and Lilly were musicians who had professional engagements during the Easter holidays.

greetings, and, dear good Rosi, many greetings and the most sincere kisses from your father who loves you. Best greetings to the dear Doktors, the Ludwigs, Albert and Lily, and everyone else—Hugo.

My Dear Ones!

Perhaps my idea is correct, and we will be made happy by good reports from you during the holidays, dear Clara, and the other dear ones. That would at least contribute greatly toward the beautification of the feast.[234] The most important and satisfying thing for us is that we hear that all our dear ones are well. Dear Rosi, the recent pictures that we have of you are especially valuable today, and the good photographs are a constant source of renewed joy for us. Hugo has already given you a report on the happy events in the family. We assume that in the meantime both the Pauls are completely well again and that all is in the best of order with the dear Doktors, the Ludwigs, and the Engelsraths. My dear ones, I send you all many warm regards, and to you, dear Rosi, many affectionate kisses. Your Clemy, who loves you all.

[At the bottom of the page, in another hand.]

My Dear Ones!

This letter came today[235] and I am sending it on at once by airmail because I can imagine, dear Rosi, how much you wait for it. Please send me your address. Easter went by very well, but with much work for Arnold and Lilly. I warmly embrace and greet all of you. From your Clara. Arnold and Lilly send heartfelt greetings.

---

[234] Passover began on April 2, 1942.
[235] Clara did not date her note, so we don't know how long Hugo's March 27 letter took to reach Zurich.

This photograph of Rosi may be a copy of one that Clemy mentions in her note of March 27, 1942.

Kew Gardens
April 15, 1942

Dear Rosi,
    A letter of March 5 just came from my sister [Clara]:[236]
    "This morning an answer came from Hugo, dated February 13. Please tell dear Rosi that her parents, praise God, are well. They got through the cold days all right since they had good heating. Hugo writes that it is now

---

[236] It took over five weeks for Clara's letter from Zurich to reach her brother Ludwig in New York. It's not clear why Clara summarized Hugo's letter instead of forwarding it to Ludwig for Rosi.

the second anniversary of their sojourn. The introduction[237] was on the whole not sympathetic, and that has not changed. Today, though, we would be grateful if things remained unchanged until peace arrives soon and brings us to our goal. After a long time a reassuring report came from Dina Schweizer. We have heard nothing from Franz since his departure.[238] Clemy writes that her thoughts are always with her dear Rosi, and she hopes that she is living there as her parents would wish her to live, that she doesn't try to do too much and takes care of her health. Have you heard anything from Erna? Both parents send Rosi their warmest kisses and their greetings to the Doktors, to Ludwig's family, to the Engelsraths, and both the Pauls."

Clara and Lilly send their special regards to you. Warmest greetings from all of us—Ludwig.

[3023-1+2A-√ 1061/z]
[Undated; estimated to be April 16, 1942.]

My Dear Ones All Together!

Our joy was great when the postman, dear Clara, handed us your letter. It became immeasurably greater when we saw, dear Rosi, that once again you had contributed to it with your Sunday note, shortly before *Purim*.[239] That was a nice beginning to the week, and on that Monday we were just counting the twelfth day of the *Omer*.[240] Today, Thursday, we now want to answer your dear letters. First,

---

[237] Hugo means their temporary detention in Amsterdam.
[238] By this time, Hugo knew, probably through Dina, that Franz had been deported to a concentration camp.
[239] *Purim* fell on March 3, 1942, so Rosi's letter had taken six weeks to reach them through Clara in Zurich.
[240] In 1942, the twelfth day of the Omer would have been on April 13, a Monday, and Hugo is writing on Thursday, April 16, 1942. Given this specific dating and Hugo's later discussion of Passover, this letter could not have been written in May, despite the penciled "May 1942" in the upper right corner in another handwriting. Perhaps Rosi penciled in the date she received the letter.

dear Clara, we must express our appreciation of your beautiful and cordial writing style and thank you for all your kindness. It is not sentimentality; our nerves badly need a kind word of encouragement. It is quite natural that one is no longer as cheerful and happy as formerly. Today we have this problem and tomorrow we have that other problem—our lives are dominated solely and exclusively by the seriousness of the times. Even in normal times it is always a cause for joy to hear of good things in a letter from one's relatives. What, then, in this present time, does a report from our beloved Rosi mean to us? It's a soothing and indeed the most beneficial elixir, especially since I must renounce all alcoholic pleasures, to which I have never been averse. Mother still possessed a small supply of that kind of liqueur that you, dear Rosi, always preferred, and it was decided long ago that this would be used when Rosi's first letter arrived from Zurich. Monday afternoon our coffee guests, Aunt Frida and Trudl, were prompt, and, when they stepped into the room, your letters were fluttering upon the pastry. Mother, of course, had produced the latter a short time before, and the quality was up to the standard for which she is known, making allowance for present conditions. And so, you see, it's still possible to have a nice afternoon if the postman brings such glad tidings.

I continue with my monologues, as I began them, and I find satisfaction in them, and I fall asleep very well, thank God. The circle of my associates has grown somewhat, and as a result the conversation has become livelier and more spirited than previously. Sometimes I sit with you at the breakfast table, dear Rosi, at 7:00 the way we used to do; another time you are with me in the office; then you and Mother and I are instantly together; then I am talking with my dear Doktors, with Sigmund and Lore and also with sister Clara, etc. I think about the family hour on Saturday and my visits to Ludwig's office, and this all takes place as I lie in bed. Due to your communication, dear Rosi, which is very important for us, I can visit Henny's son again.[241] Meanwhile, we have made friends with Sigmund Baum's relatives who are here, and it is of course very important for Uncle Emil to prepare Pauline for the fact that we were compelled to make use of a second friendship. I hope everyone is well at the Doktors. As you can imagine, dear Rosi, we unfortunately have to do too much thinking and have to use a lot of sedatives. We were especially happy to hear about Ludwig's good health and about all the great things that Hanna and her sons have done. As always, I send them my heartiest greetings.

The first evening of *seder* was passed pleasantly at the Knollers', and I held the second myself among our people at home. Frida and Lenchen were there, and of course they were happy to listen to their brother because they heard once again the same melodies that they heard as children. My recital was not a pleasure because I became hoarse immediately, and Arnold and Lilly would have run away at once because they couldn't have endured it. Even though the customs by which these *seder* evenings are celebrated are not exactly laws, I still think back to *Wilhelm Meister's Apprenticeship* in which Goethe says: "It seems equally necessary to me to prescribe, and to impress upon the children, certain laws that give a degree of stability to their lives. Indeed, I am inclined to assert that it is better to err according to the rules than to err when the arbitrary impulses of our nature drive us to and fro," etc. I have always had great respect for this "degree of stability," and once, when I knowingly abandoned it, the consequences were disastrous. The main thing is that everything gets straightened out and that everything can be made good again.

Does Uncle Emil relocating his practice mean that he will have to change his place of residence? Rosi, we are

---

[241] Possibly Rosi had conveyed news about immigration paperwork for Bruno.

filled with admiration that you have even taken care of the Falcks. It is very unpleasant for us to observe so clearly that Trude is much more interested in Erna than in us. By which I don't mean to say that our relations are less cordial. It's just that I am well aware that, while our presence here does not bother her, she placed great value on Erna's earlier stay. "That's the way it goes with relationships," as a seamstress or somebody once said; I see that it's easy to forget the sayings of important personalities. From Clara's letter we may conclude that we can expect sequels from you, dear Rosi. Rosl, with her appropriate contacts, has probably already written us, and we are already happy about it. The Doktors will also have a share in this letter. Our greetings, kisses, and best wishes to them. My warmest greetings to you all, my dear ones, and may you, dear Clara and dear Rosi, be most fervently kissed by your Hugo, your father who loves you.

My Dear Ones!

This surprise was truly good for us, but also necessary, since we were longing for it more than for anything else. We were very pleased, dear Rosi, that you had spent time with Pauline and still more pleased that you get along with her. I would like to exchange the shawl—which she brought us at that time and which, as you know, we use as a coverlet when we take a noonday nap—for some stockings. I'm pleased to know that you're well and working and was pleased to hear that you were well received by Julie M[unknown full name]. and her mother. We're on friendly terms here with a family named Herrmann whose daughter works at the Committee over there. H. is the cousin of Sigmund Baum. Perhaps it might be possible for you to make her acquaintance. Thus my day and my night are passed, thinking of you and the Doktors and all the dear ones. Mela has heard nothing from her son-in-law. We finally received a closely written four-page report from Aunt Dina; she has now moved, God be praised, and is living in a single room. Her other news was less agreeable.[242]

Ruth will probably get married before *Shavuot*.[243] When we speak about you, dear Rosi, Xander does not, of course, remain unmentioned. We send him our best wishes. You, dear Clara, now have all kinds of work to do but this activity is very rewarding. My dear ones, I greet you all; my dear Rosi, receive my most heartfelt greetings and my most affectionate kisses.

[At the bottom of page.]
Dear Rosi! Many heartfelt greetings—Aunt Clara.

[Censor numbers too smudged to read.]
May 29, 1942[244]

My dear Clara, dearest Rosi, and dear Doktors,

Today is Friday and the day before yesterday was Wednesday. That was an extraordinary day. It became a holiday because, dear Clara, we were allowed to take receipt of your airmail letter, in which you, dear Rosi, and you, dear Doktors, participated in such an outstanding manner, and once again, dear Rosl, we had the opportunity of reading something from you after such a long time. Many, many thanks to all of you—to you dear Clara, for your special attentiveness, which we value very highly. I knew immediately that an interpellation[245] from Trude would arrive because while you, dear Emil, congratulate Ruth on her engagement, your lines, dear Rosi, contain

---

[242]Most likely Dina wrote about the ongoing deportations of Jews from the Nuremberg-Fürth area to concentration camps.

[243]May 22, 1942. Ruth and Philip's religious wedding took place after Shavuot, on June 16, 1942.

[244]Faintly written in pencil in the upper right corner in another handwriting. The date is accurate. This letter is the last one that Rosi received from her parents.

[245]A procedure in some legislative bodies of asking a government official to explain an act or policy, sometimes leading, in parliamentary government, to a vote of confidence or a change of government. Hugo felt he had to keep the peace.

nothing about it. I responded to the interpellation by saying that your congratulations, dear Rosi, had already been sent in a letter that had not reached us, and both aunt and cousin were satisfied with that.

Today engagements, etc., are only of significance to a very small circle, and it is not the time to make a big fuss about such matters. For that reason we commemorate the birthdays of our dear ones, for example today on the one that you, dear Emil, shall be allowed, God willing, to celebrate in good health in nine days and for which I conveyed to you my most sincere good wishes, which Clemy sent you some weeks ago. If we want to be overly cautious, my beloved Rosi, we must start celebrating your birthday today—"must" is the wrong way to put it. I do it with special love, devotion, and tenderness, but I must exert great control over my feelings and emotions so that my joy does not turn into agitation. In the final analysis everyone is an egoist, small or large. Thus we naturally would have been more than happy to have been with you on your birthday; a reunion in good health would have been our highest happiness. Nevertheless we have a measure of satisfaction and reassurance because we know, beloved Rosi, that you are, praise God, healthy and careful, that you are making a life for yourself, and that you have appropriate employment, and that you are quite satisfied with the company you keep. On the occasion of your birthday we want to express the wish and the hope that, after these hard times have ended, no new obstacles will be placed in our way and that finally the day is approaching on which we will see each other again.

We had a long report from Dina a few days ago. She is well but still has her pains. She is living at Bahnhofplatz 1 [Fürth] in a nice room, has company, and misses the possibility of dropping by the Kocherthalers,[246] etc. Cilli Fels celebrated her seventieth. [Dina] writes about everything

---

[246] Perhaps Dina could not visit the Kocherthalers because her new room was too far away or because of travel restrictions for Jews.

and was happy to hear about you and will be happy again when she gets another report. She asked whether she could have the address of my dear cousin,[247] but I thought that I did not want to burden my cousin any more and that it is quite sufficient as it is. I can report to her now about the Biermanns. She is delighted with that, which we do not begrudge her because in the end we are all to be pitied.[248] There is a notable difference between sister Clara and me; I run across former business acquaintances, nice people, who say, "For the last two and a half years you've been promising to come and have coffee with us, and you still haven't been to see us." I know that these people mean well, but they have other matters to concern them, and they find my attitude quite acceptable.

Our good father did not use quotations very much, but he did often say, "People are not always as they seem and seldom any better."[249] I've always liked that saying, and in foreign parts I'm reminded of it often, and in my isolation I'm reminded even more often of the specialness of my beloved parents. With all due objectivity, I have to say that I have seldom encountered people who were their equals in respect to pure goodness, selflessness, helpfulness, and willingness to accommodate others. To be sure there are many who are on a very different intellectual and cultural level due to their origins or their talents, but that's an entirely different chapter and has nothing to do with this particular reflection, and in that reflection, dear Emil, I often enjoy the past.

---

[247] Probably Pauline Rubens.
[248] Hugo wrote "*Rachmonien*" which seems to be a form of "*rachmones*," the Hebrew word for mercy, compassion, or pity. In the same letter he used a different form of the word, "Rachmonium," to describe Frida. "Pitiful" or "to be pitied" makes sense here, but "merciful" or "compassionate" would also work.
[249] "Die Menschen sind nicht immer, was sie scheinen, aber selten etwas Besseres." From *Nathan der Weise*, 1799, a play by Gotthold Ephraim Lessing.

For some weeks I've been receiving a little treat that is widespread here—an inflammation of the nerves, rheumatism or neuralgia, whatever it's called—starting in my right upper arm and going down to my hand. I'm on a course of injections for it, which are somewhat expensive but not painful, and I hope that warmer weather will bring an improvement. Mother has often expressed the wish that my pains could be transferred to her, but I am quite happy that I am able to stand the pain, and Mother, praise God, is still pain-free.

Frida was naturally enormously pleased with your remarks about Anna and Fips. She is also to be pitied but always in the best of spirits. I always hope that she doesn't fall down and that nothing gets broken because at the moment replacements are not to be found. Lenchen has heard nothing from the children for a long time, which is not surprising. From those who don't write or seldom write, nothing will come or will come seldom. Dear Cousin Clara, did you get Frida's letter? I am asking you because in your letter you don't confirm its receipt. To return to the subject of household linens, dear Clara, what people say is true—your linens fare much better at home than in the laundry. The various other readers of these lines will not find it easy to conceive how we got into this laundry discussion. We are very pleased to learn about Ludwig's splendid summer home. We were most interested, dear Emil, by what you say about your daughter, and we can picture her charm, and we are sincerely happy to learn how she is developing; she is, or certainly will be, just like her charming mother, who is completely wrong if she believes that I am trying to flatter her. We understand Sigmund's current situation; things are not made as in former times.

We were pleased, dear Rosi, that you and Xander enjoyed your visit at Lily and Albert's. We were very amused by your account of Albert's conversations with

Xander.[250] Dear Rosi, we have often talked about religion, and I have my own opinions in the matter. The person who is of noble character, helpful, and good, and has other good qualities as well, is not irreligious, while the person who claims to be religious but who shuns the poor and is not charitable and not helpful and who has other bad qualities—that person, in my view, is not religious. Of course, that does not exclude the possibility that someone who is religious and pious may possess many good, praiseworthy qualities. And now I have had a chat with each of you once again. Give my greetings to all our dear ones, and you, dearest Rosi, be most warmly greeted and kissed by your father who loves you and to all of you from your Hugo.
[At the bottom of the page.]
Warmest birthday congratulations and many greetings! Aunt Clara.

My dear, dearest Rosi!

In former years we always began celebrating your birthday several days beforehand. This year, as you see, we are also starting early once more. My good Rosi, you know how much I wish all things good and beautiful for you, and I know too that that's sufficient for you, and that I can be brief due to the lack of space, and also I will be sending you my congratulations again. I was, once more, enormously delighted by your words and those of dear Clara and the dear Doktors. I find it hard to believe that you can really picture the joy that they bring. Life really ought to be more peaceful. The times are disturbing for everyone and especially for people who are predisposed to nervousness. Still, one has to be grateful if one is able to hold on to one's position. I am, of course, very interested in your purchases, dear Rosi. How I would like to admire you in your little green dress and the other things,

---

[250] Albert was an ultra-Orthodox Jew and Alexander was not religious.

although of course I trust your good taste. My best wishes to Xander. I would also like to see a picture of him, at the least. Your words, dear Emil and dear Rosl, are especially interesting to us. Perhaps in the meantime you have found an apartment that is also suitable for the practice. How lovely it would be, dear Rosl, if we could have a real heart-to-heart talk. We are very happy to hear that [?] has gotten married; perhaps this [?] is the same person who came to see us once because he knew Bruno Sichel. Lily could write to us sometime. We have had good reports from her children as well as from Hertha. And now I thank you first of all, dear Clara. Carry on as well as you have done so far, and may you all, my dear ones, and you, dear Rosi, have my warmest regards and kisses from your Clemy, who loves you.

Ruth Knoller married Philip de Paauw in a religious ceremony on June 16, 1942. Trude and Ari are to Ruth's right. Carla is standing behind Philip. The other people are de Pauuw relatives.

A Nazi decree of April 29, 1942, required all Jews, even brides, to wear the yellow Jewish star.

Ruth and Philip's wedding reception at the Knollers' apartment. Ari and his mother seated; Frida (behind Ari) and Philip's sister Sara.

At the reception. Hugo and Carla standing. Seated, from left to right: Hanna de Paauw, Philip's mother; Frederika Melkman née de Paauw (Philip's youngest sister); Joseph Melkman with his son Avraham on his lap; and Clemy.

Deportations of Jews in Holland

In July 1942 the Nazis began the systematic deportation of Jews from Amsterdam's Jewish Quarter (where they had been forcibly concentrated) to extermination camps in the east. Adolf Eichmann was in charge of the operation. Four thousand young, "stateless" (mostly German and other non-Dutch) Jews were the first to be called up. The summons arrived by mail on Sunday, July 5, 1942. Carla Knoller was in this first group deported on July 15, 1942, to Auschwitz.

```
Zentralstelle für jüdische
Auswanderung Amsterdam                              N⁰  87422
  Adama v. Scheltemaplein 1
       Telefoon 97001


                        OPROEPING!

              Jeanette van Praag - Salomons
        Aan   Weesperstr. 127        L        No.
              Amsterdam

              U moet zich voor eventueele deelname aan een, onder politietoezichtstaande, werk-
        verruiming in Duitschland voor persoonsonderzoek en geneeskundige keuring naar het door-
        gangskamp Westerbork, station Hooghalen, begeven.

              Daartoe moet U op _____8.11.1942_____ om _____ uur

        op de verzamelplaats _____Adama van Scheltemaplein 1_____ aanwezig zijn
              Als bagage mag medegenomen worden:
                    1   koffer of rugzak
                    1   paar werklaarzen
                    2   paar sokken
                    2   onderbroeken
                    2   hemden
                    1   werkpak
                    2   wollen dekens
                    2   stel beddengoed (overtrek met laken)
                    1   eetnap
                    1   drinkbeker
                    1   lepel en
                    1   pullover
                    handdoek en toiletartikelen
              en eveneens marschproviand voor 3 dagen en alle aan U uitgereikte distributiekaarten met
        inbegrip van de distributiestamkaart.
              De mee te nemen bagage moet in gedeelten gepakt worden.
        a.    Noodzakelijke reisbehoeften
              daartoe behooren: 2 dekens, 1 stel beddengoed, levensmiddelen voor 3 dagen, toiletgerei,
              etensbord, eetbestek, drinkbeker.
        b.    Groote bagage
              De onder b. vermelde bagage moet worden gepakt in een stevige koffer of rugzak,
              welke op duidelijke wijze voorzien moet zijn van naam, voornamen, geboortedatum
              en het woord „Holland".
              Gezinsbagage is niet toegestaan.
              Het voorgaande moet nauwkeurig in acht genomen worden, daar de groote bagage in
              de plaats van vertrek afzonderlijk ingeladen wordt.
              De verschillende bewijs- en persoonspapieren en distributiekaarten met inbegrip van
              de distributiestamkaart mogen niet bij de bagage verpakt worden, doch moeten,
              voor onmiddellijk vertoon gereed, medegedragen worden.
              De woning moet ordelijk achtergelaten en afgesloten worden, de huissleutels moeten
              worden medegenomen.
              Niet medegenomen mogen worden: levend huisraad.
```

An example of the call-up summons such as Carla received on July 5, 1942 [provided by René Pottkamp at NIOD in Amsterdam].

September 18, 1942

Dear Rosi,

I just received a letter from my sister, dated August 20, 1942. This is the passage that refers to you: "See the reverse side...and now I have heard from Hugo, who writes that he is having financial difficulties. He asked me to write to Emil about his problem. Since I don't know his exact address, I ask you to please inform him directly or through Rosi. We wanted to send him something ourselves, but unfortunately it's impossible to do from here. Neither cash, money, nor food packages—we have really tried everything.[251] Please tell Rosi that I sent off her letter with the charming picture as soon as I got it. They will certainly be very happy when they see how well she is looking." I immediately sent an excerpt from the letter to Emil. *We hope both of you are O.K. All the best from all of us to both of you. Yours, Ludwigs.*

I think the main thing is that your parents write at all.

---

[251] It seems that the Germans restricted mail between Switzerland and Holland. In the following postcard, Hugo wrote that they have not had mail from Switzerland in some time. We do not know if they ever received the letter and picture of Rosi that Clara relayed.

[Postmarked November 5, 1942.]
From: Mosbacher c/o Sabel
Amsterdam-Z
Rijnstraat 102/I

To: Frau Melanie Engelsrath
Piazza Aumi
Cagni 3
Asti, Italy[252]
November 4, 1942

My Dear Ones!

We received your card, dear Mela, and thank you for your good wishes. Reports are now, unfortunately, coming in very sparsely, and every time there is a mail delivery we are disappointed all over again. Ernst has already sent congratulations; he regrets the separation, of course, but I believe that he can feel quite satisfied. Milroserl [Milan and Roserl] have hired a helper and succeed with her. I am astonished that they can find the funds. If we made such expenditures here, people would not place their resources at our disposal as they do. We were pleased, dear Mela, with your remark that "God willing, the personal will come more quickly than one expects." Because we know so little, we are happy whenever we do hear something from somewhere else. Our cousin in Zurich has also become very quiet. Dear Mela, may you, together with Rose and Hertha, be heartily greeted and kissed by your Hugo.

---

[252] The postcard is addressed to Mela in Asti, Italy. Mela and her daughters Rose and Hertha had escaped from Yugoslavia and were living in an Italian refugee camp near Trieste. Apparently mail delivery from occupied Holland to Italy, another Axis country, or to Yugoslavia, another occupied country, was still possible.

My Dear Ones,

Your letters always make me happy and your activities are especially interesting to me. Dear Rose, with your dexterity and good taste you will acquire the skill very quickly. I'm also sewing and there's no lack of business. We've had news from Rosi. Alexander has also written twice; it's so odd when one doesn't know one's son-in-law.[253] Thank God [G.s.D.?][254] that the Trudari have news.[255] Stay well and be warmly kissed by your Clemy.

Write again soon!

[Postmarked December 14, 1942.]
From: Mosbacher c/o Sabel
Amsterdam-Z
Rijnstraat 102/I

To: Frau Melanie Engelsrath
Piazza Aumi
Cagni 3
Asti, Italy
December 13, 1942

My Dear Ones!

Your postcards, dear Mela, reached the Trudari and us and as always we enjoyed your brief reports. We would like to reply more extensively, but we lack the zest for writing long letters and to report all that would be worth telling each other in conversation. When we write to you, usually we also write to dear Ernst from whom we had good news a couple of days ago. At this time we do not expect any mail from Rosi or the other beloved ones. Also

---

[253] Rosi and Alexander were married by a justice of the peace on July 26, 1942. No family members were present.

[254] Clemy's abbreviation is unclear, but "G.s.D." ("Gott sei Dank," "Thank God") would be appropriate in context.

[255] Clemy probably referred to the one postcard Carla wrote from Auschwitz, dated September 29, 1942.

our cousin[256] does not hear from her loved ones anymore. December 22 is the *yahrzeit* of our beloved Papa of blessed memory. I have no doubt that you remember, dear Mela. Just now Clemy said that she is so nervous today. Unfortunately one is not able to help; we've gone through a lot in a lifetime. Dear Mela and dear daughters, be greeted and kissed many times by your Hugo.

My Dear Ones,

The only happiness for us now is when news comes from you, dear Mela and Ernst. Otherwise we do not hear from anyone anymore. I regret to hear that you, dear Mela, have lost so much weight. When we meet again, we will all be thin, but your weight loss is too much. Just take good care of your health, my Erntie. I think so often of you, my dear trio. I assume that Ernal [Erna and Alfred][257] is [are] now with Lily. I hope we will hear from you again soon. Be heartily greeted and kissed by your Clemy.

[3512 5447]
Amsterdam, January 10, 1943

My Dear Ones!

Your cards of November and December arrived at almost the same time and made us very happy to hear something more from you once again. We especially welcomed the words of our dear Rose, and to her and to you, dear Mela, we say many thanks. The Knollers, of course, always get a look at whatever mail comes to us, just as we get to see theirs. Clemy is bedridden with a stomach complaint. She has to keep to a diet, which is hard for her. Nowadays we don't complain about situations like these. We just accept them and think about conditions that are

---

[256]Clara in Switzerland had not heard from her brother Ludwig in the United States, confirming a breakdown in mail service between Switzerland and the United States. Therefore Hugo and Clemy were not receiving Rosi's letters through Clara.
[257]Erna and Alfred were in Cuba, not yet able to move to the United States.

incomparably worse and more upsetting. For example, the way the Hugos at the end of a November night suddenly got in a panic as a result of being taken ill, similar to the situation, as it perhaps was with Erwin.[258] Considering that we have had nothing but suffering to report, Clemy's complaint is actually an improvement, and I'm sure she will be better in a few days. My birthday yesterday passed like any other day; Rosi probably made more out of it than we did. Your good wishes, dear Mela, made Clemy as happy as if they had actually arrived on the day itself. Perhaps a time will come again in which these events will again be given more regard and attention. Also I must add that I still did not remain ungifted: cigars, a rare item and as always something I long for, became my portion in small quantities.[259]

We got quite a laugh, dear Mela, out of your remark about sister Lily on the one hand and Aunt Delphine (Cecil) on the other. We know that the aunt died some time ago; we don't know whether Cecil is still living in the area. Dear Mela, you asked already whether Frida had heard anything from her children, and I responded promptly that she hadn't heard anything. If we don't write anything about her now, it's not due to any special reason. She is in the same frame of mind that we all are in. If we had any happy news to relate about her, we would gladly pass it on. We sincerely regret that she has always followed our lead in all her actions and plans, and that she hasn't been more independent and smarter. Imitation isn't always the right way to go; one also has to think and act independently. We must console ourselves in thinking of all the others who didn't do any better than we did.

---

[258]Hugo probably referred to a raid that Hugo and Clemy had narrowly escaped. In his March 3, 1946, letter, Ari recounted that "the bandits had been at their place several times before but left because Clemy was sick." On June 30, 1946, Ari wrote, "At the end of 1942 the bandits came for the first time to take your parents." Hugo and Clemy were aware that Erwin has been deported to a concentration camp.
[259]For the third time Hugo and Clemy commemorated birthdays in occupied Amsterdam. Clemy was fifty-six years old; Hugo was sixty-two.

However, we can't always agree with the old idea that, in the end, the good always prevails.

We've had snow for several days and it's pretty cold; still we have better heating in our room than you do. Dear Mela, we're sorry that you're having trouble with your hands. We hope that you can get relief though suitable treatment. Ari, Trude, Ruth, and her husband are all well. In time one gets used to every situation, and young people in particular endure everything better. And now, my dears, I wish you all good things, and be heartily greeted and kissed by your Hugo.

My Dear Ones!

I have become a big *Schlemilde*,[260] but I hope that my health will be better again. We are enormously pleased by your letters, and I thank you for the good wishes. No one wants to think about celebrating. Trude is not at home on Tuesday, so that she doesn't need to receive visitors. On the fourteenth we will think of Erwin. From Rosi and husband we only had two letters written shortly after the wedding and nothing more since August. On the other hand, cousin Clara wrote this week that she had received a care package from her [Rosi]. In the meantime Roserl and Milan will have reached their goal. I am very happy for Lily. If anyone hears anything, please write to us. For your hands, soak them diligently in hot and cold water. That's still the best treatment. Stay well, my good ones. Be affectionately and most heartily greeted and kissed by your Clemy.

---

[260] The feminine form of "*schlemiel*," Yiddish for "an awkward, inept, unlucky person."

Ten days later, on January 20, 1943, Hugo and Clemy were arrested, taken from their residence in Amsterdam, and sent by train to Westerbork transit camp. Clemy wrote this postcard to Ari from Westerbork on January 26, 1943.

[Postmarked January 26, 1943.]
To: Aribert Knoller
Rijnstraat 102/II
Amsterdam

From: Clemy Mosbacher
Westerbork, Barrack 55

My Dear Ones!
A short time ago Hugo wrote to the Bessems and now I am writing to you and Frida, hoping that you are still there. Naturally from Franz [261] only the money for groceries should be requested. Now you must entrust the posting of packages to someone else. This night we slept not a single minute, but that will surely improve. There is no lack of acquaintances here. We are no better or worse off than all the others. Greetings and kisses. Stay well—
Clemy and Hugo

---

[261] Apparently a different Franz who had been helping them with errands.

Hugo, hoping they would remain in Westerbork instead of being deported to Auschwitz, sent a change of address card to his sister-in-law Mela on January 27, 1943. As a result of Ari's efforts, their deportation was postponed three times.

Nothing was heard from them after this postcard. Six days later, on February 2, 1943, they were deported to Auschwitz and gassed upon arrival on February 5, 1943. Of the 107,000 people, mostly Dutch and German Jews, who passed through Westerbork between 1942 and 1945, only 5,200 survived.

TRANSPORT LIST — 255

Morpurgo-Zinger	Sarah	13.5.70	—	18 Oosterp.str.10	8.12.42
Morpurg-Morpurgo	Sara	5.2.99	"	J.Breestr.97	3.6.43
Morpurgo	Sara	20.5.31	"	Saffierstr.91	15.7.43
Morpurgo-de Groot	Schoontje	3.4.66	"	1.Kerkln.23	16.2.43
Morpurgo-Sealtiel	Schoontje	19.6.83	"	Raitzstr.27	23.1.43
Morpurgo	Sonja	16.7.34	"	N.Prinsengr.17	2.3.17
Morpurgo	Willy	16.12.99	Utrecht	illemstr.20	29.1.43
Morpurgo	Wolf	29.5.79	A-dam	N.Hoogstr.12	23.1.43
Mosbach	Abraham	21.5.79	Oude Pekela	Krootstr.317	17.3.43
Mosbach	Alfred	5.1.06	"	Tolstr.110	20.7.43
Mosbach-Nosch	Clara	9.9.81	"	V. oustr.48	10.3.43
Mosbach	Eliazar	26.7.38	N-dam	Swaanhals 330	3.8.42
Mosbach-Arends	Eva	13.10.70	Bellingwolde D 47	?	9.2.43
Mosbach	Vrederika	3.3.06	?	?	15.7.42
Mosbach	Johanna	24.11.35	A-dam	Muiderschans 98	2.7.43
Mosbach	Kurt	3.9.08	?	?	15.7.42
Mosbach	Lea	11.5.06	Bellingwolde D 47		9.2.43
Mosbach	Louis	13.4.02	N-dam	Swaanhals 330	7.3.42
Mosbach-Kochmann	Marga	2.9.09	A-dam	Tolstr.110	20.7.43
Mosbach-Wasberg	Rachel	18.10.07	Wachel	wanhals 330	3.8.42
Mosbach	Eardus	9.3.73	Bellingwolde D 47		9.2.43
Mosbacher-Adler	Clementine	20.12.86	A-dam	Rijnstr.102	2.2.43
Mosbacher	Helene	12.10.81	A-dam	Somerdijkstr.43	2.2.43
Mosbacher	Hugo	9.1.80	A-dam	ijnstr.102	2.2.43
Mosberg-Levy	Charlotte	15.4.68	"	uterpestr.57	2.2.43
Mosberg-Oppenheimer	Rosalie	28.9.78	Assen	?	23.3.43
du Mesch	Abraham	15.6.85	?	?	7.10.42
du Mosch	Esther	17.3.24	A-dam	aphierstr.60	21.9.43
du Mosch	Hermanus	16.3.69	A-dam	Jeckerstr.77	6.4.43
du Mosch	Judith	4.9.27	"	.Theronstr.6	2.3.43
du Mosch	Marianna	24.3.23	"	aphierstr.60	21.9.43
du Mosch	Meijer	8.1.93	"	.Theronstr.6	2.3.43
du Mosch	Nathan	25.10.94	"	aphierstr.60	21.9.43
du Mosch-Piers	Sara	28.3.96	"	aphierstr.60	21.9.43
du Mosch-Verdoner	Sara	8.10.99	"	.Theronstr.6	2.3.43
du Mosch	Siepora	23.7.25	"	aphierstr.60	21.9.43
du Mosch-Lootveld	Sophia	12.9.87	"	Tugelastr.136	7.10.42
Moscou	Aaron	7.12.39	?	?	12.10.4
Moscou	Abraham	15.4.72	A-dam	1e.v.d.Helstr.8	2.2.43
Moscou	Abraham	16.4.27	"	Langkatstr.12	30.3.43
Moscou-Verffer	Betje	5.11.72	"	operstr.4	15.9.42
Moscou-Haan	Betje	16.12.90	"	Achillestr.15	31.8.43
Moscou-Hakker	Betje	1.9.11	"	Hofmeijerstr.18	4.5.43
Moscou	Betty	29.8.34	"		4.5.43
Moscou	Clara	26.3.34	"	angkatstr.18	30.3.43
Moscou	Coenrad	16.4.27	"		5.3.43
Moscou	David	17.5.13	"	elistr.141	27.7.43

The portion of the February 2, 1943, transport list from Westerbork to Auschwitz showing the names of Clementine Mosbacher-Adler, Helene Mosbacher, and Hugo Mosbacher.

Aftermath—Hugo and Clemy's Family and Friends at the End of the War

Frida Mosbacher Roederer was deported in May 1943 and murdered at Sobibor on May 28, 1943.

Helene [Lenchen] Mosbacher van Gelder was deported on the same transport from Westerbork to Auschwitz as Hugo and Clemy. She was murdered on the same day, February 5, 1943.

Henriette Mosbacher Dittus and Bruno Mosbacher went into hiding in Rotterdam, but were caught, sent to Westerbork, and deported to Poland. Henriette was killed at Auschwitz on February 11, 1944. Bruno died somewhere in Central Europe on June 30, 1944.

Ari and Trude Knoller were arrested on September 29, 1943, and detained at Westerbork until February 15, 1944, when they were sent to the Albala "preferential camp" at Bergen-Belsen. Jewish prisoners at this camp had foreign passports, papers for Palestine, or the special exemption "Sperrstamp" (the Knollers had all three), and were being held by the Germans for prisoner exchanges. On January 18, 1945, they were sent to Wurzach Castle for possible exchange. The French liberated this camp on April 28, 1945. They lived at the Jordanbad Displaced Persons camp near Biberach, Germany, until early 1946, when they returned to Amsterdam. They immigrated to the United States in 1948 and then to Israel in 1955.

Ruth Knoller and her husband Philip de Paauw were sent to Bergen-Belsen on August 1, 1944. They were sent in the same prisoner exchange as Ari and Trude and spent the remainder of the war in a Red Cross camp, then the Jordanbad DP camp. They returned to Amsterdam in March 1945, to reclaim their infant son Aron (Jaapsie), whom they had left with a Dutch family. They had a second son, Michael, in 1946 and immigrated to Israel with their two sons on July 26, 1951.

Carla Knoller was deported on July 15, 1942, to Auschwitz/Birkenau and murdered there on September 30, 1942. She was eighteen-years-old.

Franz Dietrich Schweizer was deported to Riga-Jungfernhof

work camp on November 27, 1941. About 800 of the prisoners died in the winter of 1941 to 1942 of hunger, cold, and typhus. On March 26, 1942, the camp was dissolved and between 1600 and 1700 inmates were shot in nearby Bikernieki forest. The exact date of Franz's death is not known, but it probably occurred during 1942. He was thirty-one-years-old.

Ari Knoller's Post-War Letters

March 3, 1946[262]
Gaaspstraat 73/11
Amsterdam

From Aribert Knoller (Ari) to Alfons (Alphons) Adler, Irma Adler, and Clara [Mosbacher] Sichel in New York City

My Dear All,
    In front of me lies a whole stack of letters from you, which I will try to answer now, in order. But before I begin that task I want to send you, Irma, most sincere good wishes. During this past year you have had the fulfillment of your dearest wish, a reunion with your healthy son.[263] May all your other wishes come true also. May God bless you for all the good deeds you have done for us and probably for others. But most of all I wish you good health. That is still the most important thing. As dear Alfons writes, you are responsible for much, but not feeling very well. I hope you will recover fully very soon and you, too, Alfons, so you can make your daily contribution again.
    Now to your letters of January 31 (via Monheit-Engelsrath), of February 14, 18, and 19, all of which arrived in good order and we thank you for them.
    In your letter of January 31, you, dear Alfons, write

---

[262]Ruth Adler Schottman, the daughter of Alfons and Irma, translated this letter on December 30, 2009.
[263]Frank Adler, son of Alfons and Irma, served with the American Military Intelligence Division in Africa, Italy, France, and Germany; he took pictures of Ari and Trude for the family when he found them at the Displaced Persons camp in June 1945.

that it might be better if we stayed in Jordanbad. As Displaced Persons there we might have the chance to get to the United States more quickly. We knew of the 3,900 visas that were to be distributed monthly to Displaced Persons. We still don't know whether this applies to people like us in the French occupation zone or only to those in the American zone. We believe that we will benefit anyway as a result of these 3,900 visas because these will be additional visas added to the usual quota. So there should be less demand on the usual quota and our turn should come sooner. We handed in the affidavit from Emil and the questionnaire about three weeks ago. Then came another, simpler form to fill out that we quickly returned, and now we are waiting for whatever will come. We are still not sure if Emil's affidavit will be sufficient. We don't want to ask, but we have to believe it is. But we thank you for offering a relationship-affidavit. Anyway, we had to fill out on the questionnaire whether we had relatives who are American citizens. Since we did not know whether you already are American citizens, we put down Frank, among others, since we were sure of his citizenship. We put down that he is the son of my wife's brother. As to Sweden, chances of earning a living there would be good, but, as I have mentioned before, we have no passports, and for "stateless" people getting a passport is a very drawn-out process that can take many months. It is difficult even for Dutch citizens. So meanwhile we must dispense with that possibility and try to find a way of earning some money here, which is also very difficult.

I am now corresponding with Weingartner. I have presented him with my plans and have asked him for samples. I am waiting for his answer and will then decide what to do next. I could sell everything he offers if I could get the import permit. That is the most difficult part. He also wrote me he is willing to furnish an additional affidavit, but I don't want to take him up on this unless it becomes necessary.

There is no longer a local Committee, but there is a Jewish Coordination Commission. Its job consists of helping people with emigration, in affairs concerning Palestine, and in searching for missing people. This latter is usually without success.

We thank you for the pictures you sent. We were very happy with them. We here look considerably better now. We were glad to hear that dear Frank is already enrolled in college and hope with him that in the fall he will get his heart's desire and be admitted to a veterinary school. These days you are probably enjoying a visit by dear Mausi-Ruth and hope she has helped into the world many little males and females.[264]

We could not get any positive information about Carlchen. Of the first transport, with which Carla had to leave, three young people have returned so far, two boys and one girl. The boys could give no information as they had been sent to a different place. I visited the young girl. She did not know Carla and did not recognize her from a photo I brought. She had worked in the political department at Auschwitz, while Carla, at least at the time when she wrote her only letter, was in Birkenau. Whether she stayed there, we of course don't know. She [the girl] gave us very little hope, so that now we feel more depressed than before.

Weingartner mentioned to you about compensation for business losses; I have already corresponded with him about that. It is extremely difficult. With industrial diamonds I, as exporter, would have to appear, but I can't do that because I have no capital and the manufacturers want to do it themselves without a middleman. Mostly the government deals with this so there is little room for private initiative. But I will orient myself further and see if there is a possible way. The local Chamber is poorly informed.

---

[264]"Mausi" was Ruth Adler's childhood nickname. Ruth was studying genetics at Cornell University, College of Agriculture. She believes the reference is to her work breeding fruit flies.

I will also ask at my former bank. The big banks have daily experiences and should have better information.

Excuse my disorganized letter, but I am going through your letters point by point and answering in that order.

My brother-in-law Spanier has a brother there, Jakob Spanier, whose address I don't know. As far as I know, he works for one of his relatives named Neuman, who, I think, produces wool sweaters or similar articles. As soon as I re-establish contact with Spanier I will ask for the address of Neuman. You know that it is difficult to correspond with Julius.

Now to your letter, dearest Irma and Clara. I thank you very much for all your love. Trudele will answer about your news of various people from Graz.[265] She will also write about Els, who was very good to us. We have practically no more wishes for material goods. You have supplied us with so much, we don't want to ask for more. The only thing that Trude still needs very much is a corset, and for me, if possible, a dry shaver, since I don't shave with Gillette or a blade. I once asked Emil for one, but don't know if he received that letter. It could, of course, be secondhand; it would be most helpful.

Henriette and Bruno were deported rather late. They disappeared, had their own apartment in Rotterdam, but were caught due to an unfortunate incident and sent as punishment to Westerbork where we spoke with them at various times. They were able to leave the punishment-barrack, and people tried to get them freed as non-Aryans.[266] But this attempt did not bear fruit quickly enough and suddenly they were sent to Poland. Henriette was very brave and Bruno left with faith. We never heard from them again.

Hugo and Clemy were the first ones to be taken away. As you will remember, they had a room in the same house on Rijnstraat as we did. The bandits had been at their

---

[265] Alfons, Irma, and Clara lived in Graz until 1939.
[266] It's not clear why a non-Aryan would be freed. It would make more sense if Ari meant "as Aryans."

place several times before but left because Clemy was sick. On one day in Jan. of '43 there was a special campaign to get the sick ones on Rijnstraat. Trude and Frida were having coffee at Hugo's, and they had been told not to fear another visit by the bandits because they had been there so recently. Unfortunately they did come and took everyone living in the apartment, the apartment owner, renters of rooms, and another Jewish family—the actor Kurt Lilien. Trude begged to be allowed to go upstairs to our room and at least wait for me there. Luckily I was not at home. She was granted her request provided it did not take too long. Frida, who kept her things in our room, was allowed to go upstairs with her. Later she was allowed to leave for her own place. Now the criminals waited for me. Through circumstances, my absence was extended. The fellows became impatient and also said they were hungry. Trude offered them food, which they took. As this affair dragged on, Trude asked again that we might be left at home, especially since my old mother could not travel. They withdrew for consultation, and, since the person from the Jewish "Rat"-council[267] who always appeared with the bandits also asked them to let us stay at home, they finally left, but unfortunately Hugo and Clemy were gone! A lot of work was done immediately to allow them to stay in Westerbork, and this almost succeeded. We had obtained for ourselves, through bribes, a letter that postponed deportation for nine months. It cost 1000 Fl. [florin]. I did not have that much, but a friend immediately made the money available. Of course, I had told Hugo about this possibility. At first he did not even want to know about this and then he also lacked the money. After they were removed to Westerbork we continued to work on having them kept there and succeeded in getting a fourteen-day reprieve during which time we could work on a longer postponement. But one cannot count on criminals and

---

[267] A play on words as "Judenrat" was the German name for the Jewish Council.

bandits. Anyway the top bandit,[268] who now sits in custody, was in a bad mood and ordered the departure of the Hugos with many other people. So the horrible deed happened. If our efforts had succeeded, would our loved ones still be here today? We don't know. Everything depended on chance, like our rescue.

Next Lenchen had to leave, first to Vught[269] and then via Westerbork to Poland. We never heard of her again. Frida managed to stay until the order came that all who were not locked up had to report to the railroad station. She even left the day before and went to the Hollandse Schouwburg[270] where the transports were usually assembled because she was advised to do that because transports from there were not in such large numbers. That way she delayed a week, during which we supplied her with food and tried to obtain an exception for her. This was unsuccessful. She was sent to Westerbork. We tried again to help by writing Dr. Ottenstein, best friend of Ludwig Neuburger, who had a leading role in the transportation department there, and asked him to look after her. To our misfortune, the train did not stop in Westerbork but went directly to Poland so that Dr. O. could not do anything.

As I am describing all this, the terrible days and months rise up again and the worry and horror that filled us and never left. We owe our survival to a series of lucky circumstances about which I will write another time. It would be too much for today. But, believe me, those of us who remain have to carry their sorrow. I know no one who was not touched. I wrote all this so explicitly because

---

[268] Albert Konrad Gemmeker, Westerbork's commandant from 1942 to 1945. Gemmeker was put on trial in Holland in 1949. He received ten years, minus the 3.5 years he had already served.

[269] Westerbork was overcrowded so the SS concentration camp at Vught was used as a holding place for arrested Jews awaiting deportation to death camps in the east.

[270] The Dutch Theater, renamed "Jewish Theater" by the Nazis, where only Jewish artists were allowed to perform for only Jewish audiences. The Germans used it as a collection point for Jews being shipped to Westerbork.

you, dear Clara, asked me to do so. If you want, you can let dear Emil read this letter, but only if you think it won't upset him too much.

I will now let Trude have her say. I close for today with expectations of hearing from you again soon. I hope that you, dear Alfons, will recover quickly from the injury to your hand and will soon be earning money again. I know you and realize how difficult you find idleness. Whatever I might do to help you, I will do.

Sincere regards and kisses to all of you—your Ari.

All My Beloved Ones,

It is so good to be able to wish you a happy birthday again, Irma. Everything is slowly normalizing. My wishes are timeless—always the best, especially good health for you and your loved ones. I hope you won't have to continue to work so hard. It weighs on me that we are adding to your workload, and I thank you a thousand times for your help that assisted us in so many practical ways as well as emotionally. We and you should make an end of this, but if we still have some requests it is because you always write so kindly that we should let you know all our wishes. I am interested in everything you write. It helps me share your lives. Give my greetings to the "colony" from Graz, in the United States and in Palestine. At which Bachner's does Olga Strauss work? Do you have any idea about the name of Bruno's Christian girlfriend or fiancée? I know that she was employed by a bank and has some of the Hugos' things. On the whole, only a few people had luck with the so-called caretakers,[271] but one could ask. Henriette's sister, who had come to Westerbork but was not called for the night transport to Poland, volunteered to go with them. That was the one who lived in Nijmegen who was always close to her. From Michel Rosenstock [in NYC] came another package for Ruth.

---

[271]Many deported or fleeing Jews left their property in the care of Dutch Aryans who appropriated it.

Everybody is so thoughtful, and I have meanwhile already fifty [years] behind me.[272] I think of you all, especially Franzele [Frank Adler] and will never forget how he appeared to us like "a stranger from a strange land." Aunt Clara, what you wrote about Emil pains my heart—I know how close the bond between the brothers was. Everything is so horrible and gruesome.

For today, affectionate greetings and kisses—Trude.

3/II Gaaspstraat
Amsterdam
June 2, 1946

My Very Dear Ones,

We were very happy when your dear letter of May 22 arrived here and dispelled our fear that for some reason you might be displeased with us. Many thanks for the photos with which we were especially pleased. They helped us to become at least a little bit acquainted with that part of the family we don't yet know personally. We hope, dearest Rosi, that you will visit us soon by the photo-technical route. Your two boys are splendid and, dear Xander, your eyes are simply glowing with fatherly pride.

In order to stay in character, this time I am not writing shortly before the Sabbath but shortly after the Sabbath, so I have no excuse for only sending a brief greeting. And so I'm using this Sunday to take care of at least a part of my private correspondence. On weekdays, praise be to God, I no longer have as much time as I did right after our return. I do have some business to attend to now, and I'm very happy that I do. I'm not making a fortune, but it's still good to have something to do and not to have too much time to think about things. Your description of your sons, dearest Rosi, gave me a good laugh. We are having the same experience here with our grandson Jaapsie, who is always climbing around on things. Now and then he falls

---

[272]Trude had recently turned fifty-years-old.

on his nose, but I guess that's normal. You write that Stephen—like all babies—is splendid. I sense an undertone of irony there, but all babies really are splendid. One first begins to understand that when one is a grandpa. It's also interesting that you are already so acclimatized as American citizens that you talk a lot about the climate.[273] Still, rheumatism is an unpleasant business, as I learned in Bergen-Belsen when I was laid up with it for two months and couldn't eat or wash myself without help. That, at least, is all forgotten now, and I don't feel it any more.

We are in fairly regular contact with Emil's family. We are burdened with the same grief[274] and understand and comprehend each other completely. He bears his fate with a dignity that can only come from inner serenity.

I wrote to Alfons some months ago about your dear parents, as well as about Frida and Lenchen, and left it up to him whether to show you the letter or not. Apparently he preferred not to do so. We only know the following: Your parents were taken from their home on January 20, 1943. They were sent immediately to Westerbork where they stayed only a few weeks. From there they were probably sent to Auschwitz, but we do not know that for certain. In any case, we never heard from them again. I believe Alfons still has my letter and you can probably read it.

I think your parents may have mentioned that they had some belongings in Rotterdam that they had deposited with a shipping agent. At the time they were unable to get anything out of the man, I no longer know why. Do you perhaps know the name of the shipping agent? Could it be Gutmann? As far as I can remember, he was from Nuremberg. If you could give me any particulars, we could see whether anything can still be saved. I don't have a lot of hope, but we should at least make the effort.

And now, my dear ones, the very best to you and the dear children. With warmest regards—your A.

---
[273] Alexander and Rosi became American citizens in 1945.
[274] Ari referred to Carla's death and to Emil's loss of his son, Stephen.

73/II Gaaspstraat
Amsterdam
June 30, 1946

My Dear Rosi,

Many thanks for your dear letter of the nineteenth of this month, which pleased us very much. Many thanks, also in Ruth's name, for the promised package. When it arrives we will write again specially to confirm it. Ruth and Philip and their child have gone to Scheveningen for a two-week holiday; they are staying with Japie's [Jaapsie] foster mother, which is good for both parties.[275]

That Alphonse and Irma did not give you my detailed letter was not due to any bad will on their part. I had written them that I left it up to them whether to show you the letter because I did not want to upset you all over again. On the other hand, I certainly understand that you want to be told everything, and so I am complying with your wish, and I will give you as precise an account as possible, insofar as I can reconstruct the events from memory. I don't know how long you remained in contact with your dear parents, and thus I may tell you some things that you already know.

When your parents came to Amsterdam at the beginning of 1940, after being released from detention, about which you surely must be informed, they stayed with us in Beethoven Street. They quickly obtained their visas for the U.S.A., and, on the fatal Friday when the German bandits attacked Holland, they were supposed to depart for New York with the *Veendam*. All preparations had been made to travel to Rotterdam on that Friday and to embark there. But it all came to nothing, and they and Frida had to resign themselves to waiting for the end of the war. It was a terrible disappointment, but at that time no one dreamed that it would have such fatal consequences. In

---

[275] Ruth and Philip had left their infant son, Aron [Jaapsie], with a Christian foster mother prior to their deportation to Bergen-Belsen.

November 1940 we moved to Rijn Street for reasons of economy. Your parents rented a little room in the same house with the Sabel family, and so we saw each other on a daily basis. Everything went fairly well until the deportations began in July 1942. From that point on, the Dutch Jews and the other Jews who were living here never had a moment's peace. Our own little Carla was, unfortunately, one of the first victims. She, together with 1,000 other young people, mainly Germans [German Jews], had to leave on July 15. At that time we did not yet know that the so-called Jewish Council[276] was compiling the lists. It was run almost entirely by Dutch Jews, who, of course, very kindly sent the foreign Jews to their destruction first. If we had known then what we knew ten days later we would never have let our Carla go and perhaps she would still be with us today. Beginning in July 1942, transports left regularly. At first people received a summons, but fewer and fewer responded to the summonses, and they went into hiding instead, and then the raids began. Your parents made themselves as comfortable as they could. To be sure, they lived in a tiny room, but otherwise they lacked for nothing, especially in regard to food, and got by well.

At the end of 1942 the bandits came for the first time to take your parents. Kurt Lilien, a subtenant of the Sabel family who was on friendly terms with your parents, was able to bribe them and to send them away on the grounds that your mother was ill. At that time it was possible to obtain a kind of exemption stamp from the Germans, if you were employed by the Jewish Council, or were employed by a military contractor, or were the holder of a foreign passport, etc. After failing to obtain a stamp from

---

[276]Again, a play on words. The German for "the Jewish council" is "*der jüdische Rat*," though the Germans usually used "Judenrat." The German for "council" is "*Rat*"; the German for "betrayal" is "*Verrat*." Ari wrote "*der sogenannte judische (Ver)Rat*"—this can be translated both as "the so-called Jewish Council" and "the so-called Jewish Betrayal." The Dutch-Jewish leaders of the Council created the deportation lists demanded by the Nazis.

any of the Jewish authorities who were able to supply them, I was able to get a letter of exemption, valid for six months, by paying 1,000 guilders[277] to a Dutch Nazi. I didn't have the money myself, but my friends put up the money. Of course I immediately made your parents and Frida aware of this possibility, but they were not able, at least then, to raise the money. In principle this exemption worked as follows: The person applying for an exemption pledged himself to cause his relatives abroad to pay 10,000 Swiss francs to the German criminals, whereupon he was supposed to receive permission to emigrate. Everyone who got one of these letters promised, of course, to do everything possible to raise the money abroad. That the money never came was another matter, but at least for a while they left you alone.

At the beginning of 1943 the raids became more frequent, and one literally did not have a moment's peace. On a Monday toward the end of January 1943, there was yet another raid in Rijn Street, and people were telling each other that those who had been spared previously because of illness were now being taken away. On that afternoon Trude and Aunt Frida were with your parents, and I was away on business. Mr. Lilien came to your parents to reassure them, telling them that they had nothing to fear, all the more since your mother was unwell that day and lying in bed. Unfortunately he was wrong, because the doorbell rang a few minutes later, and the bandits were there with a summons for the Mosbachers. They proceeded to make a thorough job of it and said that all the Jews in the apartment had to come along, including Frida, Trude, the Sabels, and the Liliens. It was useless to argue: Everyone had to come. However, Trude and Frida had their belongings in our apartment upstairs and got permission to go and fetch them. My mother was also upstairs in our apartment. One of the criminals went upstairs with them to supervise. Trude

---

[277]The terms "guilder" and "florin" (see Ari's earlier letter) were used interchangeably.

persuaded him to wait until I came home. Due to an accident, however, I was gone longer than usual on that day, and finally, as luck had it, they went away, leaving Trude and my mother at home. Frida, who was downstairs, was able to remain free, at least on this occasion, because she did not live in the house.

Unfortunately, nothing could be done for your dear parents, and on the same day they were sent off to Westerbork. We now, for our part, tried to do everything, both possible and impossible, to arrange for them to be kept in Westerbork. That was a possibility, and indeed some people stayed there until the end of the war. The matter appeared to have been arranged, due to my having written that an exemption letter that I had obtained was being processed and would arrive within a few days. Then a new mishap occurred: The commandant of Westerbork flew into a rage for some reason and ordered that all the internees had to go, without exceptions, and all our efforts were in vain. If that had not happened, we would have been able, through our personal contacts, to arrange a longer stay in Westerbork. To be sure, I do not believe that that would have meant that they were absolutely safe. Everything depended upon so many accidents and whims that the number of those who were saved is truly infinitesimal.

We never learned where your parents were sent, but we assume that they were taken to Auschwitz since almost all the transports from Westerbork went there. Later people were also sent to Theresienstadt and Bergen-Belsen. We have never spoken with anyone who was taken away with your parents, and we also do not know if anyone ever came back, because the transports did not leave from here, but from Westerbork. As long as your parents were in Westerbork, we supplied them with plenty of packages, so that at least they did not lack anything while they were there. Unfortunately we were unable to do anything more.

Frida, Lenchen, and Henriette, together with Bruno, were sent away soon afterwards. The Dittusens [Henriette and Bruno] were last; they had gone into hiding but were caught nonetheless. We were already in Westerbork by then and spoke to them there. Dear Rosi, if you should now have any more questions, you have only to write to me. I will answer you at once as fully as possible. For today, many regards to all of you—your Ari.

[This note, now faded and hard to read, is written along the left margin of the first page of the letter.]

Dear Rosi—
Today in brief haste and in love—many thanks for your prompt dispatch—the next time there will be more, since this letter, for which you are surely already waiting, has to be sent. What profession does your husband actually have? We know so little about each other. Many good wishes to all of you—your Trude.

Aribert Knoller
73/II Gaaspstraat
Amsterdam
November 1, 1946

My Dear Baczewskis,
Many thanks for your dear lines of September 23, that I wanted to answer with my usual punctuality, but the vicissitudes of daily life prevented me. First came the holidays, then a severe attack of lumbago kept me in bed for a week, then my time was taken up by various business deals that didn't work out, and now I want to use a rainy evening to warm my feet by diligent writing, although of course I'm typing with my hands. So I don't harbor any feelings of revenge against you. I'm saving those for others, even though, regrettably, I'm powerless to do anything about them. Dear Rosi, unfortunately I must give a negative response to your question of whether we know

anyone who was with your parents in Westerbork and who has returned. We do not even know who was transported with them from Westerbork where they stayed about two weeks. However, I want to see if I can find out something about this. Perhaps the transportation lists have been found.

Our children, Ruth and Flip, want to go to *Eretz* [Israel], naturally. Even though it's not possible to go now, as enthusiastic Zionists they hope that everything will be straightened out within the foreseeable future. I hope so, too, but I don't believe it. We European Jews have lost the war all along the line, and we are not able to recover. Some individuals, perhaps, but not as a whole. We have had frequent reports from Erna. She and Marion have done well to find employment so quickly. We hope Alfred gets well soon so that he can also find something to do; it will do him good, because he has always been so extremely hardworking. In the meantime, Mela has arrived there with her daughters so that the family circle there is growing steadily larger while here it gets steadily smaller.

I got a hearty laugh from your description of your sons, all the more since we have their exact counterpart in our grandson Jaapsie. He even plays the same tricks and is absolutely adorable, just like your boys. I can well imagine that the father, when he starts telling stories about the children, puts the mother in the shade. I'm glad, dear Rosi, that, drawing on your own experience, you can be so understanding about it. Our own Ruth is looking forward to her accouchement within the next few weeks, and we hope that everything will go well.

Dear Xander, I want to give you my special thanks for your efforts in the plastics matter; I just hope that you didn't lose too much time over it. If you have anything that needs attending to, I would be glad to hear about it.

And now my better half will take the floor. Many warm and sincere regards from your Ari.

[Handwritten note along the bottom and left margin of the page.]

My Dear Ones,

The bit about the better half can be ignored; we are equal. Rosi-child, your dear lines were a great pleasure for us, and the descriptions of the splendid boys were a still greater one. I hope, dear Xander, that you have found a steady job again—in America, changing jobs does not appear to be such a tragedy. It's wonderful that Erna is living near you for the time being and you will be able to talk to each other from time to time. We are now the shabby leftovers in Europe and have to wait until our time comes. I imagine that when you want to go out in the evening, that the old aunt is phoned and then she looks after your children. Otherwise there isn't much to report. I am constantly knitting woolens for the coming child and for Jaapsie and am going to become an expert at it yet. My spoken English, unfortunately, is still very halting. Ari comforts me. He believes that, when I get over there, it will come naturally. *Nous verrons!*[278] Give Tony and your little angel each an extra kiss. Your Trude embraces you in love.

---

[278] "We will see!"

Mentioned in the Letters

This list is meant to provide the reader with quick identification of names that appear more than once and that have some significance in the letters. Most people are listed as they are referred to, usually by first name.

Frequently Mentioned

The Doktors—Emil Mosbacher and his wife Rosl née Neumann. Emil, Hugo's younger brother, was an obstetrician. Emil, Rosl, and their children Lore (Marianne) and Sigmund (Stephen) emigrated from Germany on October 20, 1938. The family lived in New York for over a year while Emil qualified to practice medicine in the United States. They then moved to Toledo, Ohio, in May 1940, where Emil opened a medical practice. Rosl's mother, Jettchen Neumann (Mother Jettchen), joined them in the spring or early summer of 1940.

Frida Roederer—Hugo's sister who was very close to Hugo and Clemy. In November 1937, Frida visited her daughter Anna in the United States on a six-month visitor's visa. Anna and her husband Philip White pleaded with her to stay, but Frida returned to Germany in April 1938 because Hugo had signed for her and she didn't want to get him in trouble. Also, she missed Hugo and Clemy. She left Germany with them in February 1940 and lived near them in Amsterdam. Frida's stepsons, Ludwig Neuburger in Montevideo (Uruguay) and Fritz Roederer in New York, along with the Whites in Oakland, California, did their best to get Frida a South American visa while she was in occupied Amsterdam, but none of their efforts succeeded. Frida was deported in May 1943 and murdered at Sobibor on May 28, 1943.

Trude (Trudl) and Ari Knoller—Trude was Clemy's half-sister and Hugo's niece. The Knoller family left Berlin in 1937 and were living in Amsterdam when Hugo and Clemy arrived there in early 1940. Trude and Ari survived Bergen-Belsen, returned briefly to Amsterdam, immigrated to the United States in 1948, and in 1955 joined their daughter Ruth and her family in Israel.

Also Mentioned

Albert Engelsrath—the second husband of Lily Neurath née Adler, Clemy's sister. Albert was originally from Zagreb, Yugoslavia.

Albrecht—Rosi's boyfriend in Nuremberg. He left Germany and lived safely somewhere in Europe. He settled in Sweden after the war and became a rabbi.

Alexander (Xander) Baczewski—a refugee from Vienna who met Rosi at a Broadway cafeteria in October 1940, shortly after she arrived in the United States. They married on July 26, 1942. Alexander was a chemist, and Hugo and Clemy often refer to him as "the chemist" in their letters. Alexander had been arrested in Vienna when Hitler invaded Austria. He was first sent to Dachau, then to Buchenwald. He was released from Buchenwald in January 1939 and was given ten days to leave Germany. He arrived in New York on June 1, 1939.

Alfons Adler—Clemy's brother, who immigrated with his family to the United States in 1939.

Alfred Falck—the husband of Erna Adler, Clemy's half-sister.

Anna White née Roederer—Frida's daughter who immigrated to Oakland, California, with her husband Philip White and their infant son Leon in 1936.

Anthony Sudweeks—the infant Rosi cared for while she was in England.

Apeldoorn—a Jewish home for the mentally ill located outside Amsterdam.

Bruno Mosbacher—was murdered in the Holocaust somewhere in Central Europe.

Carla Knoller—the younger daughter of Ari and Trude Knoller who was deported to Auschwitz on July 15, 1942, and murdered at Birkenau on September 30, 1942.

Ces (Cecile) Mosbacher—Hugo's cousin who lived in England and whom Rosi met there in 1939/1940.

Clara Fenigstein née Mosbacher—Hugo's cousin and Ludwig's sister. She lived in Zurich with her husband Arnold and daughter Lilly and survived the war.

Clara Sichel née Mosbacher—Hugo's older sister who

received a visa because her son Bruno was an American citizen. Clara arrived in the United States on December 23, 1938. She lived with her daughter Irma in South Carolina, but made extended visits to Emil and Rosl in Toledo, Ohio. She moved to New York City in 1942.

Committee—The Committee for Jewish Refugees in the Netherlands was established in 1933 to provide financial aid, emigration advice, and lodging to the stream of German and later Austrian, Czech, and Polish Jews seeking safety in Holland. After the German occupation of Holland on May 10, 1940, the Committee was no longer able to operate independently and was subsumed by the Nazi-controlled Joodse Raad (Judenrat).

Dina Schweizer—the mother of Emil Mosbacher's first wife, Anna. She was deported from Fürth on October 9, 1942, and died at Theresienstadt on October 18, 1942.

Don Mosbacher—Hugo's older brother who died in 1909. He had been living in Amsterdam but died in Fürth. The circumstances are unknown.

Ella Cohn Goldberger—a friend of Clemy's who was also in Amsterdam with her husband and daughter. There is no mention of the family after June 1941.

Els (Elisabeth) van Gelder—Hugo's niece, the daughter of Helene Mosbacher and Philip van Gelder. Els worked at the Committee for Jewish Refugees in the Netherlands. It is likely that she sent her two children to England before she escaped to Lisbon in the summer of 1940. She eventually made her way to England and later lived in Geneva.

Emil Mosbacher—an older, wealthy cousin of Hugo's, who lived in England and who paid for Rosi's passage to the United States. He provided immigration affidavits for Hugo and Clemy and helped them financially while they were in Amsterdam.

Erna Falck née Adler—Clemy's half-sister and Hugo's niece. In early 1939, the Falcks left Berlin, entered Belgium illegally, and lived in Brussels until the Germans occupied Belgium in May 1940. Alfred was arrested as an "enemy alien" and sent to Saint Cyprien prison camp in southern France. Erna and her daughter Marion fled occupied Belgium, taking a train to southern France where Alfred was interned. Although extremely ill, Alfred escaped Saint Cyprien. They procured visas for Cuba and departed in December 1941 on the SS *Guinea*, one of the last boats to leave Europe. Erna, Marion, and Alfred Falck moved from Cuba to the United States in August 1946.

Ernst Engelsrath—the husband of Mela, Clemy's sister. He was deported from Yugoslavia and murdered at Auschwitz in May 1943.

Erwin Adler—Clemy's brother. He moved from German-occupied Graz, Austria, to Yugoslavia in 1940. He was arrested at some point in 1942 and died in a concentration camp in Yugoslavia or murdered at Auschwitz in 1943. No definite record exists.

Eva Goldberger—Ella Goldberger's daughter who was in Clemy's sewing class.

Fellheimer, Herman—Hugo's good friend who remained in Nuremberg. He was deported on November 29, 1941, to Riga-Jungfernhof. The date of his death is unknown.

Frank Adler—the son of Alfons and Irma Adler. After immigrating, he served in the United States Army in Europe and found Ari and Trude Knoller in a Displaced Person's camp on June 15, 1945.

Franz Dietrich Schweizer—a close friend of the family and cousin of Emil's first wife, Anna Schweizer. He was deported from Fürth on November 11, 1941, to Riga-Jungfernhof and died there, probably in the winter of 1941/1942.

Freddy (Alfred) van Gelder—Helene Mosbacher's son and Els' brother. He and his family escaped occupied Amsterdam in the summer of 1940, presumably to England. The details are unknown.

Fredl Adler—Clemy's brother. He and his wife Lusi were in New York City by 1941.

Frida Maier—Hugo's cousin who immigrated to the United States, probably in late 1935 or early 1936, and helped many family members with documents, money, etc.

Fritz Roederer—Frida Roederer's stepson, whose mother died in childbirth. He was an infant when Frida married his father, Gustav Roederer. Fritz immigrated to the United States in early 1940.

Hammelburgers—friends from Nuremberg. The parents and one daughter left Germany; their other daughter Fanny was murdered at Auschwitz.

Heddy—wife of Jacob Fleischmann who was Hugo's first cousin. The Fleischmanns lived in Nuremberg and the two families were close. Jacob died in September 1938. Heddy and her younger son Ludwig immigrated to Chile in August 1939. Her older son Paul immigrated to Argentina in 1939 and to the United States in 1967.

Helene (Lenchen) van Gelder née Mosbacher—Hugo's sister who married Philip van Gelder, a Dutch Jew, and was living in Amsterdam before the war. She was deported on the same transport as Hugo and Clemy and murdered at Auschwitz on the same day, February 5, 1943.

Henriette (Henny) Mosbacher Dittus née van Raap—the widow of Don Mosbacher, Hugo's older brother. Henriette was a Dutch Jew. She was murdered at Auschwitz on February 11, 1944.

Hertha Engelsrath—the younger daughter of Mela and Ernst Engelsrath.

Hichenberg—possibly Hugo's former business partner and also a family friend, someone well known to Rosi. Hugo quotes his sayings. He had died by the time of these letters.

Ida Rau—Hugo's cousin who lived in Würzburg. She was deported to Izbica on April 25, 1942, and murdered there.

Irma Adler née Sichel—the daughter of Clara Sichel née Mosbacher and thus Hugo's niece, who was married to Clemy's brother Alfons Adler. Irma, Alfons, and their children Frank and Ruth left Graz on February 15, 1939. They spent ten months in Holland due to a problem with Frank's papers. Visas were finally granted, and they sailed from Rotterdam on November 24, 1939. The Reform Synagogue of Columbia, South Carolina, helped them find work and housing. Irma and Alfons relocated to New York City at the end of 1941 or beginning of 1942.

Jettchen Neumann—the mother of Rosl Neumann, Emil Mosbacher's second wife.

Johanna (Hanna) Mosbacher—the wife of Ludwig Mosbacher.

The Joint—the American Jewish Joint Distribution Committee

(often called "the Joint" or the JDC) is a worldwide Jewish relief organization established in 1914 in New York. During the years of Nazi persecution, the Joint provided emergency aid for stranded refugees, covered travel expenses and landing fees, and secured accommodations and visas for countries of refuge. With the United States' entry into the war, the JDC was no longer permitted to operate legally in enemy countries, but JDC representatives channeled aid to Jews living under Nazism, while trying to secure permanent refuge for them in the United States, Palestine, and Latin America [adapted from Wikipedia].

Lily (Valerie) Neurath Engelsrath née Adler—Clemy's older sister. Lily and her husband Albert moved from Vienna to Zagreb in April 1940, then to Italy, Lisbon, and finally to the United States in late February or early March 1941. Lily's sons Hans and Paul Neurath and their families arrived in the United States in 1938 and 1939, respectively. Paul was able to expedite his parents' immigration through connections he had in Washington.

Lina—the Mosbachers' Gentile maid in Nuremberg.

Ludwig Mosbacher—Hugo's first cousin who left Germany for England in June 1939. He, his wife Johanna, and their sons Alfred and Eric were in England when Rosi arrived there on June 12, 1939. The family immigrated to the United States in April 1940.

Ludwig Neuburger—the son of Gustav Roederer's first wife who was raised by Frida and Gustav. He immigrated to Montevideo, Uruguay.

Luise (Lusi) Adler—the wife of Fredl Adler, Clemy's brother.

Marianne (Lore) Mosbacher—the daughter of Emil and Rosl Mosbacher.

Mela (Melanie) Engelsrath née Adler—Clemy's oldest sister lived with her husband Ernst and their daughters Hertha and Rose in Zagreb, Yugoslavia. Rose's husband, Leo Weinberger, was arrested shortly after the German occupation of Yugoslavia on April 6, 1941. Hertha escaped to Italy in 1941. Mela and Rose left in 1942, once Rose was certain that Leo was dead, probably in the mass murders at Jadovno concentration camp in August/September 1941. Ernst was too ill to travel, so he went into hiding with a Gentile family. Mela, Rose, and Hertha were in

Italian refugee camps when the Germans occupied Italy on July 25, 1943. They escaped to Switzerland and finally immigrated to the United States in October 1946.

Michel and Selma Rosenstock—cousins, probably on the Adler side, with whom Rosi briefly lived when she first arrived in the United States.

Mirko (Zvonimur) Engelsrath—Albert Engelrath's son from a previous marriage. He and his wife Valerie reached the United States on August 20, 1940, shortly after Rosi arrived. Mirko enlisted in the United States Army in 1943 at the age of thirty-six.

Paul Engelsrath/Elgart—the son of Mela Engelsrath, Clemy's older sister. Paul and first wife Vally left Vienna in 1939, settling in Los Angeles in 1941.

Paul Neurath—the son of Clemy's sister Lily. He and his family left Vienna in 1939.

Paula Schweizer—the mother of Franz Schweizer. Paula was among the patients evacuated from Apeldoorn Jewish Mental Hospital and sent to Auschwitz. On January 21, 1943, the Nazis began the deportation of about 1,100 patients and fifty nurses. There were no survivors. Paula's date of murder is listed as occurring on January 25, 1943.

Pauline Rubens—a distant Mosbacher relative who was living in Chicago. Emil located her, and she helped members of the family with immigration affidavits and money. She sponsored Rosi, Hugo, and Clemy, although Hugo and Clemy were never able to use their American visas.

Philip de Paauw (Flip)—a Dutch Jew who married Ruth Knoller in 1942 in Amsterdam.

Philip van Gelder—Helene Mosbacher's ex-husband and Els' father, a Dutch Jew. He survived the war.

Philip [Seligsberger] White (Fips)—Frida's son-in-law, the husband of Anna Roederer. The Whites immigrated to Oakland, California, in 1936. Philip changed his name to White shortly after he arrived.

Rose Weinberger Karliner née Engelsrath—Mela Engelsrath's daughter.

Roserl Engelsrath née Neurath—Lily Engelsrath's daughter.

Roserl and her husband Milan Engelsrath escaped from Yugoslavia and lived in a refugee camp in Rovigno, Italy, from March 18 until August 18, 1942. A note on their camp records indicates that they immigrated to Paraguay, but there is a question mark after the note. They arrived in the United States on April 13, 1945.

Ruth Knoller (later de Paauw)—the eldest daughter of Trude and Ari Knoller. She and her husband Philip survived Bergen-Belsen and eventually immigrated to Israel on July 26, 1951, with their two sons.

Ruth Schottman née Adler—the daughter of Alfons and Irma Adler.

Sabels (Eugen and Else)—the family who rented a room at 102 Rijnstraat to Hugo and Clemy. They were arrested at the same time as Hugo and Clemy and murdered at Auschwitz.

Sigmund (Stephen) Mosbacher—Emil's son from his first marriage, to Anna Schweizer. He joined the United States Army in June 1943 and served as a staff sergeant in the 8th Armored Division in Europe. He died "while rescuing a comrade under fire" during an Allied operation in Germany on April 2, 1945. He was twenty-one-years-old.

Tuchmann—the senior partner in Montangesellschaft A. Tuchmann & Co., Hugo's metal distribution firm. His widow was in England when Rosi was there, and she immigrated to the United States shortly before Rosi did.

Veendam—the Holland America Line ship that Hugo and Clemy were ready to board on May 12, 1940.

Vieyra—Isadore Vieyra and his wife were Dutch Jewish immigrants in New York who employed Rosi from October 1940 until May 1941. Rosi did light housekeeping and cooking for them in the afternoons, after her factory job.

Emigration and Immigration Visa Requirements

Documentation Required for Emigration from Germany

After 1937, Jews needed the following documents from German authorities to leave the country.
1. Passport.
2. Certificate from the local police noting the formal dissolution of residence in Germany.
3. Certificate from the Reich Ministry of Finance approving emigration, which required:
   a. Payment of an emigration tax of 25 percent on total assets valued at more than 50,000 Reichsmark. This tax was due upon the dissolution of German residence.
   b. Submission of an itemized list of all gifts made to third parties since January 1, 1931. If their value exceeded 10,000 Reichsmark, the gifts were included in the calculation of the emigration tax.
   c. Payment of a capital transfer tax of 25 percent (levied only on Jews) of assets, in addition to the emigration tax.
   d. Certification from the local tax office that there were no outstanding taxes due.
   e. Certification from a currency exchange office that all currency regulations had been followed. An emigrant was permitted to take 2,000 Reichsmark or less in currency out of the country. Any remaining assets would be transferred into blocked bank accounts with restricted access.
4. Customs declaration, dated no earlier than three days before departure, permitting the export of itemized personal and household goods. This declaration required:
   a. Submission of a list, in triplicate, of all personal and household goods accompanying the emigrant, stating their value. The list had to note items acquired before January 1, 1933; those acquired since January 1, 1933; and those acquired to facilitate emigration.
   b. Documents attesting to the value of personal and household goods, and written explanations for the necessity of taking them out of the country.

c. Certification from a currency exchange office permitting the export of itemized personal and household goods, dated no earlier than fourteen days before departure.

With the preceding documents, an emigrant could leave Germany, if and only if he or she had valid travel arrangements and an entrance visa for another country. After the union of Germany and Austria in March 1938, an emigrant from Austria holding an Austrian passport had to apply for a German exit visa before he or she was permitted to leave the country.

Documentation Required for Immigration to the United States

1. Visa application (five copies).
2. Birth certificate (two copies).
3. The quota number must have been reached. (This established the person's place on the waiting list to enter the United States.)
4. A Certificate of Good Conduct from German police authorities, including two copies respectively of the following:
   a. Police dossier.
   b. Prison record.
   c. Military record.
   d. Other government records about the individual.
5. Affidavits of Good Conduct (required after September 1940).
6. Proof that the applicant passed a physical examination at the U.S. Consulate.
7. Proof of permission to leave Germany (imposed September 30, 1939).
8. Proof that the prospective immigrant had booked passage to the western hemisphere (required after September 1939).
9. Two sponsors (close relatives preferred). The sponsors must be American citizens or have permanent resident status, and they must each have filled out an Affidavit of Support and Sponsorship (six copies notarized), as well as provided:
   a. Certified copy of his or her most recent federal tax return.
   b. Affidavit from banks regarding his or her account.
   c. Affidavit from any other responsible person regarding the

sponsor's other assets (an affidavit from the sponsor's employer or a statement of commercial rating).

Adapted with permission from "For Jews Desperate to Flee, There Were No Easy Options" from *Memory & Action*, United States Holocaust Memorial Museum magazine, Spring 2016, p. 5.

Rosi Lisbeth Mosbacher Baczewski
(1916-2009)
by Judith Vasos Baczewski

Rosi in the 1940s and in 2005.

I wish my mother-in-law Rosi were here to help me write the story of her life. Fortunately, she left behind many stories, letters, photos, and documents to help me. Though it has been three years since her death, her letters to me and the stories she told me remain vivid in my mind.

Rosi, born on July 14, 1916, in Nuremberg, Germany, spent the first twenty-three years of her life in her birthplace, in the close-knit Orthodox Jewish world of her parents, Hugo and Clementine (Clemy) Mosbacher, and an extended family that considered the Mosbacher home a center for family activities. Relatives joined them for dinner on many occasions, and Rosi remembered having to "kiss so many relatives good night." She was an only child and close to her many aunts, uncles, and cousins. She felt safe and well cared for, especially by her father with whom she had a special connection. Everyone loved her father, she said, for his kindness, willingness to listen, and wonderful sense of humor. She often remarked that he could be funny without being cruel. She described her parents as "such good people."

Clemy and Rosi in Graz, Austria (1918).

Her father was born in Fürth but moved to nearby Nuremberg when he married Clemy in 1911. He was a partner in a metal firm and was very friendly, outgoing, and at home in Nuremberg. Clemy, on the other hand, was less at ease and a bit shy, having been raised in the small town of Mürzzuschlag in Austria.

Despite the love and safety of her family and even before Hitler came to power, Rosi was exposed to anti-Semitism. She walked to school over the Kettensteg, a suspended footbridge that she described as "wobbly and scary." Waiting for her by the bridge on most days was a young Gentile boy who yelled "dirty Jew" and spit at her. As an adult, she wondered why she hadn't changed her route to school and why people, even young people, hated Jews so much.

Rosi's school years were disrupted by Hitler's ascension to power in 1933. She was sixteen or seventeen and enrolled in the Lyzeum Findelgasse. There were ten other girls in her class, but she was the only Jew. Her friends told her, "If we talk to you, shake your hand, invite you home, our fathers will lose their jobs." A few days later, Rosi left school, gave private English lessons, and "pondered her future."

Rosi's (second from left) last year in school in
Lyzeum Findelgasse, 1933.

She became active in Kameraden, a somewhat political Jewish youth group that also sponsored activities like hiking, camping, and swimming. She made close friends in the group, and it must have helped fill the gap left by leaving school. Eventually she took business training courses and worked in a Jewish kindergarten for six months. Then she took a job as a bookkeeper that resulted in her receiving German social security payments some forty years later. Her gift for working with the young led to her next job in a home for difficult children. Later she enrolled in a Jewish teacher-training school in Würzburg.

Rosi (sitting in front row) with friends in Jewish youth movement Kameraden.

Rosi in Würzburg, 1937.

Hugo was also confronted with increasingly violent anti-Semitism in 1933: On July 20, he and about 300 other men in Nuremberg were picked up by SA storm troopers and forced to cut grass with their teeth on a sports field. Rosi recalls that even during this time he kept his sense of humor and good nature and frequently said, "Well, at least our heads stay on" or "At least we still get mail."

Rosi was at school in Würzburg on November 9, 1938, when her mother phoned to say that Hugo had been arrested during the pogrom against Jews in all parts of Germany that would come to be called Kristallnacht. She returned to the family home, a third floor apartment at Hallerstraße 27, bringing a Greek dessert wine as a gift for her mother, Aunt Frida, and the maid, Lina. A mob had been to the apartment and cut the legs off all the tables and china cabinets. The women were scared and crying. They had been canning rose hip jam when the mob entered, and there was red jam on the carpets, walls, and furniture and broken glassware everywhere. Rosi remembered looking at this scene of destruction and vowing never to become attached to material objects.

It was impossible to stay in the apartment that night. They slept at the Jewish Home for the Aged and returned home the next day to clean up. As a further harassment and humiliation, they were given only one garbage bag to hold all their damaged possessions. A neighbor, an officer in the German Army, saw them cleaning and offered to help—a kind and courageous act that left a deep impression on Rosi.

Hugo was taken to Dachau, a concentration camp outside Munich. Hundreds of other men who had been dragged from their homes or arrested on the streets during Kristallnacht were also imprisoned there. He was kept in Dachau for forty-five days and released on December 19, 1938. Jews were ordered to pay for the destruction of their homes, businesses, and synagogues during Kristallnacht. Rosi also remembered having to deliver the family's silverware and other valuables to a municipal office that seized them on behalf of the Reich.

Hugo returned from Dachau to find that the Adas Israel Orthodox synagogue on Essenweinstraße, the family's congregation for almost thirty years, had been destroyed. He was dismissed from his twenty-seven-year job as a junior partner in the metal firm because of a Nazi decree prohibiting Jews from employment.

Kristallnacht marked a major turning point for Jews in Germany. Many of them left Germany for other countries. Rosi had already applied for an American visa three months earlier. Hugo's cousin, Pauline Rubens in Chicago, was her sponsor, promising to provide for Rosi so she would not be a financial burden on the United States. On the affidavit, the reason given by Mrs. Rubens for bringing Rosi to the United States was "the discrimination by the German government against non-Aryans."

Frida, Clemy, and Rosi walking in the environs of Nuremberg.

Rosi's teacher-training program in Würzburg ended when Nazis closed the school in January 1939. In her later life she was never able to make a career of being a children's social worker partly because the Nazis had twice terminated her schooling. She returned to Nuremberg to live with her parents and Aunt Frida Roederer née Mosbacher on Hallerstraße and to wait for her quota number for immigration to the United States.

On April 1, 1939, the Nazis forced the family to leave their apartment and move to a "Jew House" at FürtherStraße 16 as subtenants of a Schmitt family. According to the May 17, 1939, census, there were eight people listed in the Mosbacher household: Rosi, her parents, Aunt Frida, Lina the maid, and three unrelated Jews. These crowded conditions were an enormous pressure on the family.

The Nazi pressure on the Jews also increased in other ways. Males were forced to add "Israel" and females "Sara" to their names. Jewish passports were each stamped with a large "J." More and more places and activities—such as schools and jobs—were forbidden to Jews. As the persecution escalated, Jews continued to leave Germany however they could, including, eventually the Mosbachers.

In June 1939, Rosi was able to leave Nuremberg for England to work as a maid for the Heron family in Welwyn Garden City, Herts, near London. She was twenty-three, young enough to work, and the Herons, a liberal-minded family who took in refugees, offered her a job. War broke out on September 1, 1939, and, with fears of a German attack on London, the Heron family made arrangements for Rosi to seek safety in the home of their relatives in Penzance in the south of England. Rosi stayed in Penzance for several months and returned to the London area in early 1940 to work for the Sudweeks family in Ealing. She took care of the Sudweeks' baby, Anthony. Her plan was to continue working for them until she received her visa for the United States, and then she would go to New York and reunite with her parents who expected to be there soon.

However, conditions in Nuremberg worsened. Hugo and Clemy felt unable to wait any longer for their quota number and visas to the United States. It was widely believed that there would be a German invasion of the west and all exit routes from Germany would be closed. Rosi said it was not like her parents to enter Holland illegally and thought that someone must have talked them into doing it. Hugo wrote in a letter from Amsterdam that "When your house is on fire—you jump."

With valid exit visas to leave Germany and immigration quota numbers for their American visas, they deregistered as residents of Nuremberg. On February 18, 1940, they left for Holland where they intended to stay briefly with family members, complete their visa paperwork at the United States Consulate in Rotterdam, and make arrangements to sail to the United States. Neither Rosi nor any other family member knew of Hugo and Clemy's plan until they learned of their arrest at Oldenzaal, a Dutch border town known to be helpful to refugees fleeing persecution. They had crossed the border on foot and entered Holland illegally. Many Jews from Germany had fled to Holland, a neutral country. The Dutch government was unable to accommodate all the refugees. Their official policy was to send them back to Germany, but they allowed Hugo and Clemy to stay in Holland under detention because they would only be there a short time while they made arrangements to leave for the United States.

Hugo and Clemy were separated and detained in Amsterdam, Hugo in a police station and Clemy in a women's shelter. They corresponded with Rosi during their two months of detention. When they were released on April 21, 1940, they booked passage on the S.S. *Veendam* to sail from Rotterdam to the United States on May 12, 1940. Two days before their scheduled departure, the German Army invaded the Netherlands, took control of the country, and canceled all exit visas.

Hugo and Clemy were trapped in Amsterdam. They lived in a room with kitchen privileges in the River District of Amsterdam, a neighborhood where many Jews lived. During their three years in Amsterdam they wrote over one hundred letters to Rosi. The letters were censored by the German authorities so Rosi was never clear what her parents were actually experiencing and feeling. From historical records we know that the Jews in Holland eventually suffered the same restrictions and oppression they had had to endure under the Nazis in Germany.

Rosi received her long-awaited immigration visa in London on July 26, 1940. She left from Liverpool and arrived in New York on the S.S. *Scythia* on August 12, 1940. Hugo and Clemy were very happy to learn she had arrived safely in New York and wrote of their hopes to join her.

She was very much on her own in New York, even though a number of relatives and a few friends from Germany were also living there. Most were penniless and unmoored in this new world, as Rosi was. She found work, a place to live, and, soon after, while waiting in a cafeteria to meet a date, she met her future husband, Alexander Baczewski, who was also waiting for his date.

Neither date showed up. Rosi and Alexander spent the evening getting to know each another. Alexander was a refugee from Vienna and had been imprisoned in Dachau and Buchenwald after the Anschluss. They dated for two years. Alexander, although Jewish, was not observant, but the Orthodox Hugo wrote to Rosi that what mattered was what kind of a man he was, giving his blessing to their marriage. Rosi wanted to wait for her parents' arrival before marrying, but they wrote her to go ahead with the wedding without them. They were married in New York on July 26, 1942, with no family members at the wedding; they hired someone to be their witness.

Rosi and Alexander wrote letters to her parents but lost touch in December 1942. Communication had become much more difficult after Germany declared war on the United States and mail between those two countries was curtailed. Letters were sent to friends and relatives in neutral countries such as Switzerland who would try to forward them. And, once the Nazis began deporting Holland's Jews to Auschwitz in July 1942, communication to the outside world became almost impossible.

Cousin Ruth White, Rosi, Alexander, and the Greek judge who officiated at Judy and Tony's wedding, October 3, 1982.

Rosi became pregnant with her first child, Anthony, named for Anthony Sudweeks, the child she had cared for in England. Hugo and Clemy would never know of Tony's birth in August 1943 nor the birth of their second grandchild, Steven, born in October 1945. In January 1943 Hugo and Clemy were arrested and taken to Westerbork. Two weeks later they were deported to Auschwitz where they were gassed upon arrival on February 5, 1943. Rosi learned that her parents were no longer in Westerbork in early 1943 through Clara Mosbacher, a cousin in Switzerland. She did not learn of their deaths until after the war.

Rosi in Manhattan.

Rosi and Alexander settled in Kew Gardens, Queens, New York, where many other Jewish refugees lived. Surviving family members came to New York after the war, and Rosi was devoted to them. She used to say she was so good to her relatives because she had no parents. The Baczewski home became a center of family activity, much as her parents' home in Nuremberg had been.

Rosi loved New York, her family, her work as office manager and German translator for Jordan & Hamburg, patent attorneys.

She was filled with gratitude that she had made it safely to the United States and said she never wanted to return to Germany. When my husband Tony and I visited Germany in 1989, however, she gave us a long list of places she wanted us to visit in Nuremberg: each place she had lived (Maxfeldstraße 16A, Großweidenmühlstraße 2, her favorite, and Hallerstraße 27); Labenwolf-Lyzeum (her first school); the old castle in the passageways of which she and her friends had played; and the cemetery in nearby Fürth where Hugo's parents, Sigmund and Karoline Mosbacher, were buried. We visited these sites, took photographs, and tried to imagine Rosi's life in Nuremberg, the center of Nazi rallies and activities, the city where Julius Streicher published his fiercely anti-Semitic newspaper *Der Stürmer*, the city she had been forced to flee.

From Rosi's photo book of the 1930s. Großweidenmühlstraße 2 was her favorite home. She could see Nuremberg's river, the Pegnitz, from her room. She lived there 1927–1936.

Hugo and Rosi on the balcony of their Nuremberg apartment in Großweidenmühlstraße.

Rosi and Alexander were married for over forty years, and Rosi always said that each year together was better than the last. After his death in January 1983, she took trips to China, Russia, Czechoslovakia, and every year went to a spa in Ixtapan, Mexico, where she befriended a group of women her age, Gentiles originally from Germany. Tony saw her openness to these women as a sign of his mother's ability to recognize that not all Germans were the same.

In 2004, at age eighty-eight, she reluctantly retired from her job with Jordan & Hamburg. A few years later she left New York where she'd lived for sixty-four years and came to San Francisco to be near her sons. She moved into the Rhoda Goldman Center, a Jewish assisted-living center where her cousin, Anna White née Roederer, lived. Her fax machine, typewriter, and computer came with her, and she continued to do German translations for Jordan & Hamburg. She missed New York a great deal, but was comforted by the company and support of her sons and daughters-in-law. And she discovered the nearby Murano cafe where she enjoyed three of her favorite things: a cup of espresso, a sweet, and a cigarette.

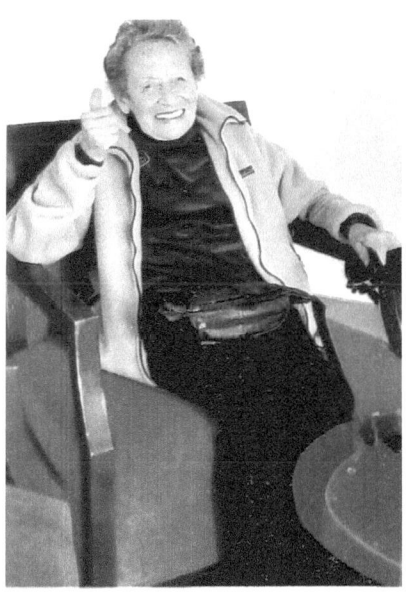

Rosi in January 2005, after her move to the Goldman Center.

She lived at the Rhoda Goldman Center for five years and died there, peacefully, in her sleep, on December 1, 2009. Tony and I and several other relatives had visited Rosi two days before she died. We brought her two of the over one hundred letters her parents had written her from Amsterdam, letters she had saved for almost seventy years. She beamed when she saw them and said, "It's too bad you never met my parents—they were such good people." She read the letters to herself in German and then to us in English. At the end of our visit she said, "Don't throw the letters away." We told her of our plans to have the letters translated and published, and she was pleased.

Rosi's wish was to be buried in New York next to Alexander. We made the arrangements she wanted. Her body was sent as "precious cargo" to New York, met by a rabbi at the airport, and taken to the Vaad of Queens where the traditional Taharah was performed by women of the community. Her body was washed and purified, prayers and psalms were recited, and then she was wrapped in a shroud. The women stayed with her body and continued to say prayers until time for the graveside services. At the cemetery, Rabbi Chaim Schwartz led us through a traditional Jewish burial service. Jordan & Hamburg closed for the day, and the entire office staff was at the service for Rosi. Her long-time Kew Gardens neighbors were there along with members of her family.

From left: Steve, Judy, Rosi, Maureen (Steve's wife), and Tony on Rosi's ninetieth birthday at Judy and Tony's home in Oakland, California.

Rosi, Judy, and Rosi's cousin, Ruth Schottman, two days before Rosi died.

She lived to be ninety-three. She survived the Nazis, exile, and great loss, and rebuilt her life in a new country. We miss her and will always admire her courage and her ability to focus on positive things such as the goodness of her parents and the deepening joys of her marriage. She was able to see that not all Germans were alike and greatly appreciated New York, her job, and particularly her family.

This article first appeared on www.rio.homepage.t-online.de/

Stolpersteine/Stumbling stones in honor of Hugo Mosbacher, Clementine (Clemy) Mosbacher, and Hugo's sister, Frieda[279] Röderer. Hier Wohnte translated means Here Lived.

The stones were laid on October 1, 2015, in the sidewalk at 27 Hallerstrasse, Nuremberg, Germany, where the family freely lived from 1936 to 1939, before they were removed to a Jew House by the Nazi regime. Hugo, Clemy, and Frieda fled to Holland in 1940 and were murdered by the Nazis in 1943: Hugo and Clemy in Auschwitz and Frieda in Sobibor.

Hugo and Clemy's grandson, Tony Baczewski, and his wife Judy Vasos, arranged with the Stolpersteine project and the city of Nuremberg to install the memorial stones.

Many thanks to our Nuremberg friends who joined us at the ceremony to lay the stones, read Kaddish for the family, and celebrate the lives of Hugo, Clemy, and Frieda.

And many thanks to the artist, Gunter Demnig, who conceived of this deeply personal and moving way to honor the many victims of Nazi atrocities.

---

[279]Frida is the spelling of her name in the letters. Her family members use Frieda and wanted that spelling on her Stolpersteine in Nuremberg.

Hallerstrasse 27, Nuremberg.
Photo courtesy of Hubert Rottner, Coordinator Stolpersteine Nuremberg.

> For more information about the stumbling stone project, visit www.stolpersteine.com.
>
> The video, *My Grandparents, Hugo and Clemy Mosbacher: From Nuremberg to Auschwitz* by Tony Baczewski, can be seen at youtube.com and at www.judyvasos.com.
>
> Other articles and videos about Rosi and her family are available at www.judyvasos.com
>
> The article titled "Only One Day Away from Rescue" published in the *Nurenberger Zeitung* about Hugo and Clemy and the stumbling stones can be read at www.judyvasos.com.

Resources

Boas, Jacob. *Boulevard Des Misères: The Story of Transit Camp Westerbork*. Hamden, Connecticut: Archon Books, 1985.

Friedlander, Saul. *Nazi Germany and the Jews: Volume I: The Years of Persecution, 1933–1939*. New York: Harper Perennial, 1997.

Friedlander, Saul. *Nazi Germany and the Jews: Volume II: The Years of Extermination, 1939–1945*. New York: Harper Perennial, 2007.

Gilbert, Martin. *The Holocaust: A History of the Jews of Europe during the Second World War*. New York: Holt, Rinehart and Winston, 1986.

Hillesum, Etty. *An Interrupted Life: The Diaries of Etty Hillesum, 1941–43*. London: Jonathan Cape Ltd., 1983.

Jewish Virtual Library website: www.jewishvirtuallibrary.org/jsource/Holocaust/.

JewishGen website: www.jewishgen.org. The Jewish Gen website provides invaluable online databases and resources for researching Jewish family history.

Kaplan, Marion A. *Between Dignity and Despair: Jewish Life in Nazi Germany*. Oxford: Oxford University Press, 1998.

Moore, Bob. *Victims and Survivors: The Nazi Persecution of the Jews in the Netherlands, 1940–1945*. New York: Arnold, 1997.

NIOD [Netherlands Institute for War, Holocaust, and Genocide Studies]: www.niod.nl. NIOD maintains archives and carries out historical studies on the Second World War.

Presser, Jacob. *Ashes in the Wind: The Destruction of Dutch Jewry*. London: Souvenir Press, 1968.

Rijo website: http://www.rijo.homepage.t-online.de/en_nu_index.html Susanne Rieger and Gerhard Jochem maintain an extensive website dedicated to Jewish life and history in Nuremberg, Fürth, and environs. The site provides invaluable Holocaust records and documents.

Schwab, Henry. *The Echoes That Remain: A Postal History of the Holocaust.* Weston, Massachusetts: Cardinal Spellman Philatelic Museum, 1992.

United States Holocaust Museum website: www.ushmm.org.

Verdoner, Yoka, and Francisca Verdoner Kan. *Signs of Life: The Letters of Hilde Verdoner-Sluizer from Nazi Transit Camp Westerbork, 1942–1944.* Washington, DC: Acropolis Books, 1990.

Wikipedia contributors, "History of the Jews in Germany," Wikipedia, The Free Encyclopedia: en.wikipedia.org/w/index.php?title=History_of_the_Jews_in_Germany&oldid=676194209.

Wyman, David S. *The Abandonment of the Jews: America and the Holocaust, 1941–1945.* New York: Pantheon Press, 1984.

About the Author

Judy Vasos is a historical detective who lives in Oakland, California, with her husband, Tony Baczewski, and Ruby, their fifteen-year-old Norwich Terrier. Judy's years of experience with social work, freelance writing, and creation of family history books led her to the belief that most people are waiting to hear the words "tell me" to reveal their personal story. Her passion is to listen and record those stories. She grew up in the Midwest surrounded by a large extended family of aunts, uncles, cousins, and grandparents full of love and stories. They brought family history alive, played a crucial role in helping her through rocky times, and gave Judy and her five siblings an appreciation of unconditional love.

www.ingramcontent.com/pod-product-compliance
Lightning Source LLC
Chambersburg PA
CBHW020416010526
44118CB00010B/279